THE CIVIL WAR LETTERS

OF

Colonel Hans Christian Heg

Edited by

THEODORE C. BLEGEN

NORWEGIAN-AMERICAN HISTORICAL ASSOCIATION
NORTHFIELD, MINNESOTA
1936

PREFACE

Colonel Hans Christian Heg of the Norwegian pioneer settlement at Muskego, Wisconsin, led a regiment of immigrant soldiers, recruited chiefly in the Badger State but also in Illinois, Iowa, and Minnesota, to the battlefields of the South in the Civil War. This volume is made up mainly of the letters, hitherto unpublished, that he wrote to his wife and children from January 16, 1862, shortly after the organization of the Fifteenth Wisconsin Volunteer Infantry, to September 18, 1863, the day before the battle of Chickamauga, in which, as the commander of a brigade, he met his death. Some of these personal records are presented in full, some in the form of abstracts, and some merely through excerpts. Supplementing them are a few communications from Colonel Heg that found their way into the columns of a Milwaukee newspaper. A biographical essay supplies a background for the interpretation of the documents.

One group of Heg letters, comprising about ninety items, is in the possession of the State Historical Society of Wisconsin. A larger body of Heg letters — some 130 in number — is owned by Mrs. A. R. Van Doren of Summit, New Jersey, a great-granddaughter of the colonel. Through the courtesy of the State Historical Society of Wisconsin and of Mrs. Van Doren, all these letters have been made available for transcription and publication by the Norwegian-American Historical Association. For this privilege, the Association proffers its sincere appreciation.

The Association desires also to express its hearty thanks to Mr. Magnus Swenson of Madison, Wisconsin, Mr. Arthur Andersen of Winnetka, Illinois, Mr. J. A. Holmboe of Oklahoma City, Oklahoma, Mr. Olaf Halvorsen of Huntington Park, California, Mr. O. M. Oleson of Fort Dodge, Iowa, and

Mr. G. G. Martin of Pacific Palisades, California, who sub-
scribed generously to a special fund that made possible the
printing of this volume.

In the course of the preparation of the book, valuable as-
sistance has been received from Dr. Knut Gjerset, curator
of the Norwegian-American Historical Museum, Decorah,
Iowa; Miss Alice E. Smith, curator of manuscripts, State
Historical Society of Wisconsin, Madison; Mr. Waldemar
Ager of Eau Claire, Wisconsin, the author of *Oberst Heg og
Hans Gutter* and of many articles on the Fifteenth Wiscon-
sin; Mr. Albert O. Barton of Madison, Wisconsin; Mr. Birger
Osland of Chicago; Mr. Karl T. Jacobsen, librarian, Luther College Library, Decorah, Iowa; Dr. Luther M. Kuhns,
historian of the Evangelical Lutheran Synod of Nebraska,
Omaha; Professor Agnes M. Larson of St. Olaf College,
Northfield, Minnesota; Mr. Kenneth M. Stampp of the University of Wisconsin; Mr. Herbert Kahler of the National
Park Service, Fort Oglethorpe, Georgia; Mrs. H. L. Howard
of Chicago, a niece of Harvey Britton, a sergeant in the Fifteenth Wisconsin; and finally Mr. Tollef Sanderson of Harmony, Minnesota, and his mother, Mrs. Sophia Jacobson
Sanderson, who is a niece of Mrs. Hans C. Heg. I desire
to express my gratitude for this assistance, which brought
to light several photographs of Colonel and Mrs. Heg and
other interesting pictures, made available for my use transcripts of various letters and articles published in early Wisconsin newspapers, furnished biographical material on the
Heg family, and supplied many other useful items of information. Finally, I may be permitted to make a bow of
appreciation to Mrs. Arthur Katz of St. Paul, who served
as my editorial assistant, compiled the index, and helped me
in that harrowing drudgery euphemistically called "seeing
the book through the press."

THEODORE C. BLEGEN

UNIVERSITY OF MINNESOTA
   MINNEAPOLIS

CONTENTS

ILLUSTRATIONS

THE CIVIL WAR LETTERS
OF
COLONEL HANS CHRISTIAN HEG

COLONEL HANS CHRISTIAN HEG

A BIOGRAPHICAL ESSAY

The story of Hans Christian Heg runs from 1829 to 1863. It begins at the hamlet of Lier, near Drammen, in south-eastern Norway. It ends on the field of Chickamauga in northern Georgia. Into the intervening thirty-four years are packed a series of varied experiences that link one life with characteristic movements in the " epic of America."

The elements in Colonel Heg's career have a wide sweep — a boyhood in the Old World, a transatlantic migration, contact with the American westward movement, the taste of frontier life in Wisconsin, identification with a community that cradled some of the more significant developments among an immigrant people, an overland trek to the gold fields of California, life in the mining camps of the West, a return to the community near Lake Michigan, a career in local and state politics, leadership of a regiment of Scandinavian immigrants in the Civil War, and death in a great battle of that war. His achievements are well known among Norwegian-Americans — for whom his name is in some sense a symbol of the contribution made to America by their pioneer ancestors — but they are little known outside that circle. One will look in vain for his biography in the dictionaries of distinguished Americans. The significance of his career is not to be sought in nation-wide fame or extraordinary achievement. Though he ultimately commanded a brigade in the Civil War, he was, after all, only a minor figure in that gigantic conflict. His importance lies rather in the fact that his life story typifies processes of transition that have marked the lives of thousands of immigrants.

Even among people of his own blood, Heg has been virtu-

1

ally unknown as a personality. He has indeed been accorded the honors of a hero, but appraisal too often has become apotheosis, and with the passing years he has taken on the aspect of a bronze statue. Yet, through all the years since he fell at Chickamauga, his own letters of the Civil War, warm, human, interesting, packed with shrewd observation and detail, and disclosing both his virtues and his faults, have been preserved. These letters, published for the first time in the present volume, tell their own story. They portray the man and soldier, and they record the history of a regiment. They require little amplification or comment, but their meaning and value cannot be fully understood unless they are read in the setting of Heg's career. They constitute the last chapter of a human story. In the light of the earlier chapters the last takes on a significance that it would not possess if it stood alone.

1

Hans Christian Heg was born on December 21, 1829, about four and a half years after the pathfinders of Norwegian emigration to America had sailed out from Stavanger in the sloop "Restauration." He was one of four children in the family of Even Hansen Heg, a shrewd and prosperous innkeeper who was a devout follower of the teachings of Hans Nielsen Hauge, the apostle of Norwegian pietism.

The Hegs were in close touch with the movement of emigration from its early stages. They lived at Lier in the vicinity of Drammen, a small town on the Christiania fjord, not far from the national capital. America and its opportunities were among the most interesting topics of the day in that corner of the world. As early as 1824 a local Drammen newspaper had published a series of descriptive articles on America, a land "for the present and the future."[1] Two men of Drammen left for America in 1825, the same year that saw the beginnings of emigration from southwestern

[1] *Drammens Tidende*, October 7, 14, 21, November 1, 1824.

Norway.² In the thirties Drammen was a center of emigration interest; there Ole Nattestad's book telling of his journey to distant Illinois was published in 1839, and in the spring of the same year Ansten Nattestad, who had himself seen the glories of America, led a party of more than a hundred and thirty emigrants from Drammen to New York.³ The year 1839 saw the departure for America of two very good friends of the Hegs — Søren Bache and Johannes Johansen, the former a son of Tollef Bache, the leading Haugean in that part of Norway. The letters of these two men were awaited with anxious interest by the Heg family during the ensuing winter, for Even Heg was playing with the idea of migration to the New World.⁴ In 1839 another emigrant party, composed for the most part of people who had failed to secure accommodations aboard the vessel that had carried Ansten Nattestad and his following, set out under the leadership of one John Nelson Luraas. They took passage from Göteborg, Sweden, to Boston, where it is said that the immigrants from the "high north" occasioned no little surprise. "The foreign language of the emigrants, their clothes, and their customs were marveled at," wrote an observer, "but the visitors were even more astonished to find that people who came from a land so near the ice region as Norway looked like other human beings." ⁵ Luraas and his party made their way to Milwaukee and later established a Norwegian settlement on the shores of Muskego Lake in Waukesha County, Wisconsin. This was the beginning of one of the best known Norwegian communities in the United States — the community with which the Heg family soon was to be identified.⁶

² Theodore C. Blegen, *Norwegian Migration to America, 1825–1860*, 49 (Northfield, Minnesota, 1931).
³ An English translation of Nattestad's book, " Description of a Journey to North America," has been published by Rasmus B. Anderson in the *Wisconsin Magazine of History*, 1:149–186 (December, 1917). On the emigrant party led by Ansten Nattestad, see *Norwegian Migration to America*, ch. 5.
⁴ *Norwegian Migration to America*, 118–119.
⁵ *Billed-Magazin* (Madison, Wisconsin), 1:7 (November 14, 1868).
⁶ *Billed-Magazin,* 1:6–10; *Norwegian Migration to America*, 115–118.

Bache and Johansen also found their way to the West.
They made a searching investigation of the prospects for
settlers; late in December, 1839, they wrote jointly a long
letter to their friends in Norway which was published in full
in a Drammen newspaper.[7] They presented no favorable
picture of conditions in the Fox River settlement of Illinois,
where they found living conditions miserable and malaria
prevalent; but, after a tour of inspection, they were able to
promise immigrants good land and favorable conditions in
Wisconsin. In the summer of 1840 the two investigators,
who had returned to Illinois, again pushed into Wisconsin;
they went to the Muskego settlement, but selected land on
the shores of Wind Lake in what later became Norway
Township of Racine County. As a result of this move, the
Norwegian settlement tended to expand southward into Norway and other townships of Racine County, where land conditions were better than in the first settled area; but the
colony as a whole continued to be known as Muskego.[8]

The stage was now set for the coming of the Heg family.
In the spring of 1840 Even Hansen Heg, encouraged by reports from Bache and Johansen, sold his Norwegian property and became the leader of a group of emigrants, including
his wife and his four children, from Drammen and other dis-
tricts. They set sail from Drammen on May 17 in the same
vessel that had carried the Nattestad party the year before.
The "Emilie," after touching at Göteborg, where a cargo of
iron was secured, made the long, eleven-week voyage to New
York. From the eastern metropolis, the immigrants followed the usual route to the West, going by river and canal
to Buffalo, and thence by steamer on the Great Lakes to
Milwaukee. Heg's objective was Muskego.[9] On August 28
Søren Bache made the following entry in his diary:

[7] *Tiden* (Drammen), March 3, 1840.
[8] *Billed-Magazin*, 1:11; and Søren Bache, Diary, entries for the summer of
1840, beginning June 3. This diary, which covers the period from 1839 to 1847,
is being translated by Professor Andreas Elviken of Temple University, Philadelphia, and is to be published by the Norwegian-American Historical Association.
[9] *Norwegian Migration to America*, 126–127. A manuscript journal by Ole

I heard the voices of Even Heg and Johansen outside and our servant boy came rushing to report that Even Heg had arrived. I hastened to meet them and great was the joy in meeting such old friends in so distant a land. Even Heg and his companions had arrived in the morning at Milwaukee, and guided by a Norwegian he had come on to meet us. Luckily we were able to treat him to a fresh fish that our boy had caught and to a cup of tea. After the meal we finally had to go to bed, but because our house was so little we had to move the bed outside and make up beds on the floor. But there was little sleep that night, for there was an unceasing flow of questions and answers.

So the Heg family came to Wisconsin. And they arrived when Hans was "just the age to be impressed with all the strange things seen on the voyage and in the new home."[10]

Hans was in fact only eleven years old when he reached Muskego, and there, amid characteristic frontier conditions, he passed the remaining years of his youth. It was a typical pioneer immigrant community.[11] The settlement occupies, however, a place of special importance in the history of the Norwegians in the United States, "not because of prosperity — in the forties it was scourged with sickness, its land was not the choicest Wisconsin land, and in its material achievements it did not equal certain other midwestern settlements — but because it was a 'mother colony' to numerous other settlements and because it witnessed during the forties and the fifties some significant beginnings in the field of Norwegian-American religious, social, and cultural activities."[12] In most of these beginnings Hans Heg's father played a part, for he had not lived long at Muskego before

Trovatten telling of this migration is in the possession of Mr. Halvor Skavlem of Janesville, Wisconsin, and a photostatic copy is owned by the Minnesota Historical Society.

[10] Joseph Schafer, "Hans Christian Heg," in *Wisconsin Blue Book*, 1933, p. 37–38.

[11] See Albert O. Barton, "Muskego, the Most Historic Norwegian Colony," in *Scandinavia*, 1:22–29 (January, 1924); H. R. Holand, "Muskego," in *Symra*, 3:187–196 (1907); *Billed-Magazin*, 1:10–13; Rasmus B. Anderson, *First Chapter of Norwegian Immigration, 1821–1840; Its Causes and Results*, 266–284 (Madison, Wisconsin, 1896); and the writer's *Norwegian Migration to America*, ch. 5.

[12] *Norwegian Migration to America*, 129–130.

he won, through the force of his character, his religious zeal, and a substantial economic status, the position of the acknowledged leader of the community. Like most of the immigrants who went to Wisconsin, he became a farmer. Soon after his arrival he bought the farm of Luraas, the leader of the settlers of 1839.[13] In the larger story of immigrant pioneering, this was no ordinary farm. It was an immigrant station on the road to the West and was the Mecca of hundreds, perhaps thousands, of immigrants searching for new homes in the American West.[14]

A pioneer once said of the Muskego community, "This settlement was the journey's goal for the majority of the emigrants and it thus became a common assembling place and point of departure for most of the older colonies in America. It was later that the settlers went directly from their native land to the newer settlements in Wisconsin, Iowa, and Minnesota."[15] Even Heg won renown alike for his hospitality and for his resourcefulness and sagacity as an adviser and helper to the immigrants who stopped at Muskego to get their bearings. The problem of receiving new immigrants was difficult to meet both because they were so numerous and because often their funds were exhausted when they arrived. In 1843 Heg erected a large barn that seems to have been used as a kind of free hotel for immigrants. The small cabins of the settlers could not accommodate the swarms of newcomers who passed through Muskego on their way to Koshkonong and other settlements. How pressing the problem was may be understood by noting that at one time in 1843 — a time when incidentally an epidemic was sweeping the colony — every cabin had to house from fifteen to twenty persons. Heg threw his barn open to all, not only in 1843 but every summer, when throngs of immigrants clamored for shelter. It served as the temporary home of large parties of newcomers during the first days

[13] Anderson, *First Chapter of Norwegian Immigration*, 276.
[14] *Billed-Magazin*, 1:12–13.
[15] Quoted in *Billed-Magazin*, 1:11.

and weeks of their new life in America.   During this period
they would consult with Heg and other Muskego settlers and
prepare for the next stage of their journey.   A part of the
schooling of Hans Heg was undoubtedly gained through his
contact with the immigrant stream that flowed past his very
door.[16]

The Heg barn was not merely a haven for new arrivals.
It served also as a social and religious center for the Muskego
community.   In the period before a church was built in the
settlement, lay services were held in the barn, and frequently
Even Heg himself preached.   When Claus L. Clausen, the
pioneer minister, arrived at Muskego, he preached his first
sermon in the barn; and in 1843 he organized a congregation
within its commodious walls.   Sunday-school classes were
also held in the building and Clausen confirmed his first class
of children there in 1844.   A double wedding was held on
one occasion in "Even Heg's new, home-sawed, oak frame
barn."   The structure was called into use as a hospital when
cholera and malaria desolated the colony.

Hans Heg was "a charter member of the new Scandi-
navian-American civilization which was growing up in Wisconsin prior to the Civil War," [17] and naturally he was close
to many events that are celebrated in the story of the Norwegians in America.   One of these was the building of the
first Norwegian Lutheran church in the United States, begun in 1843 and completed two years later.   Even Heg, in
fact, donated the ground on which this historic edifice was
erected.[18]   Another   happening   that   may   have   impressed

[16] Perhaps the most significant record of social and economic conditions in the
Muskego settlement is the diary of Søren Bache.   *Billed-Magazin*, 1:12–13,
tells about Heg's barn.   See also George T. Flom, *History of Norwegian Immigration to the United States*, 160–161 (Iowa City, 1909); Anderson, *First Chapter of Norwegian Immigration*, 278–279; H. G. Stub, " Reminiscences from By-
gone Days," in *North Star* (Minneapolis), 4:12–27 (January–February, 1922);
J. W. C. Dietrichson, *Reise blandt de norske Emigranter* (Stavanger, 1846 —
reprinted at Madison, Wisconsin, 1896); J. A. Bergh, *Den norsk lutherske Kirkes
Historie i Amerika*, 11, 15–20 (Minneapolis, 1914); and J. Magnus Rohne, *Norwegian American Lutheranism up to 1872*, 45 ff. and *passim* (New York, 1926).
[17] Schafer, in *Wisconsin Blue Book*, 1933, p. 38.
[18] Rohne, *Norwegian American Lutheranism up to 1872*, 79.

Hans Heg was the Muskego manifesto of 1845; his father was one of its leading signers. The settlers in the Wisconsin colony were indignant over the extent and bitterness of the anti-emigration propaganda being circulated in Norway and over the misrepresentation of American conditions that seemed to fill the newspapers of the home country. In January, 1845, eighty men of Muskego therefore addressed an open letter to the people of Norway that was later published in the leading newspaper of Christiania. The pioneers conceded immigrant discouragement, need, sickness, and suffering, but they affirmed their faith in America as a haven for the oppressed of Europe. They drew a striking contrast between the conditions that nineteenth-century immigrants faced and the far more severe trials that the seventeenth-century founders of Virginia had met. These men of Muskego found certain compensations in the New World. "We live," they asserted, "under a liberal government in a fruitful land, where freedom and equality are the rule in religious as in civil matters, and where each one of us is at liberty to earn his living practically as he chooses." Through these opportunities, they concluded, "we have a prospect of preparing for ourselves, by diligence and industry, a carefree old age. We have therefore no reason to regret the decision that brought us to this country." [19]

Hans became known in the Muskego community as an alert and active boy. He attended the common schools, but there is no evidence that a thought was ever given to the possibility of a higher education for him. As the son of an enterprising father whose home was a cultural center for the community, however, he had good opportunities, and he seems to have used them to advantage.[20]   Living in a settle-

---

[19] *Norwegian Migration to America*, 209–211. The manifesto has been turned into English and published by S. B. Hustvedt under the title "An American Manifesto by Norwegian Immigrants," in *American-Scandinavian Review*, 13: 619 (October, 1925).

[20] A valuable source of information on Heg's career is Knud Langeland, "Oberst H. C. Heg," in J. A. Johnson, *Det Skandinaviske Regiments Historie* (La Crosse, Wisconsin, 1869). On Heg's boyhood, see especially p. 103. Langeland was an intimate friend of Heg.

ment in which Norwegian was generally spoken, he naturally retained a fluent command of the language he had learned as a child. But he also learned to use English with ease and no little force; and it is of some interest to note that his Civil War letters were written in the language of his adopted country. Frequently Muskego settlers accompanied parties of newly arrived immigrants to settlements in the interior of Wisconsin; and thus Hans made many trips to the Jefferson, Rock, and Koshkonong prairie settlements.[21] Such an experience was not formal education, but it must have played its part in widening the mental horizons of a keenly observant boy. It is reported that some years before Hans became of age he held positive views on the question of slavery and its spread. This is not difficult to believe; his father's home was the cradle of the Norwegian-American press and the newspaper there published in the late forties served as a Norwegian-American organ for the Free-Soil movement.

Even Heg was one of the founders and publishers of the Muskego paper, the first Norwegian newspaper published in the United States. It was called *Nordlyset* (The Northern Light).[22] In the middle forties the Norwegians in the West had begun to interest themselves in the possibility of a newspaper of their own. They felt the need of a press printed in their own language and projected from their own cultural background. It would be, they thought, a focus for common interests, a medium for exchange of ideas, an instrument for promoting knowledge of American conditions and easing the transition of immigrant to citizen, and an ameliorating influence in frontier life. It might also serve to define political standpoints and to advance the social and political recognition of the immigrants.

[21] Knud Langeland, *Nordmœndene i Amerika; Nogle Optegnelser om de norskes Udvandring til Amerika*, 46 (Chicago, 1889).
[22] Carl G. O. Hansen, "Pressen til Borgerkrigens slutning," in J. B. Wist, *Norsk-Amerikanernes Festskrift 1914*, 10 ff. (Decorah, Iowa, 1914); Albert O. Barton, "The Beginnings of the Norwegian Press in America," in Wisconsin Historical Society, *Proceedings*, 1916, p. 190–196.

The ferment of such ideas seethed most actively in the home in which Hans Heg grew up. Even Heg, Søren Bache, and James D. Reymert, all three prominent in the Muskego community, had considered the establishment of a newspaper as early as 1845. Two years later it became a reality, the necessary funds having been supplied, for the most part, by Bache and Heg. The three men were joint publishers, and Reymert served as editor. The first number, printed in Heg's cabin on July 29, 1847, announced that the purpose of the venture was to enlighten the Norwegian immigrants, who could not as yet readily read the American newspapers, concerning the history and government of the country; to present general news of social and religious interest; and to purvey information about happenings in the old country. Its American tone was emphasized by the inclusion of a translation of part of the Declaration of Independence; by the publication of " a few remarks by Daniel Webster, member of Congress, and one of the most keen-minded American citizens "; and by a cut of the American flag at the head of the editorial column. At the outset the paper made a declaration of political neutrality, but in September, 1848, it placed the names of Van Buren and Adams, the candidates of the Free-Soil party, at its masthead. The original motto of the paper, " Freedom and Equality," blossomed into " Free Land, Free Speech, Free Labor, and Free Men." [23] *Nordlyset's* importance to Hans Heg lies not merely in the fact that it took a definite stand on the outstanding issue of the day and gave specific information about American politics, but also in the circumstance that its publishing office — the young man's own home — became the political center of the community. This center was visited by many candidates for office who sought the support of the paper with a view to winning the " Norwegian vote." Hans was eighteen years old when *Nordlyset* was established; in its

[23] *Nordlyset*, July 29, 1847. Files of this paper are in the libraries of Luther College, Decorah, Iowa, and of Luther Theological Seminary of St. Paul, Minnesota.

offices his own talent for politics began to develop; and later he became an active local worker for Van Buren.[24]

II

Politics yielded temporarily, however, to the lure of adventure. Gold was discovered in 1848 in the Sacramento Valley, and the following year witnessed a remarkable rush of gold hunters to California. In 1849, at the age of twenty, Hans Heg, with three companions, joined the army of forty-niners. The four young men,[1] equipped with a solid wagon and two yoke of oxen, started on the overland trek on March 26. They "should be quite safe on their forthcoming long, inconvenient, and tedious journey," it was stated in *Nordlyset* when their departure was announced, for "as far as human understanding and planning may avail, they have taken every precaution."[2]

They reached Hannibal, Missouri, on April 6, and then pushed on to St. Joseph, where Heg found time, on April 29, to write to his brother Ole. "We had bad roads in places," he explained, "and worst of all, the bridges all along were washed away by ice, but aside from this, everything went quite well." The party had secured an additional yoke of oxen and intended soon to buy yet another, so that in all they would have four yoke for the long trail westward. Prices had been high on the way from Hannibal to St. Joseph, Heg pointed out, but at the latter place they were much lower, "the reason being that there are here quite a few who have become discouraged with the journey and are now selling out at less than half price." He evinced in his letter a certain flair for observation. "Cholera and smallpox are raging severely in this city at present," he wrote, "and it is rumored that the Indians are not very well satisfied with having so many people traveling through their country this

[24] Langeland, in Johnson, *Det Skandinaviske Regiments Historie,* 104.
[1] According to *Nordlyset,* March 26, 1849, the party consisted of Engebret and Halvor Rosvald, Magnus Hansen, and Hans Christian Heg.
[2] March 29, 1849.

summer. Many, therefore, become frightened, pack up their belongings, and set out for home. Not a few immigrants headed for California have been attacked by cholera since they came here, but most of them, however, are known to be addicted to drinking." The gold rush was a mighty movement. "It is impossible to say with any degree of certainty," he wrote, "how many will be crossing the Missouri River for California this year — some say ten thousand, others, forty thousand wagons. I believe, however, that the latter figure is excessive, although there are a tremendous number of them." [3]

At Savannah Landings so great a throng was waiting to cross the Missouri that the young men were delayed a few days. Heg tells in a letter written to his brother from that place on May 2 of buying "a yoke of oxen before leaving St. Joseph at a price of $55.00 and a horse for $30.00." "We have not as yet formed any company, but we thought of joining the other wagons from Wisconsin when we have crossed the Missouri River. Our health is good and we are in fine spirits. The reports from California are exceptionally favorable, yes, favorable enough to encourage the most disheartened person." They had come to the dividing line between civilization and wilderness. "We are now camped on the banks of the Missouri River, where on the one side, as far as the eye can penetrate, one sees only the wild Indian land through which our journey goes to California; and on the other side, one sees the white man's dominions with attractive-looking tents spread over the entire country. It is actually a beautiful sight." [4]

The little company of gold seekers from Muskego eventually got across the Missouri and struck out for the farther West. They made their way to Fort Laramie and thence to the Green River, a distance of four hundred miles, in the course of which no grass for the oxen was found. They

[3] Heg's letter is printed in *Nordlyset*, May 17, 1849.
[4] *Nordlyset*, October 11, 1849.

reached South Pass on July 4 and Salt Lake City on July 16. A letter that Heg wrote from Fort Laramie has apparently been lost, but on July 17 he wrote to his brother from the Mormon capital, and this letter is preserved in the columns of his home newspaper. Commenting on South Pass, he said that his party "had here the most beautiful road that we ever could wish for, and we would have passed by the summit without noticing it, had we not known its exact location. It was so cold during the night that the water in our tent froze, and there was snow all about us."

Heg went on to tell of the journey beyond South Pass: "When we approached Green River, we discovered that the majority of the immigrants had gone by the northern route, namely by Fort Hall, but we decided to follow the southern route, because this one is the shortest. Yet, since there is here a desert seventy miles long, most of the immigrants had decided to go by way of Fort Hall. We discovered, however, when we came to Fort Bridger, that the Mormons had found a new route on the north side of Salt Lake, where there was abundant water and grass. We will doubtless follow this route from Salt Lake." As Heg and his friends pushed westward, they began to hear reports about the riches of California. "A few days ago," Heg wrote from Salt Lake City, "we met many Mormons who had been at the gold mines last summer; and they assured us all that we could find enough gold if we only were able to endure the hard work that is connected with digging and washing out the gold. They said that ordinarily one is able to make from four hundred to a thousand dollars a week. This is good comfort to us, and we bear the inconveniences of the journey with patience in the hope of winning compensation once we get there. We have kept up our courage and feel well, though some of the immigrants have suffered from the so-called 'mountain fever.'" [5]

[5] *Nordlyset*, October 11, 1849. A diary kept on the journey and later by Engebret Rosvald (Solveson), later known as Engebret S. Roswell, has been

At length, after many adventures and hardships, the Wisconsin argonauts reached their destination. Heg remained in the West two years, experiencing the usual vicissitudes of fortune of the gold miners. Unfortunately, his letters from California, save one, have not been preserved, and we have little detail about his life in the mining camps. In one letter, written at Weaversville evidently in the spring of 1850, he has left a partial record of this period: " We have been very actively engaged during the whole winter in digging gold. But it is becoming scarce, and little is found. Last fall, when we arrived, we built a log house, ten feet square in size, equipping it with a good fireplace, etc. . . . I and H. have worked together since we came here in September, and we have saved one thousand dollars, besides our expenses, which have amounted to about three hundred dollars. . . . In my opinion, the best part of the gold crop has now been harvested, and those who come out next year will find themselves much disappointed." [6]

After Heg had spent many months in the West, and when he was just beginning to have considerable success in his mining ventures, he received news from home that his father had died on August 17, 1850.[7] His mother had died eight years earlier, and he now felt that it was clearly his duty to return to Wisconsin and to assume charge of the home farm and the care of his sister and his younger brothers. Accordingly, in 1851 he returned to Muskego.[8]

The gold digger now adopted the prosaic duties of a farmer; he took over his father's farm of three hundred and twenty acres. In 1851, shortly after his return, he married Gunild Einong, the daughter of a Norwegian immigrant of

deposited with the Norwegian-American Historical Association. It is little more, however, than an itinerary and account book. With it is a manuscript written by Halvor Rosvald (Roswell) giving biographical information about himself and his brother. These materials were lent to the Association by Mr. Herbert Roswell of Mauston, Wisconsin, a grandson of Halvor.

[6] Quoted by Langeland, in Johnson, *Det Skandinaviske Regiments Historie*, 104.

[7] *Democraten* (Racine, Wisconsin), August 31, 1850.

[8] Sketch in *Emigranten* (Madison, Wisconsin), September 12, 1859, p. 2.

1843.[9] He was then twenty-two years of age and had already won in his community the respect not only of the Norwegian settlers, but also of many of the native Americans. Politics, of which he had had a taste before going to California, again attracted him, and he soon entered the local political arena. A writer who knew Heg personally declares that his political views were influenced by the "freedom, equality, and the spirit of brotherhood" of the frontier. There can be little doubt that there was a considerable measure of democracy in the pioneer society of Muskego, and it is not difficult to understand why Heg, who seems to have had a sturdy faith in freedom, should have made his political debut as a Free-Soiler. In 1852 he was put forward as a Free-Soil candidate for a seat in the Wisconsin state assembly. The contest was three-cornered, for both the antislavery Whigs and the Democrats had candidates in the field. The Democrat, Thomas West, was elected by a small majority over Heg.[10]

Defeat thus blocked the direct road to state politics for Heg, but he opened for himself an indirect road to the larger field by entering into the political and civic work of his own community. At the same time he won a valuable school-ing in practical politics in those basic units of American government, the township and the county. In 1852 he was made supervisor in the town of Norway, Racine County, and he also became a justice of the peace. Two years later he was chosen chairman of the board of supervisors, and in 1855 he was re-elected to this position. As chairman of the town board he was also a member of the county board; and in 1855 he was made one of three commissioners to superintend the Racine County Poor Farm in the western district. Two years later he was again selected as a poorhouse commissioner, but he now found himself too busy to retain the town office, a post to which he had the satisfaction of seeing

[9] For a sketch and characterization of Mrs. Heg, see supplement II, *post*, p. 249.
[10] Langeland, in Johnson, *Det Skandinaviske Regiments Historie*, 104; *Emigranten*, September 12, 1859, p. 2.

his brother elected. He appears to have discharged faithfully the duties of the various local offices that he held, and
with their successful execution he gained the confidence of
increasing numbers of citizens.[11] Heg's local political career
now swung open the door to state politics. In the autumn
of 1857 he was a delegate from Racine County to the Republican state convention at Madison. A group of Norwegians met in Madison and proposed the nomination of Heg
for a state office as a recognition of the Norwegian element
in Wisconsin, which just then was flocking to the support
of the new party. Though a Wisconsin congressman, John
F. Potter, of bowie-knife fame, spoke in the convention for
Heg, the latter was able to secure only a few scattered
votes.[12] He therefore returned to his round of local activities. In 1859 he determined to give up the immediate supervision of his farm, removed to Waterford, and there, in
company with two native Americans, conducted a mill and
a general merchandise store.[13]

Heg's stay at Waterford was, however, of short duration.
Political recognition of a substantial character came in his
nomination by the Republican state convention of 1859 as a
candidate for the office of state prison commissioner of Wisconsin. Heg accepted this nomination and traveled about
the state, making political addresses in Norwegian in the
Norwegian settlements and in English elsewhere. He emphasized the slavery issue. The Norwegians, he said, leaving one of the most beautiful lands in the world, came to
America because it was a free country, whose principles
struck a responsive chord in their hearts. They were for the
most part working people with deep antislavery convictions.
"I went aboard the Republican ship when she was launched,"
he declared in an address at Madison. "I was aboard when
she made trips up Salt River. I am still aboard, but I be-

---

[11] A summary of Heg's career in local politics is presented in *Emigranten*,
September 12, 1859, p. 2. See also *History of Racine and Kenosha Counties*,
315, 329 (Chicago, 1879).

[12] *Emigranten*, September 12, 1859, p. 2.

[13] Langeland, in Johnson, *Det Skandinaviske Regiments Historie*, 105.

lieve she is now heading toward a very different port. But whether she be destined for one port or another, so long as she sails under true Republican colors, you can rely upon finding me among the working members of her crew." [14]

Many Germans and Scandinavians in the middle fifties believed that the Republican party was tainted with Know-Nothingism. This feeling declined after 1855, but it was slow to disappear. In 1856 a Norwegian newspaper published at Madison maintained that the Know-Nothing element in the state Republican party was strong enough to control the state convention of that year and it urged Scandinavians to have nothing to do with the party.[15] *Emigranten*, the most influential of the Norwegian-American newspapers, affiliated with the Republican party, however, and staunchly defended it from attacks by other Norwegian newspapers.[16] In 1857 both the Republican and Democratic parties in Wisconsin adopted strong planks against nativism, but charges persisted, especially from the Germans.[17]

It is in part against this background that Heg's winning of a place on the Republican ticket of 1859 must be interpreted, though he had fairly earned leadership and responsibility. His nomination was undoubtedly a Republican bid for Scandinavian support. It must be remembered that in Wisconsin, where foreign voters held the balance of power, nativism, as Dr. Schafer puts it, has been "a threat instead of a present political danger." [18] Political recognition of racial groups was forwarded by the desire of politicians to erect buffers against charges of nativism. Heg himself frankly regarded his nomination as a compliment to the Norwegians

---

[14] Heg's nomination is reported in *Emigranten*, September 5, 1859, p. 2. See also the same paper, October 3 and 10, 1859. The Madison address as reported in the September 10 issue is based upon a report in the *State Journal*.

[15] *Den Norske Amerikaner*, April 19, May 3, 10, and 31, 1856.

[16] See, for an example of such an attack, *Nordstjernen* (Madison, Wisconsin), July 22, 1857.

[17] See Ernest Bruncken, "The Political Activity of Wisconsin Germans 1854–60," in Wisconsin Historical Society, *Proceedings*, 1901, 197 ff. An excellent general account of "Know-Nothingism in Wisconsin" by Joseph Schafer appears in the *Wisconsin Magazine of History*, 8:3–21 (September, 1924).

[18] Schafer, in *Wisconsin Magazine of History*, 8:12.

and effectively maintained in his campaign speeches that the Republicans were not nativistic.[19]   Some of the comments on Heg made by contemporary newspapers are of interest. The Milwaukee *Free Democrat* said, "Mr. Heg is completely Americanized, speaks English as clearly and fluently as a native citizen." [20]   In some quarters it was even alleged that Heg was so completely Americanized that he had become indifferent to the Norwegians.[21]   In his addresses, however, he expressed pride as well as deep interest in the Norwegian backgrounds of the immigrants. *Emigranten* called attention to the confidence that the Norwegians in Heg's own community had in him and characterized the charge of indifference as a "Norwegian-Democratic Yankee trick." [22] At the subsequent election he received a majority of 2,673 over his Democratic opponent, Henry C. Fleck.   In attaining the office of state prison commissioner, Heg appears also to have won the distinction of being the first Norwegian immigrant elected to a state office in the United States.[23]   What was of greater significance to him than this, however, was the fact that the campaign had made him well known throughout the state of Wisconsin.

At Waupun, where Heg in his new official capacity took charge of the state prison, he displayed considerable administrative ability and also gave evidence of a deep interest in the perplexing problems of human conduct that confronted him.   He introduced improvements in the machinery operated by the prison and improved the system of prison labor. After a visit to the Illinois penitentiary at Joliet, he opened cooper and broom shops at Waupun.   He quickly appre-

---

[19] *Emigranten*, October 10, 1859, p. 2, quoting from the *Wisconsin State Journal*.

[20] Milwaukee *Free Democrat*, September 14, 1859, quoted in *Emigranten*, September 26, 1859, p. 2.   See also *Emigranten*, October 3, 1859, with extracts from the *Waupun Times* of September 21, the Watertown *Volkszeitung* of September 24, and the *Free Democrat* of September 19.

[21] *Emigranten*, October 31, 1859, p. 2.

[22] *Emigranten*, October 31, 1859, p. 2.   This issue also contains a report of an address by Heg at Monroe, Wisconsin, in which he answered taunts of nativism.

[23] *Emigranten*, November 21 and 28, 1859.

ciated the need of removing his position from the domain of politics. In one of his reports he declared his opposition to the practice of electing prison commisioners every two years, and favored appointment with permanent tenure. After careful study, he advocated the principle of the indeterminate sentence, later generally adopted. His reports contain some statements that deserve quotation. "The penalty of the law," he wrote, "is justly due to its transgressor, but in the midst of deserved wrath, it is God-like to be merciful." He opposed brutal disciplinary methods. "Experience," he said, "has confirmed my conviction that a mild and merciful application of the rules of discipline is sufficient in all cases to reduce the most hardened offenders to obedience." He believed that prisons were established not merely for the punishment of offenders, but also "to reclaim the wandering and save the lost." "Nothing," he declared, "will arouse the virtuous aspirations of a fallen man so powerfully as the conviction that it still lies in his power to regain the rights he has forfeited, and that he yet can be respected by society as a fellow-man." [24] His administration of the prison seems to have rated high in respect to honesty, efficiency, and economy, and there was no doubt of his renomination as the political campaign of 1861 drew near.[25]

III

The year 1861 marked the conclusion of Heg's services as prison commissioner, however, as in fact it marked the interruption of normal careers in every part of the country. President Lincoln's call for volunteers for the task of preserving the Union met with a stirring response through all the North, among immigrants as well as among native-born, and regiment after regiment was recruited, organized, trained, and sent off to the front. Men of Scandinavian

[24] State Prison Commissioner, *Annual Report*, 1860, p. 1, 2, 7.
[25] Considerable information about Heg's administration, with anecdotes and stories illustrating his methods, is in "En Tur til Wisconsins Statsfængsel," in *Emigranten*, August 3 and 9, 1861. See also Langeland, in Johnson, *Det Skandinaviske Regiments Historie*, 105–106.

blood joined the colors with enthusiasm in Wisconsin, Minnesota, Iowa, Illinois, and other states in which they had but recently settled. Scandinavian names are to be found in the rosters of many regiments that were raised in the Northwest.

As the process of recruiting got under way, however, it became evident that many of the immigrant citizens of the West wanted to serve, if possible, in regiments made up of their countrymen and commanded by officers of their own blood, and this desire evoked a sympathetic response from high officials. When, for example, a call came to Wisconsin on August 20, 1861, for five additional regiments, Governor Randall made an official request that one of these regiments be composed of Germans.[1] The Ninth Wisconsin was organized as a German immigrant regiment, and the Eleventh Wisconsin was preponderantly Irish. A movement seems to have been started in the first months of the war to raise a Norwegian regiment in Wisconsin. Governor Randall's special invitation to the Germans probably influenced J. A. Johnson, a Norwegian of Madison, to open a roll on August 31 for the recruiting of a Scandinavian company, calling for at least eighty-three men; and two weeks later *Emigranten* announced that this call had met with an eager response.[2] Meanwhile, both Johnson and Heg had taken under consideration the possibility of organizing a Norwegian, or Scandinavian, regiment. Heg had informed Johnson of his intention to go to war and had in fact already handed his resignation as prison commissioner to the governor, who refused to accept it. From the beginning, Heg had been warmly interested in the cause. As early as April 26 his name headed a list of Waupun subscribers for the benefit of families of volunteers.[3] On May 7 he offered the convict

---

[1] *Emigranten*, August 26, 1861.
[2] *Emigranten*, September 2, 16, 1861.
[3] William DeLoss Love, *Wisconsin in the War of the Rebellion*, 131 (Chicago, 1866), with a reference to the *Waupun Times* of April 26, 1861.

labor at Waupun to be utilized in the making of uniforms. "We are ready to take hold at any time," he wrote.[4] As plans for the proposed Scandinavian regiment took form, it was decided to have Heg's name presented for renomination in the state Republican convention in the belief that such action would add to his prestige and stimulate recruiting.[5]

On September 25, 1861, a meeting of leading Scandinavians was held at the state capitol in Madison, and at this gathering it was formally decided to raise a regiment. A letter was dispatched to Governor Randall informing him of this decision and petitioning for the appointment of Heg as colonel. This document was signed by J. A. Johnson, C. F. Solberg, B. W. Suckow, S. Samuelson, K. J. Fleischer, and Chr. Winge.[6] "The undersigned," they wrote, "as a Committee, appointed by a meeting of Scandinavians from different parts of the State, assembled here at Madison today — have been assigned the duty of informing Your Excellency that said meeting has passed a resolution to raise a Scandinavian Brigade for the war now pending in this our adopted Country; And that we recommend the following Gentlemen to be appointed as follows: Hon. Hans C. Heg as Colonel; K. K. Jones as Lieut. Col." They closed the letter by expressing their belief that "a movement like this for the defence of our Country and our Flag will meet the approbation and support of the Government."

The governor was in full sympathy with the project, and on October 1, 1861, a commission as colonel was issued to Heg.[7] He was renominated for the office of prison commissioner with acclaim.[8] In declining the honor, he called for

[4] H. C. Heg to W. H. Watson, May 7, 1861. Ms. in Civil War papers from governor's office, in the possession of the State Historical Society of Wisconsin.
[5] Johnson, *Det Skandinaviske Regiments Historie*, 15 ff.
[6] The letter, dated September 5, 1861, is in the Civil War Mss. from the governor's office, in the possession of the State Historical Society of Wisconsin.
[7] *Emigranten*, October 7, 1861.
[8] The Madison *Wisconsin State Journal*, Janesville *Daily Gazette*, Milwaukee *Free Democrat*, and other newspapers are quoted on Heg and his renomination, in *Emigranten*, October 7, 1861.

the selection of a "courageous, liberal, and humane man" in his place.[9] He then devoted himself energetically to securing a vigorous response to the call for volunteers. The selection of Heg as Colonel was greeted with approval in both the English and the Norwegian newspapers of Wisconsin. A typical Norwegian-American editorial, taken from *Emigranten*, reads: "Young, powerful, and attractive, honorable, unimpeachably honest, to a high degree considerate of the welfare of his subordinates, with a splendid fund of practical, sound sense, and with the increased knowledge of men and things which his work as a state official has given him, he is the best man of all the Norwegians in America whom we know to lead such an undertaking. Our countrymen can gather about him as their chief with unqualified trust."[10]

Recruiting officers were chosen and promptly began their work in the Norwegian settlements. In the Norwegian as well as in the English newspapers effective aid was given the campaign. *Emigranten*, in particular, devoted much space to the proposed regiment and to the cause of the North. Late in September there was published in this Madison newspaper an appeal by ten leading Scandinavians to the people of their blood in the United States to help make the organization of the regiment a success.[11] Southern victories showed plainly that only by a united and powerful effort could the Union be saved; the proposed regiment gave the Scandinavians of the West a unique opportunity to enter the army; and finally, it was pointed out, other racial elements in the population were taking similar steps, and the Scandinavians could not permit themselves to be outmatched by the Germans and the Irish. In supporting this appeal editorially, *Emigranten* called for the organization of "at least one regiment."[12] It should be added that *Emigranten* made

[9] *Emigranten*, October 14, 1861.
[10] *Emigranten*, October 7, 1861.
[11] *Emigranten*, September 30, 1861. The call was addressed particularly to able-bodied Scandinavians. It was signed by H. C. Heg, Adolph Sorenson. Knud Langeland, J. A. Johnson, K. J. Fleischer, Chr. Winge, S. Samuelson, Ole Torgersen, C. F. Solberg, and Chr. Colding.
[12] *Emigranten*, September 30, 1861.

Extrablad af "Emigranten" No. 40 og 41.

Opraab.

Landsmænd!

Vort adopterede Lands Regjering er i Fare. Hvad vi som Frimænd ogsaa i vort gamle Fædreland har lært at elske — vor Frihed — vor Regjering — vor Selvstændighed—trues med Tilintetgjørelse.

Bør det os ikke som brave og dygtige Borgere at give en Haandsrækning til at forsvare vort nye Fædrelands Ret og vore Familiers Hjem? Landsmænd — det hører Eder til at svare!

Guvernøren af Wisconsin har bemyndiget Oprettelsen af et skandinavisk Regiment til de Forenede Staters Tjeneste. Jeg har erholdt Ansættelse som dets Oberst. Jeg har besluttet at forberede mig til at antage den mig saaledes overdragne Post. Vi tiltrænge et Tusind Mand — Norske, Svenske og Danske, at organiseres under Navnet den "Første Skandinaviske Brigade."

Fremad da, Landsmænd — lader os vise, at ogsaa vi elske vort nye Fædreland — at ogsaa vi ere rede til at forsvare vor Regjering, vor Frihed og vort Lands Enhed.

Regimentets Officerer ville blive Mænd, som tale de skandinaviske Sprog. Saaledes gives ogsaa den Skandinav Anledning til at indgaae i Tjenesten, som endnu ikke taler det Engelske.

Guvernøren af Wisconsin har tilsikret os al mulig Hjælp og vil gjøre Alt for at udruste os saa godt som noget af de hidtil afreiste Regimenter. Regimentet ønskes fuldt snarest muligt. Leirpladsen vil blive Madison.

Madison, 6te October 1861.

Hans C. Heg.
Oberst.

Den skandinaviske Brigade. "Chicago Journal" fortæller: "Kaptain Andrew Torkildsen her af Byen er især med at oprette et Kompagni til den skandinaviske Brigade, som ligger i Leir ved Madison, Wis. Kompagniet vil blive kaldet St. Olafs Rifles. Rekruteringskontoret er No. 44 North Wells Street. Kapt. Torkildsen er kjendt af Mange her i Byen, hvor han en Tid har været Politiofficiant, og vil neppe have stor Vanskelighed ved at faae sit Kompagni istand. Brigaden, hvortil det skal høre, skal bestaae hovedsagelig af Norske, Danske og Svenske. Hr. K. K. Jones, der længe har boet i Chicago og Manitowoc, er af Guvernør Randall udnævnt til dens Oberstløitnant."

Vi haabe Regimentet vil komme til at bestaae ikke blot "hovedsagelig," men udelukkende af Norske, Svenske og Danske. Halvandet hundrede Tusinde Norske og hele den svenske og danske Befolkning burde ikke tiltrænge Nogens Hjælp til at stille et Regiment i Marken.

Skandinaviske Frivillige. La Crossebladet "Republican" for 28 Sptb. siger: "H. N. Soelberg, Esq., er især med at oprette et Kompagni af Skandinaver, og det seer ud til, Kompagniet snart vil komme istand. De, som ønske at slutte sig dertil, bør melde sig til Hr. Soelberg. De Norske ere rolige og ordentlige og vil gjøre gode Soldater. Bring istand et Regiment af dem, de ere rede til at gaae og vente kun paa en Chance."

Soelbergs Kompagni vil komme til at høre til det skandinaviske Regiment.

Oberst Heg. Guvernøren af Wisconsin har udnævnt Hon. Hans C. Heg til Oberst og Kommandør for første skandinaviske Regiment. Heg har taget mod Udnævnelsen. Den nye Oberst har et godt Navn blandt de Norske overalt i Landet. I to Aar har han til almindelig Tilfredshed bestyret den vanskelige, halvt militære Post som Statsfængsels-Kommissær for Wisconsin, og da Statskonventionerne vare forsamlede forrige Uge, opstillede baade den republikanske og Unionskonventionen ham enstemmigen til Gjenvalg. Han kunde være vis paa uden nogen Anstrengelse fra sin egen Side at blive gjenvalgt med en umaadelig Majoritet; men Bevidstheden om, at alle andre Hensyn, som nu kunne tilsidesættes, bør sættes tilside for Unionens Sag, bragte ham til at opgive det sikkre og indbringende Embede for Krigstjeuesten. Vi kan ikke noksom ønske det vordende Regiment til lykke med dets Oberst. Ung, kraftig og kjæk, ærekjær og urokkelig redelig, i høi Grad omhyggelig for sine Underordnedes Vel, med en fortræffelig praktisk sund Sands og med den forøgede Kjendskab til Mænd og Ting, som hans Virksomhed som Statsembedsmænd har givet ham, vil han være den Bedste til at staae i Spidsen for et saadant Foretagende af alle de Norske, vi kjende i Amerika. Vore Landsmænd kunne samle sig om ham som deres Chef med ubetinget Tillid. De vil hverken komme til at beklage sig over deres Behandling som Soldater eller behøve at frygte for, at det norske Navns Ære ikke skal være i gode Hænder.

Fremmede Officerer i de Forenede Staters Tjeneste. Et stort Antal udmærkede europæiske Officerer ere i Løbet af Høsten komne over til Amerika og have tilbudt Præsidenten deres Tjeneste. Blandt de mere fremragende af dem nævnes den sidste franske Konges Sønnesønner Greven af Paris og Hertugen af Chartres, som med Kaptains Rang ere blevne ansatte som Adjudanter ved McClellans Stab. De have begge erholdt en fuldstændig militær Uddannelse og skildres som særdeles dygtige Officerer. De gjorde den Betingelse ved sin Ansættelse, at de ei maatte opføres paa Lønningsrullerne. John Fitzroy de Courcy, Major i den engelske Armee, er bleven ansat ved McClellans Stab med Oberstløitnants Rang. Major de Courcy kommanderede et tyrkisk Regiment under Krigen paa Krim. Major Valentine Bausenwein, Adjudant hos Garibaldi under Krigen i Italien, er bleven udnævnt til Major ved det 58de Ohioregiment. Han havde særdeles smigrende Anbefalinger fra Garibaldi at fremvise. Baron Ernest von Vegesack, Kaptain i den danske Armee, er bleven ansat med Kaptains Rang, men er ei endnu bleven anviist nogen Tjeneste. Løitnant Oscar Hultman er bleven udnævnt til Kaptain og anviist Tjeneste ved General Blenkers Stab. Han har tjent under de franske Krige i Algier, hvor han vandt Æreslegionskorset. Oscar Brabender er ogsaa bleven ansat ved Gen. Blenkers Stab. Han har tjent med Udmærkelse i den kongelige Garde i Preussen.

Endvidere har Præsidenten udnævnt forhenværende Admiral i den merikanske Marine, Zerman, til Kaptain i den amerikanske Marine. Kaptain Zerman er sat under General Fremonts Befaling og menes at ville faae en Kommando paa Missisippi-Flotillen. Han har forhen tjent ogsaa i den tyrkiske Marine.

(Et Brev.)

Frivillige det eneste rette Slags Soldater i denne Krig.

Kjære Fætter Paul. Du skal have saa mange Tak for Brevet Dit, men angaaende den Tingen, Du fornemmelig skriver om, nemlig om ikke Regjeringen burde holde Session Landet rundt og udskrive Soldater, da troer jeg rigtig, Du tager feil; og for det Tilfælde, at der skulde være Andre af din Mening, saa vil jeg svare Dig gjennem "Emigr." for at slaae saamange Fluer som muligt med eet Smæk.

Du siger, min kjære Paul, at dette frivillige Stel ikke bringer Folk fort nok i Krigen, og det glæder mig rigtig paa Dine Vegne, at Du synes saa, for det viser Din Iver for en stor og god Sag; men forresten saa synes jeg dog, Folket har Hjertet paa rette Sted. Regjeringen har paa en fer Maaneder reist en Armee paa en halvtrediehundrede Tusinde Mand, uden at have tvunget en eneste Mand af dem til at gaae. I hvilket andet Land har Du seet det gjort? Og mon ikke det er omtrent saa fort, som Regjeringen har været god for at antage dem? At organisere og indrette en Armee koster Tid, Penge og Arbeide og kan ikke gjøres Alt paa engang. Seer Du, det er ikke her som i Europa, hvor en heel Deel af Landets Marv er bleven udsuget i Fredstid til at holde store Armeer parat bestandig. Vi have her levet under heldigere Omstændigheder, fritagne saavel paa Grund af Landets Beliggenhed som ogsaa paa Grund af vor Regjeringsform for de evindelige Krige, der plage den gamle Verdens Nationer og gjøre slige Ting fornødne. Vor Regjering har hverken behøvet at støtte sig til eller hvile paa Bajonetter, saaledes som de europæiske. For Øieblikket maa den vistnok gjøre det; men det er kun et forbigaaende Tilfælde, som aldrig har hendt før og maaskee aldrig vil indtræffe igjen, naar vi rigtig faaer kvalt Oprøret. Og selv i nærværende Tilfælde vilde det været et Spørgsmaal, om en stor fast Krigsmagt, fix og færdig forud, vilde været gavnlig. Havde Krigsmagten været Unionen tro, da vilde det været all right; men naar det betænkes, hvormeget Buchanans Regjering benyttede den lille Krigsstyrke, vi havde, til at styrke Oprøret, saa maa det befrygtes, at havde vi havt en stor Krigsstyrke, da vilde Oprørerne været stærkt nok strax til at omstyrte Unionen.

Men saa siger Du ogsaa, at hvis Folk kommanderedes til Krigstjeneste ved Session, da vilde Mange gaae, der ere ligegyldige eller hvis Samvittighed nu lader dem i Tvivl om, hvad de skal gjøre. Det er udentvivl sandt, kjære Paul, men efter min Mening maa de fleste slige Folk have en meget daarlig Samvittighed og er ikke værd at have med. Den Mand, som er ligegyldig i disse Tider, han er sandelig en Usling, der skulde sendes til Patagonien eller Kamschatka jo før jo heller, og den Mand, der er tjenestedygtig og kunde afsee Tid og Leilighed til at gaae i Krigen, men lader være, fordi han ikke veed, hvor langt han bør gaae for sit Land, han har sandelig saa liden Kjærlighed til Fædrelandet og saa lidet Begreb om sine sønlige Pligter mod det, at han ikke er værd at være Borger. Det er derfor efter min Mening kun liden Grund til at foretrække Udskrivning for frivillige, især under nærværende Omstændigheder.

Jeg holder paa Frivillige, og Hovedgrunden derfor, jeg kan gjerne sige Dig den reentud, er at Regjeringen holder paa Frivillige. Jeg har stor Tillid til vor nuværende Præsidents Klogskab og Fædrelandssind, og jeg maatte have meget klare Grunde for min Menings Rigtighed, naar jeg ikke skulde bøie min Mening for hans i Noget, som angaaer Regjeringens Politik og Forholdsregler i denne Krig. Jeg seer i Bladene, at da Guvernøren af Iowa syntes, det gik lidt sløvt med Frivillige, saa telegraferede han til Washington, med Spørgsmaal om han skulde begynde at udskrive Soldater; men Regjeringen svarede ham:

"Nei. Vi maa stole paa Folkets Fædrelandssind."

Du seer deraf, at Regjeringen har besluttet at stole paa Frivillige, og hvilket Nonsens er det da ikke af Dig, der vil efter bedste Evne understøtte Regjeringen, at præke om det Modsatte. Du kan troe, den Sag er bleven nøie overveiet i Washington, og at Regjeringen har kloge og fædrelandssindede Grunde for sin Beslutning. Vort Fædreland Unionens Frelse afhænger nu, næst Gud, af de Frivillige, og jeg siger Dig, de vil frelse den, der vil ikke være ligegyldige eller tvivlende Døgenifte nok til at forhindre det.

Jeg gjentager, at min Hovedgrund til at ansee Frivillige for den eneste rette Slags Soldater i denne Krig er, at det er Præsidentens Mening. Men der er forresten Grunde, min kjære Ven, som Enhver selv let kan tænke sig, skjøndt det maaskee ikke er saa let for en simpel Mand at udvikle dem klart. Dog maa her kommer Regjeringens Svar til Guvernøren af Iowa mig tilhjælp: Vi maa alene bruge Frivillige, thi "vi maa stole paa Folkets Fædrelandssind", hedder det. Hvad vil nu det sige? Intet mindre end dette, at under nærværende Omstændigheder er det at stole paa Frivillige det Samme som at stole paa Folkets Fædrelandssind, — at ligesaa fornødent som Fædrelandssind er til at frelse et af Borgerkrig splittet Land, ligesaa fornødne ere nu frivillige Krigere til at frelse Unionen. Det kan synes noget stærkt, min kjære Ven, men forsaavidt jeg for Nærværende kan overskue vore Forholde, synes det mig aligevel klart, og jeg skal sige Dig hvorfor.

Vor Regjering har vel Udskrivningsretten, enhver amerikansk Stemmeberettiget mellem 18 og 45 Aars Alder er, som Du veed, værnepligtig; men, saavidt mig er bekjendt, er den aldrig bleven brugt. Den lille faste Armee, der har været nødvendig til at forsvare de vestlige Grændser mod Indianerne, har været samlet ved frivillig Hverving, og hele Militstjenesten har været frivillig. Den amerikanske Borger er derfor ikke, saaledes som den Værnepligtige i Europa, voret op med Bevidstheden om, at han i en vis Alder skal indkaldes til en vis Tids tvungen Krigstjeneste. Blandt et Folk med saa udstrakt borgerlig Frihed og slig Vane til at opponere som det amerikanske, kunde Udskrivning derfor til ingen Tid pludselig indføres uden Klager, Misfornøielse og Modstand fra mange Hold. Og

An Extra Number of *Emigranten*, Issued to Promote Recruiting for the Fifteenth Wisconsin

up a special number composed of articles dealing with the Fifteenth Wisconsin and the Civil War in general and circulated it widely as an aid to recruiting.[13]

Throughout the autumn of 1861, several calls were written by Colonel Heg and spread broadcast. It is interesting to note that he appealed to the Scandinavians, not merely to the Norwegians. He asked for a thousand men — Norwegians, Swedes, and Danes. "The officers of the regiment," he explained, "will be men who speak the Scandinavian languages. Thus an opportunity to enter the service is afforded those Scandinavians who do not yet speak English." "The government of our adopted country is in danger," he wrote.[14] "That which we learned to love as freemen in our old Fatherland — our freedom — our government — our independence — is threatened with destruction. Is it not our duty as brave and intelligent citizens to extend our hands in defense of the cause of our country and of our own homes?" A few weeks later he declared that for young men there never had been "a better opportunity to fight for a noble cause, to win an honored name and proud memories for the future, and an experience that could not be had elsewhere." He asked, "Shall we Scandinavians sit still and watch our American, German, and English-born fellow citizens fight for us without going to their aid?" He closed his appeal with these words: "Come, then, young Norsemen, and take part in defending our country's cause, and thus fulfill a pressing duty which everyone who is able to do so owes to the land in which he lives. Let us band together and deliver untarnished to posterity the old honorable name of Norsemen."[15]

It is of interest to recall that almost simultaneously Hans Mattson addressed an appeal to the Scandinavians of Minnesota "to rise with sword in hand, and fight for our adopted country and for liberty." The call phrased by the Min-

[13] The special number was made up from the issues of October 7 and 14.
[14] *Emigranten*, October 7, 1861.
[15] *Emigranten*, November 18, 1861. Six hundred men had already volunteered for service in the regiment at the time Heg published this appeal.

nesota Swede resembled that of the Wisconsin Norwegian.
"The land which we, as strangers, have made our home,"
he wrote, "has received us with friendship and hospitality.
We enjoy equal privileges with the native born. The path
to honor and fortune is alike open to us and them. The law
protects and befriends us all alike. . . . Let us prove ourselves worthy of that land, and of those heroes from whom
we descend." [16]

The recruiting and organization of the Fifteenth Wisconsin went forward rapidly under the supervision of Colonel
Heg. The regiment was assembled at Camp Randall, Madison, in December, 1861; and by the following February its
numbers had reached the necessary minimum.[17] The prospective soldiers had their first taste of military life at Camp
Randall, their experiences being typical of those of all the
thousands of Wisconsin soldiers who were there prepared
for service in the South. In February, 1862, there were
about three thousand men at the camp, two other regiments
being also in process of organization. Much time was devoted to drill, in the elements of which the men of the
Fifteenth were reported to be well grounded before their
departure from Madison.[18] Gradually the regiment was
built up to a strength of about nine hundred, and its officers
awaited orders to start for the South.

Though an attempt had been made to recruit the regiment as a Scandinavian unit, it was preponderantly Norwegian, with only a sprinkling of Swedes, Danes, Germans, and
native-born Americans. Not a few of the soldiers of the

[16] Mattson's appeal appeared in *Hemlandet* of Chicago and.is translated in
his *Reminiscences : The Story of an Emigrant*, 60 (St. Paul, 1891). *Emigranten*
for September 16, 1861, contains an advertisement calling attention to the organization of one or possibly two companies in Goodhue County, Minnesota,
for the Third Minnesota, the regiment of which Mattson later became colonel.

[17] *Emigranten*, December 23, 1861. and January 20, February 3 and 10, 1862;
Bersven Nelson, "Optegnelser fra Borgerkrigen," in Waldemar Ager, *Oberst
Heg og hans Gutter*, 16–17 (Eau Claire, Wisconsin, 1916). The Nelson narrative (p. 15–61) covers the entire period of the service of the Fifteenth Wisconsin and is a valuable source of information.

[18] *Emigranten*, February 17 and 24, 1862; Nelson, in Ager, *Oberst Heg og
hans Gutter*, 16.

Fifteenth were immigrants who only a few weeks earlier had trod on American soil for the first time. Bersven Nelson, for example, reached La Crosse from Norway on July 16, 1861; less than four months later he was a soldier of the Fifteenth Wisconsin.[19] Most of the recruits, however, came from the old Norwegian immigrant communities. Nearly all joined before the Fifteenth was ordered south, though some entered later.[20] Iowa, Minnesota, and Illinois, in addition to Wisconsin, were well represented. Heg himself had visited certain Norwegian settlements in all four of these states during the recruiting campaign. In October, 1861, for example, he visited successively Chicago; Cambridge and Pleasant Springs, Wisconsin; Decorah, Iowa; and Fillmore and Houston counties, Minnesota. Captain Grinager of Company K was from Freeborn County, Minnesota, and the majority of his company were from Minnesota and Iowa. In Company A there were many soldiers from Chicago and other parts of Illinois. It is evident, therefore, that the regiment was more than a Wisconsin regiment, that it was in fact a regiment of the Northwest.[21] Typical of the names of Colonel Heg's soldiers were Olsen, Hansen, Peterson, Johnson, Thompson, and Ericksen. There were five Ole Olsens in Company F; Company E boasted three Ole Ericksens; and Company B had three Ole Andersons. In the regiment as a whole there were no less than 128 men whose first name was Ole.[22] The names chosen for the regimental companies were unique and interesting. Among them were the St. Olaf Rifles, the Wergeland Guards, Odin's Rifles, the Norway Bear Hunters, the Scandinavian Mountaineers, Heg's Rifles, the Rock River Rangers, and Clausen's Guards.[23]

[19] Nelson, in Ager, *Oberst Heg og hans Gutter*, 15–16.
[20] See *Roster of Wisconsin Volunteers, War of the Rebellion, 1861–65*, 1:804–829 (Madison, 1886). A. L. Lien, "Liste over nordmænd blandt Wisconsin tropper i borgerkrigen: IV, 15 Regiment Wis. Vol. Inf.," in *Samband*, no. 72, p. 339–358 (April, 1914) is unreliable.
[21] See *Emigranten*, October 14 and 21, 1861.
[22] *Roster of Wisconsin Volunteers*, 1:804–829.
[23] On C. L. Clausen, for whom Clausen's Guards were named, see *post*, p. 69, n. 21.

When the regiment left for St. Louis on March 2, 1862, the Madison station was thronged with hundreds of friends and relatives assembled to bid goodbye to the soldiers.[24] Upon the arrival of the Fifteenth Wisconsin at Chicago, it was met by the members of Nora Lodge, a Norwegian society, who entertained the soldiers and presented them with a flag "having, on the one side the American colors, and, on the reverse the American and Norwegian arms united, the Norwegian being the picture of a lion with an axe, on a red field." The flag bore the inscription "For Gud og Vort Land" (For God and Our Country).[25]

After a very brief stop in Chicago the regiment departed for St. Louis. It soon became a fighting unit in the army of the West. During the next three years the Fifteenth Wisconsin took part in the operations of the Union forces in Missouri, Kentucky, Mississippi, Tennessee, Alabama, and Georgia.[26] Near the end of the war, when its surviving members were mustered out of service, they were veterans of more than a score of severe engagements and innumerable skirmishes. Among the more important landmarks in the regiment's history are Island No. 10, Perryville, Murfreesboro, Chickamauga, Chattanooga (Missionary Ridge), Re-

[24] A long account of the departure of the regiment for the South, by C. F. Solberg, the editor of *Emigranten*, is in that paper for March 17, 1862. Solberg accompanied the regiment as a correspondent of his own newspaper. See also Nelson, in Ager, *Oberst Heg og hans Gutter*, 17.

[25] P. G. Dietrichson, "The Fifteenth Wisconsin, or Scandinavian Regiment," in O. N. Nelson, ed., *History of the Scandinavians in the United States*, part 1, p. 155 (2d edition, Minneapolis, 1904). *Cf. Emigranten*, March 17, 1862. The flag in question is now preserved in the Norwegian-American Historical Museum at Decorah, Iowa.

[26] Much has been written in the Norwegian language about the Fifteenth Wisconsin. The first history was J. A. Johnson, *Det Skandinaviske Regiments Historie* (1869), which incorporates an excellent account of Heg by his friend Knud Langeland. O. A. Buslett, *Det Femtende Regiment Wisconsin Frivillige* (Decorah, Iowa, 1895, 696 p.), is an entertaining and well-written narrative, but is hardly to be relied upon for details. P. G. Dietrichson, *En Kortfattet Skildring af det femtende Wisconsins Regiments Historie og Virksomhed under Borgerkrigen* (Chicago, 1884, 32 p.), is a sketch which has also appeared in English (see preceding n.). Waldemar Ager, *Oberst Heg og hans Gutter*, is valuable for the narrative of Bersven Nelson, the diary of Morten J. Nordre, and approximately one hundred Civil War letters written by soldiers of the Fifteenth Wisconsin. There are also chapters by Mr. Ager on some of the battles in which

saca, New Hope Church, and Kenesaw Mountain. By the end of its service in the Civil War the Fifteenth Wisconsin had lost by death nearly a third of its original enrollment.[27]

IV

The history of the Fifteenth Wisconsin and the biography of Colonel Heg are merged from that spring day when the train carrying the immigrant soldiers steamed out of the Wisconsin capital until the battle of Chickamauga, a year and a half later. With the exception of a few brief leaves of absence, Heg was constantly with his regiment and brigade during that time — in camp, on the march, and in battle. His own letters tell informally the story of commander and soldiers, of campaigns and battles, of field and camp; they convey the atmosphere of soldiering in Civil War days; and there is little need to anticipate the tale they unfold. The very fact, however, that they are the unreserved record of his thoughts and emotions, poured out in the intimacy of family letters, filled with pictures swiftly sketched amid the swirl of events, crowded with personal detail, and flavored with a deep family affection, makes it necessary to read them in their larger setting. The man must be considered in the light not only of his own letters but also of other historical records.

What manner of man was this immigrant son of the frontier who took up the sword? Colonel Heg was a young man. He was, in fact, less than thirty-four when, at the end, he led his brigade into the smoke of Chickamauga. He was

the regiment participated and on other aspects of its history. Mr. Ager has published many articles on the Fifteenth, among which may be noted "The Fifteenth Wisconsin," in *American-Scandinavian Review*, 3:325–333 (November–December, 1915). He has also used the story of the regiment as a partial background for his novel *Gamlelandets Sønner* (Oslo, 1926). Selections from letters written by Dr. S. O. Himoe, the surgeon of the Fifteenth, are in Luther M. Kuhns, "An Army Surgeon's Letters to His Wife," in Mississippi Valley Historical Association, *Proceedings*, 1913–14, p. 306–320.

[27] Ager, in *Nordmands-Forbundet*, 9:162–169. According to Mr. Ager, the percentage of losses sustained by the Fifteenth Wisconsin was 33.04. See also Charles E. Estabrook, *Wisconsin Losses in the Civil War*, 74–79 (Madison, 1915).

tall and straight, heavily bearded, strong, and vigorous. His quiet demeanor, taciturn manner, and sternness as a discipli- narian have concealed from public view the boyish ardor with which he went to war; the desire for glory, for himself and for his regiment, that burned deep within him; and his joy in the danger and excitement and praise that fell to his lot as leader of regiment and brigade.

These qualities, accompanied by a sturdy faith in himself and by a very marked tendency to boast, are revealed in his letters.   There was a strain of Peer Gynt in the man which the records have not disclosed hitherto.   Reading between his lines, one can readily understand that he frequently wrote as he did in order to encourage and strengthen his wife, who had a fatalistic conviction that the war would make her a widow.[1] He tried to soothe her anxiety by picturing himself as a hero marching down the lane of glory. Yet something more than this rings out in his assertions — some quality compounded of the individualism of a self-made leader, of a frontiersman's arrogance, of youth facing ad- venture but freighted with responsibility, and of psycho- logical elements deeply rooted in his past.   He would not give up the war and the opportunity it brought him for winning distinction "even for the greatest pleasure in the world."[2] "I never fail in courage," he assures Gunild. "You will not hear that I have ever played the coward."[3] "If Bullets do not kill me," he writes, "I am pretty sure I can stand it as well as anybody, and a good deal better than the most of those who are in the Army."[4]   Again and again he defers request for leave of absence, explaining that "the boys" would be demoralized if he were not present.   "Ev- erybody says this Regiment would not be worth anything under any body els[e]."[5]   The commanding general is "very

[1] See Heg's letter of September 5, 1862.
[2] April, 1863.
[3] December 28, 1862.
[4] August 18, 1862.
[5] April 1, 1862.

anxious I should not go away for a few days, and you must make up your mind to be disappointed again."[6]   That Heg had genuine resources of courage is evident, not indeed from the ebullience of his claims, but from the unmistakable calm fortitude that underlies his entire narrative.   His descriptions of battles are vivid and unerring in selection of detail, but he seems to be instinctively casual about his own discomforts, his own narrow escapes. The testimony of comrades and fellow officers leaves no doubt of the tough strength of his fibre.

He believed in his own competence.   "I have a good deal to do in organizing my new command," he explains to Gunild.   "The fact is I have been put in command of this Brigade for the purpose of making it more efficient — and I am going to try my best to do it."[7]   "I have done more for the government," he exclaims in one letter, "than any man that has gone from Wisconsin."[8]   And his pride in the Fifteenth Wisconsin knew no bounds.   "The 15th imortalised itself yesterday," he wrote after a battle.[9]   "We have won a reputation now, that will be hard to beat."[10]   "It is admitted that our exploit was the best during the fight."[11] As the regiment met test after test, however, and as Heg and his soldiers grew more experienced in the rigors of war, the colonel himself became more sober in his reports of events.

In all his pride in the Fifteenth and confidence in himself, the young crusader never forgot the Wisconsin home at Waterford, where his wife and children awaited his messages. The prevailing note was his desire to reassure Gunild about his safety, to undermine her instinctive apprehension of disaster.   "I am all right myself and I hope you will not trouble

[6] May 10, 1862.
[7] May 1, 1863.
[8] August 5, 1862.
[9] December 27, 1862.
[10] December 28, 1862.
[11] The phrase occurs in a letter of October 15, 1862, written after the battle of Perryville.

yourself about me too much." [12]   He anticipates the ending
of "this misserable war," and the coming of a time when
"we shall yet have a chance to enjoy life together." "If
you should not get another letter for a week, you must not
feel uneasy." [13] "Do not fret too much for me — take good
care of yourself and trust me to my luck." [14] "I hope you
will be [brav]e enough to keep up good courage." [15] He compliments her on the cheerful tone of a recent letter, explains
that he cannot "come home honorably by resigning," and
adds, "The greatest consolation a man has, is to know that
every thing is right at home." [16] It "is not so hard for me,"
he writes as he tells her of the busy round of his life as an
officer, "as it is must be for you, who are at home alone." [17]
But rewards will crown patience, and he tells her that when
the ordeal has passed he will take her on a trip to Norway.[18]

In the press of great affairs, he remembers his children and
their needs. "Tell Hilda to go down to the Store and buy
her a new pair of shoes — and it will make her Toe well
again." [19] "You must learn to ride horseback on the mare,"
he tells Edmund, "and I will let you keep her for your
pony." [20] Writing from Island No. 10 he says, "When I
come home I want to see Edmund ride on his new saddle,
and his pony." [21] In the South he secures a wonderful new
pony and sends it home to the boy.[22] He is interested in
Hilda's progress with the piano and wants to know if her
"little fingers" have "learned to play on it yet? When I
come back next time I expect to have you play *Old John
Brown* for me." [23] He writes that he would like "especially

[12] June 24, 1862.
[13] July 3, 1862.
[14] August 31, 1862.
[15] September 2, 1862.
[16] August 25, 1862.
[17] April 1, 1862.
[18] August 5, 1862.
[19] July 9, 1862.
[20] March 23, 1862.
[21] May 5, 1862.
[22] September 26, 1862.
[23] June 14, 1862.

to see that little rat *Elmer* that you write so much about."
And near the end of his soldiering, in the summer of 1863,
he pauses to say, "I have more anxiety about having Edmund & Hilda receive a good education than anything
els[e]."[24]

Not the least interesting aspect of Colonel Heg's letters
is the picture that they build up, through the accumulation
of detail, of a wife and family at home in war time. The
colonel pauses in his military occupation to give counsel to
Gunild about the crops. "I would advise you," he writes,
"to have your part of the wheat brought down to Palmer
and Moes Mill — and put in there and draw it out in Flour
as you need it. The Oats you must not thresh, but feed it
to the sheep — in the Bundle. Potatoes and such things you
know what to do with."[25]

Heg made his soldiers feel that he trusted their courage
and competence, and he took inordinate pride in their ex-
ploits.[26] He believed that strict discipline and an unweary-
ing vigilance in attending to the details of routine were
essentials in drilling his men for the ordeals that they faced,
and when he took command of a brigade he did his best to
build up its morale. In unofficial hours he could prove a
friendly and jovial companion. Veterans of his regiment
liked to recall, in later years, his ability to drive away discouragement and to stimulate self-confidence. He himself
was well aware of his talent. "Many of the boys in the
Regiment, especially the officers," he wrote casually in one
of his letters, "feel homesick and dull — but, I generally
have to cheer them up. When any of them gets the blues
they generally come to me and get cured."[27]

Heg's belief in the importance of a cheerful morale, as well
as his broader views of the war, found expression in a public
letter that he wrote on February 15, 1863, near Murfrees-

[24] October 23, 1862; June 29, 1863.
[25] August 5, 1862.
[26] Ager, *Oberst Heg og hans Gutter*, 249
[27] September 5, 1862.

boro.[28] This was an acknowledgment of gifts for sick and
wounded soldiers received from a soldiers' aid society in
Norway and Raymond townships, Wisconsin. His men, he
wrote, had risked their health and lives for a cause vital to
all. Appreciation at home was both an encouragement and
an incentive to the soldiers. "Our army is bound to crush
this terrible rebellion, if the people of the North will only
stand by the army, and by all their power encourage the soldiers." There "is nothing equal to encouragement from
home. . . . If a mother has a son, or a wife a husband in
the army, her encouragement to him to do his duty, is worth
more than anything else; her continual complaints, whinings
asking him to 'come home' etc., has more to do with creating discouragement and finally sickness and disease than the
hardships he has to endure." On the central issue Heg's
views were emphatic. "I can see no daylight in any other
direction than a suppression of the rebels by us. It is nothing else than simply this. Death and destruction to us, and
our government, or their subjugation. The latter must be
accomplished, no matter what the sacrifice may be — life,
property, or anything else." If Heg at times reminds one
of Peer Gynt, he had also something of Brand in his spirit.

The opening scenes in the regiment's service are vividly
pictured in Colonel Heg's letters. Forts Henry and Donel-
son had been captured in February and the next northern
objective was Island No. 10 in the Mississippi, near New
Madrid, at the southern Missouri boundary. Some of Heg's
early letters were written aboard the steamboat "Graham."
He met Commodore Foote, whose gunboats were aiding in
the campaign against the Confederate fortress. He describes
the commodore as "a real fine old gentleman, very sociable,
and appearantly a very brisk, smart man."[29] Heg's troops
had their first "smell of powder" on a little expedition to

---

[28] The letter, addressed to "Mr. Adland," is printed in the *Milwaukee Sentinel*, March 30, 1863. It is reprinted post, p. 219.
[29] March 23, 1862.

Union City which resulted in a brush with the enemy and the capture of supplies and " trophies." [30]   On April 9 the colonel reports the Union occupation, two days earlier, of the strategic Island No. 10.   In later letters Heg revels in his responsibilities as " acting brigadier general " on the island.

As the summer and autumn of 1862 wore on, the letters disclose Heg and his command moving from place to place — Island No. 10, Union City, Trenton, Corinth, Iuka, Franklin, Nashville, and Louisville.   The routine of camp and march is described; the regiment — reduced in size, for two companies were left at Island No. 10 — wins standing as a well-drilled unit; and Heg himself acquires valuable experience as an acting brigadier general — at one time commanding, in addition to his own regiment, the Twenty-second Missouri, and the Seventh Wisconsin and Second Illinois batteries. Through this period his mind ranges over a variety of subjects.   The Confederates, he thinks in June, " are perfectly used up here in the valley of the Mississippi." [31]   He welcomes the draft and exclaims, " We will make some of these fellows come out who have laid at home sucking their thumb." [32]   He finds an additional outlet for his energy in planning to raise a second Scandinavian regiment, and he gets permission from Governor Alexander Ramsey — who delivered a Fourth of July address to the brigade — to recruit soldiers in Minnesota.[33]

On July 30 he wrote to Reymert, " One more Scandinavian Regiment ought to be raised in Wisconsin and Minnesota.   This war is a stern reality and will undoubtedly last a long time.   The country will need the services of all good and capable men."   He had asked the government to allow him to go home to aid in raising the regiment.[34]   A few days

[30] April 1, 1862.
[31] June 24, 1862.
[32] July 14, 1862.
[33] July 23, 1862.
[34] Heg to Reymert, Cairo, July 30, 1862. A copy of this letter is in the archives of the Norwegian-American Historical Association.

later, on August 3, he wrote Gunild that he had had a long talk with General Grant about raising another regiment and had found the general sympathetic with the idea.

On September 26, ten miles from Louisville, Heg stops to describe a series of forced marches of more than four hundred miles — one phase of Buell's race against Bragg for Louisville — and assures his wife that, notwithstanding the severity of these marches, he is "as tough and strong as ever." Writing a second letter on the same day he gives an amusing picture of the soldiers of the Fifteenth marching through the streets of Louisville singing Norwegian songs.

The letters of September foreshadow the coming of large-scale fighting; and on October 8, 1862, the regiment took part in the battle of Perryville, the northern troops fighting under Buell, the southern under Bragg.[35] It was a tense moment when the order came to advance. "I called the men together," wrote Heg, "gave them such advise as I thought proper, and spoke to them a few minutes. Everybody was anxious to go ahead, and with much earnestness promised to do their best. Forward then we started." The colonel, coming to the crest of a hill, saw for the first time the spectacle of a great battle in progress. "The smoke and dust filled the air a great deal — and a constant rattle of cannon and muskets, and now and then came a ball whistling by me so near that I would sometimes bow my head down without hardly knowing it myself." The regiment made an effective charge, but, remarkably enough, none of its soldiers were killed. In telling of the engagement Heg pauses to say, "You have no Idea how much the people down here are suffering. It is awfull. Wemen and children, left homeless, and fatherless by thousands." In the same letter: "I hope Edmund has his pony now. I am waiting to hear from him."[36]

Perryville was the prelude to even harder ordeals. "We fought yesterday for 4 hours," wrote Heg on December 27

[35] See Ager, "Slaget ved Perryville," *Oberst Heg og hans Gutter*, 181–184.
[36] October 13–15, 1862.

from the Knob Gap battlefield, near Nolensville, "after having marched during a heavy rain, through mud knee deep some places." In this fight, he writes, "I charged with my Regiment up to a Battery and captured one Brass Cannon, 7 Horses, 3 Prisoners and one Caison — and what is the best of all — not one man wounded." And at Murfreesboro, or Stone River, from December 30 to January 2, the regiment, fighting in the Army of the Cumberland, went through its greatest battle up to that time.[37] Eighty-five members of the Fifteenth were killed or wounded and thirty-four missing. Among those killed was Lieutenant Colonel McKee. Colonel Heg, though he had his horse shot under him and was himself injured by the fall, went unwounded. His regiment was on the federal right, which was turned back by a sharp and furious Southern attack. The troops, after a hard first day's fight, spent the night on the battlefield. "It was a cold frosty night," wrote Heg, "and as I walked along my little regiment, watching the men sitting on the rocks and cold ground shivering from frost, I could not help but think how little the people at home know of the suffering of the soldier." The fight was renewed the next day and continued on January 2. "I have passed through thus far unhurt and Providence will yet bring me safely through the struggle," Heg wrote a few days later, after Bragg had withdrawn. "I have been in the thickest of the fight and led my men whereever they have fought." His letters of January 4 and 6, in which he tells of this battle, are among the most memorable in the entire collection. "While every field officer under my command did his duty faithfully," wrote the commander of the brigade, "Colonels Alexander and Heg, in my opinion, proved themselves the bravest of the brave."[38] It may be added that in this battle Heg "lost a splendid Horse &

[37] Ager. *Oberst Heg og hans Gutter.* 185–199.
[38] On this battle, see *War of the Rebellion, Official Records of the Union and Confederate Armies,* series 1, vol. 20, part 1, p. 282; Dietrichson, in Nelson. *History of the Scandinavians in the United States,* part 1, p. 158–159; Langeland. in Johnson, *Det Skandinaviske Regiments Historie,* 107.

Saddle, my Blankets and Bedding, my sachell with all my cloths." He had nothing left "except what I have on me," and so he asked the faithful Gunild to send him a new supply of clothing as promptly as she could.[39]

In February, 1863, Colonel Heg commanded temporarily the second brigade, and on May 1 he was placed in permanent command of the third brigade of the first division, twentieth army corps. His own regiment was at the same time transferred to this brigade.[40] He remained for some months, his troops inactive, near Murfreesboro, and his letters for this period, though interesting, have little military incident to report. Heg visits General Rosecrans, who had relieved Buell after Perryville; he keeps his brigade well disciplined and ready for movement; he watches springtime in the South and notes that the "Birds and Frogs are singing as they do up in Wisconsin in April"; he tries his hand at poetry, but his verses apparently have been lost; he dreams of having his wife visit him at his camp; he worries about copperheadism in the North and sounds a grim warning of what the soldiers will do to the copperheads once they have put down the rebellion; and he occasionally goes out on foraging or scouting expeditions. On March 4 his brigade engaged in an expedition from the vicinity of Murfreesboro to Shelbyville. At one point Heg, accompanied by a few of his men, stole up through woods hoping to surprise some mounted rebel pickets stationed on a main turnpike. When within some twenty or thirty yards of the unsuspecting pickets, he sent two men on a dash to capture them without firing a gun, and this they succeeded in doing. Another picket post was surprised and one man and several horses were taken. Heg was delighted with the exploit, which was accomplished near a rebel camp containing some four thousand soldiers. "The idea," he wrote to his wife, "of capturing a cavalry Picket Post, with infantry is what is

[39] January 6, 1863.
[40] Buslett, *Det Femtende Wisconsin Frivillige*, 295.

interesting."[41]   This adventure helped to relieve the bore-
dom of inactivity for Heg.   The weariness of camp life,
coupled with Gunild's anxiety and her reiterated pleas for
his return, caused his mind to turn again and again to
thoughts of leave of absence and of possible resignation of
his commission.   In his letters he predicted with unfailing
optimism an early end of all fighting; he betrayed little
knowledge or understanding of the larger aspects of the
Civil War; he played with the idea of going home permanently in the fall of 1863, but deep in his consciousness he
seemed to retain the determination to stay on until the war
was over; he was intensely ambitious and interested in the
prospect of being promoted to a brigadier-generalship, and
in some of his letters he even told his wife that unless the
promotion came, he would resign in the fall; yet, much as he
chafed under inactivity, he felt an irresistible lure in the life
of an officer.   Whether active or inactive, cheerful or discouraged, he kept up an unceasing stream of letters to his
wife and children, never losing his enormous interest in the
multifarious details of home.

In the summer of 1863 the inactivity that had succeeded
Murfreesboro ended, and Heg's brigade participated in the
campaign that led to Chickamauga.   His letters tell of
marches in June and July, as Rosecrans faced Bragg, and
on August 29 his brigade had the distinction of being the
first to cross the Tennessee River, a feat accomplished in an
early morning maneuver.   Pontoon boats were put in place
at Caperton's Ferry; the brigade crossed; and as the cavalry
of the enemy withdrew, Heg's men occupied the southern
bank of the river.   "At 7 oclock in the Morning all was
ready," he wrote.   "My whole Brigade in the Boats.   We
went over expecting every moment to be shot at, But
all went well.   We were the first accross the River and moved

---

[41] See Heg's letter of March 5, 1863. His official report of the affair is in
War of the Rebellion, series 1, vol. 23, part 1, p. 138–139; see also Johnson, *Det
Skandinaviske Regiments Historie*, 45.

right up on the Mountain without any fighting a[nd] very little skirmishing. A few Rebs were captured." [42] Some days later the brigade moved into Alabama in what Heg interpreted to be a phase of an effort by Rosecrans to encircle Bragg. Two army corps, under McCook and Thomas, were in fact striking at Bragg's communications with Atlanta. The approach of a great battle was foreshadowed in the letters that Heg wrote in September, and on the eighteenth he penned his last message to Gunild. "The Rebels are in our front and we may have to fight him a Battle — if we do it will be apt to be a big one." In characteristic vein, he begs his wife not to feel uneasy for him. "I am well and in good spirits — and trusting to my usual good luck. I shall use all the caution and courage I am capable of and leave the rest to take care of itself." The thought of going home engaged his fancy and he wrote, "The ' Gen.' will call and see you the first thing you know — probably surprise you." A few hours after he made this whimsical promise, he rode into the turmoil of Chickamauga.

Chickamauga was a bloody battle marked by savage fighting at close quarters, full exposure to enemy fire, advance and withdrawal through underbrush and in the open, repeated attacks and counterattacks, tremendous losses. On the first day the Fifteenth Wisconsin, serving in Heg's brigade, Davis' division, twentieth army corps, lost seven officers and fifty-nine enlisted men; on the second day the losses brought the total to one hundred and eleven.[43] So small, in fact, was the number of its survivors that the regiment probably would have gone out of existence but for the opportune arrival of the two companies that had been garrisoned at Island No. 10.

It is no easy matter to form a clear picture of Chickamauga. In its smoke and confusion there are brief instants,

[42] Heg's letter of August 30, 1863. See also *War of the Rebellion*, series 1, vol. 30, part 1, p. 485, 496–497; and Michael H. Fitch, *The Chattanooga Campaign*, 59 (Wisconsin History Commission, *Original Papers*, No. 4).
[43] Fitch, *The Chattanooga Campaign*, 130–131.

however, when figures and masses take definite form, and the records enable one to catch glimpses of Heg and his brigade. The Fifteenth Wisconsin had been sent forward on the first day with the Eighth Kansas at its left, both supported by a second line that included the remainder of Heg's brigade. In the sharp fighting that followed, the Kansas regiment was obliged to withdraw, leaving the Fifteenth unsupported on the left and compelling it also to fall back. An Illinois regiment was brought up; the lines were re-formed; and a charge was made against the enemy. The Confederates, yielding some two hundred yards, promptly countered, forcing the Illinois troops back; and the Fifteenth suddenly found itself between the fire of friends and foes.[44] It was forced to retire as best it could. Colonel Heg was in the thick of the day's fighting. His coolness and ability to spur men on to hard effort did not desert him in the stress of battle. When the Twenty-first Illinois arrived, the lines had been broken. Colonel Heg rode forward, waved his hat to the soldiers, and ordered them to follow him. They stormed forward, cheering as they charged, and won a brief advantage.[45] A correspondent of a Cincinnati newspaper watched the fighting and has left a report of it:

The Third Brigade, Colonel Heg commanding, had hardly advanced fifty yards when the enemy suddenly opened on it a destructive fire. The Second Brigade had not yet formed into line, but was rapidly doing so, three regiments to the right and one on the left of the Third Brigade; all some thirty yards to the rear. The troops of the Third Brigade pressed vigorously forward, firing promptly and with coolness, as they advanced. Its flank, however, was exposed; a wide gap being between it and the troops on the left; its right was the extreme right of the troops in this vicinity. The firing at this time was terrible, and the stream of wounded to the rear was unprecedently large. Bullets tore through the ranks; grape and cannister flew whistling among the brave men, but they stood their ground, not yielding an inch.

[44] Dietrichson, in Nelson, *History of the Scandinavians in the United States*, part 1, p. 160; *War of the Rebellion*, series 1, vol. 30, part 1, p. 498–499.
[45] Johnson, *Det Skandinaviske Regiments Historie*, 108.

In vain the rebel hosts pushed forward; in vain they brought fresh troops — the desperate valor of the men resisted every effort to drive them back. For three quarters of an hour this small brigade held them at bay. But its flanks, those weakest points of an army, were exposed, and the enemy struck at these, and pouring through its gap on the left and right, subjected it to a terrible enfilading fire. Colonel Heg, the brave brigade commander, reluctantly gave the order to fall back, and the men slowly retreated, until they reached Carlin's Brigade, loading and firing as they went. Here the Third Brigade again reformed and the division again united, charging the enemy, driving them until it had reached the ground occupied by the Third Brigade before it fell back. For a quarter of an hour they held this position, the rebels massing column after column and hurling them with desperate valor against their thrice decimated ranks.[46]

"Throughout all those hours of severe danger and exposure," wrote one of Heg's captains, "Colonel Heg was ever prompt at his post, always courageous and self-possessed."

Not once did he falter or swerve from his duty. . . . His comrades fell at right and left, still he rallied on. From noon until sundown he was constantly exposed to the fearful fire of the enemy. It was at this hour, when his day's work was so nigh done, that a ball from a sharpshooter's rifle pierced his bowels, causing the mortal wound. He did not stagger or fall, but even when death stared him in the face, full of life and ambition and true to his manliness, he once more rallied his men, and rode on for about a quarter of a mile. Loss of blood enfeebled him, and he was obliged to give up his command. He was taken to a hospital, where he passed the weary night in suffering.[47]

Heg's successor as brigade commander, Colonel John A. Martin, wrote in his official report that the brigade was "cheered on by the gallant, but unfortunate, Colonel Heg, who was everywhere present, careless of danger." [48] He pictures stubborn fighting in which the brigade formed and

[46] A report to the *Cincinnati Commercial* reprinted in the *Wisconsin State Journal*, October 30, 1863. In essentials the account is similar to that of Colonel John A. Martin, Heg's successor as commander of the brigade, dated September 28, 1863, and printed in *War of the Rebellion*, series 1, vol. 30, part 1, p. 528–531.
[47] Albert Skofstad of Company D, writing to the *Milwaukee Sentinel* on October 20, 1863. His letter was reprinted in the *Wisconsin State Journal*, October 27, 1863.
[48] *War of the Rebellion*, series 1, vol. 30, part 1, p. 529.

advanced again and again, only to fall back. "Almost half of the brigade was killed or wounded. Colonel Heg was mortally wounded; but the remnants of the brigade, falling back to a fence a short distance in the rear, held the enemy in check until re-enforcements came up and relieved them, when they fell back across an open field, taking position in the edge of a forest behind a log barricade." [49]

Several officers of the Fifteenth Wisconsin visited their fallen chief on the night of September 19. One of them told the colonel that he had heard of his gallantry during the battle and that the boys of the Fifteenth would have been glad to see him. "Tell my boys of the Fifteenth," Heg replied, "that I kept myself where I was needed and that I knew they did not need me." [50] To Lieutenant Colonel Johnson he said that "he was glad that the Fifteenth had held their places like men and had done their duty to the last." [51] His own life, he said, was given for a just cause. [52]

On the following day, September 20, 1863, shortly before noon, Colonel Heg died. [53] In the regiment and brigade his death was deeply mourned. How fully he had won the respect and affection of his soldiers is suggested by the words of a captain: "We miss him in our regiment, for he was more than a friend to us all. The influence he exerted among us will long be felt. Our hearts are crowded with sorrow." [54] Captain Skofstad paid tribute to "the magic" of Heg's

[49] War of the Rebellion, series 1, vol. 30, part 1, p. 528–531. A report by Captain Mons Grinager of the Fifteenth Wisconsin is in the same official record, p. 533–534. Some account of the Norwegian and other Scandinavian participation in the battle is given in "Skandinaverne ved Chickamauga," in Emigranten, October 12, 1863. On the wounding of Heg, see Langeland's account, which differs somewhat from Skofstad's, in Johnson, Det Skandinaviske Regiments Historie, 109; Ager, Oberst Heg og hans Gutter, 251; Fitch, The Chattanooga Campaign, 87; and a letter of Lieutenant Colonel Johnson, dated at Libby Prison, November 3, 1863, in Wisconsin State Journal, December 23, 1863.

[50] Quoted in Ager, Oberst Heg og hans Gutter, 252. This statement would seem to cast doubt upon the assertion that Heg fell in front of the Fifteenth Wisconsin while leading a bayonet charge. Ibid., 251.

[51] Quoted in Johnson, Det Skandinaviske Regiments Historie, 54.

[52] Johnson, Det Skandinaviske Regiments Historie, 109.

[53] Wisconsin State Journal, October 27, 1863.

[54] Captain Skofstad, in Wisconsin State Journal, October 27, 1863.

"power to dispel gloom and sorrow," and was impressed by the fact that this power did not desert him as he lay dying. "The same peaceful atmosphere which surrounded him in life did then. From the nature of his wound his sufferings were severe, but he uttered no complaint."[55] General Rosecrans is reported to have said, "I am very sorry to hear that Heg has fallen. He was a brave officer, and I intended to promote him to be general."[56]

It is not within the province of this essay to follow further the history of the Fifteenth Wisconsin. It played a brave part in the second day's fighting at Chickamauga. Lieutenant Colonel Johnson was taken prisoner and conveyed to Libby Prison, from which he later escaped and made his way back to the regiment to be its colonel. The Fifteenth Wisconsin was present at the taking of Missionary Ridge and it participated in the advance of Sherman from Chattanooga to Atlanta. Meanwhile, however, the body of its organizer and first leader was brought back to Muskego. He was buried with fitting honors in the churchyard of the pioneer community to which, twenty-three years before, he had come as an immigrant boy from Norway.

His state mourned with his home community when the news of his death became known. The *Wisconsin State Journal* echoed scores of newspaper comments when it said, "The State has sent no braver soldier, and no truer patriot to aid in this mighty struggle for national unity, than Hans Christian Heg. The valorous blood of the old Vikings ran in his veins, united with the gentler virtues of a Christian and a gentleman."[57] A meeting of Norwegians held at Madison on October 3, 1863, adopted resolutions of tribute to Colonel Heg, whose death was mourned "not as a loss sustained by individuals only, but as a loss inflicted upon a people who loved and respected him for his unswerving honesty, excel-

[55] *Wisconsin State Journal*, October 27, 1863.
[56] According to Captain Grinager. See Johnson, *Det Skandinaviske Regiments Historie*, 55–56.
[57] *Wisconsin State Journal*, September 29, 1863.

lent ability and exalted patriotism, whom he so honorably and faithfully represented, and who will ever cherish his memory with the deepest and sincerest affection." [58]

So the son of old Muskego passes from the scene — a hero who died for his country. Time has enhanced his fame, his name has become a symbol, and his achievements are commemorated in monuments. At Chickamauga a pyramid of cannon balls marks the spot where he fell. There also a monument to his regiment has been raised. In Madison, on the grounds of the state capitol, stands a heroic statue of Colonel Heg, portraying him in uniform, head bared, eyes looking into some far distance. The sculptor, Paul Fjelde, in this bronze has interpreted Heg as a man of courage and action whose vision seems to seek distant horizons. Replicas of the statue, the original of which was presented by Norwegian-Americans to the state of Wisconsin in 1926, have been erected at Lier, Heg's native village in Norway, and in the old Muskego community of Wisconsin.

It is time, however, for another kind of monument to Colonel Heg, one that will perpetuate the man himself, not on a pedestal and in one unchanging mood, but on the plane of warm, human relations and in the varied, sometimes contradictory, moods of life itself. Such a monument is offered in his own letters to his wife and children. Mrs. Heg preserved and cherished them through all the years until her death in 1922, at the age of eighty-eight. Her daughter, Mrs. Charles N. Fowler of Elizabeth, New Jersey — the Hilda Heg of the letters — in 1928 presented to the State Historical Society of Wisconsin one group of Heg Papers, approximately ninety in number and including, in general, the more interesting and valuable of Colonel Heg's letters. At the same time Mrs. Fowler presented his watch, uniform, and various other Civil War articles. Through the generosity and courtesy of that institution the letters were made available for publication in this volume.

[58] *Wisconsin State Journal,* October 7, 1863.

It was supposed that the group of letters thus placed in the permanent keeping of the Wisconsin society comprised all the Heg Papers that had been saved. The work of preparing them for publication had been completed when the editor, searching for Heg photographs and other incidental materials, fortunately learned of the existence of a large number of Colonel Heg's letters in the possession of Mrs. A. R. Van Doren of Summit, New Jersey, a granddaughter of Mrs. Fowler and a great-granddaughter of Heg. Mrs. Van Doren has kindly put this group of letters — approximately 130 in number — at the disposal of the editor of this volume. This important accession of material necessarily altered the scope of the proposed publication. While the Wisconsin Historical Society's collection includes the more significant letters, some of the letters in the second group are of special interest and importance, and these have been printed in full. Many others, however, proved to be repetitious of views and information presented in other letters and seemed of negligible general interest. It has been found feasible, therefore, to represent these, for the most part, in the form of abstracts or through excerpts. In revising the volume a similar treatment has been accorded some of the letters in the first group. Colonel Heg's own words have been quoted wherever it seemed desirable to do so. Much of the material, however, is summarized by the editor. By means of the method followed, the volume has been kept down to a reasonable size, has avoided the wearisome repetition that the full publication of the letters would have made inevitable, and yet has reported upon every item in the collection. The book is, in a sense, a combination of documentary publication *in extenso* and the calendaring of a collection. Typewritten transcripts and also a set of filmslides have been made of the Van Doren manuscripts, and they may be consulted by any reader or investigator who desires more detail than is given through the abstracts and excerpts. The editor ventures to express the hope that eventually the Van Doren manuscripts will be merged with the Heg Papers now in the possession of the Wisconsin Historical Society. Meanwhile, filmslides of the manuscripts in question have been deposited with the Wisconsin institution as well as in the archives of the Norwegian-American Historical Association.

Dr. Louise Phelps Kellogg, in commenting upon the first group of letters, declared that they gave " an unusual and intimate account of the experiences and war reactions" of Colonel Heg.[59] This characterization should apply with even greater force to the collection as an entire unit, embracing both the Wisconsin Historical Society group and the Van Doren manuscripts. The letters, taken in their chronological sequence, constitute in effect a diary covering the Civil War experiences of Hans Christian Heg.

THEODORE C. BLEGEN

University of Minnesota
Minneapolis

[59] *Wisconsin Magazine of History*, 12:229 (December, 1928). In writing this sketch, I have made considerable use of the material presented in my article " Colonel Hans Christian Heg " in the *Wisconsin Magazine of History* for December, 1920, and I desire to express my thanks for this privilege to the editor of that periodical. A word should be added as to the editorial method followed in publishing the letters. As a convenience to readers, I have capitalized words at the beginnings of sentences where Heg failed to do so, supplied periods where they were left out, in some instances clarified the punctuation, and corrected palpable slips of the pen. Misspellings of words, on the other hand, have been allowed to stand. In instances where less than the full text of a letter is printed, I have italicized my own words, whereas all the words printed in roman letters are direct quotations from Heg. It happens that Colonel Heg himself occasionally underlined a word. In order to avoid confusion in my abstracts and summaries, when confronted by such a word I have followed the original literally by underlining it. On the other hand, in all letters printed in full, the conventional editorial practice is followed: words underlined in the originals are represented by italics. All the letters derived from manuscripts are autograph letters signed. Those designated as " Van Doren Mss." are from the collection belonging to Mrs. Van Doren; all the others are from the group of letters in the possession of the State Historical Society of Wisconsin. In a few instances, these manuscript records have been supplemented by letters that originally appeared in newspapers. In each case the exact source has been indicated.

THE LETTERS OF COLONEL HEG

I. FROM MADISON TO ISLAND NO. 10

To Gunild, January 16, 1862

[Van Doren Mss.]

CAMP RANDALL.   Jan 16th 1862

DEAR GUNILD.

I promised to write often, but I have not had time till to day.   Everything is going off right now, they all seem to be very glad to get me up here.   I took command yesterday for the first time.

Doctor Himoe has got his papers all right.[1]   I have got Anton Skofstad in as 1st Lieutenant, in the Waupun Company, and he will soon be up here.

Christian Tanberg is 2^d Lieutenant, and Campbell is Captain.

I guess Albert will feel good when he gets his commission.[2]

Give my love to all the children and Hans Wood, have Hans write to me often.[3]   We have about 800 men now.

Your own

HANS

[1] Dr. Stephen O. Himoe of Lawrence, Kansas, was the surgeon of the Fifteenth Wisconsin from November 11, 1861, to November 13, 1863. He was born in Norway in 1832, migrated with his father to Wisconsin in 1845, studied medicine at the St. Louis Medical College, and set up practice in Kansas. Before he was assigned to the Fifteenth Wisconsin he was on the staff of the Fifth Kansas Cavalry. The change was made doubtless because he was of Norwegian origin and because his wife was Andrea Heg Himoe, a sister of Colonel Heg. Andrea was a pioneer school teacher in Wisconsin. She taught the common school of the Norway settlement in 1855–56. Selections from a collection of some two hundred Civil War letters written by Dr. Himoe are published by Luther M. Kuhns in "An Army Surgeon's Letters to His Wife," in Mississippi Valley Historical Association, *Proceedings*, 1913–14, p. 306–320.

[2] In his first mention of Skofstad, Colonel Heg mistakenly writes " Anton." Albert Skofstad became captain of Company D on April 20, 1862, succeeding Charles Campbell of Waupun, who resigned. Skofstad proved a competent officer. A biographical sketch of him appears in Johnson, *Det Skandinaviske Regiments Historie*, 121.

[3] Hans Wood was employed as a farm aid and general assistant to Mrs. Heg while her husband was at the war. It is evident from many allusions to Hans in Heg's letters that he was a close friend of the colonel.

To Gunild, January 22, 1862
[Van Doren Mss.]

Chicago. I have just been in and had a talk with General Jim Lane.[4] We have made arangements, I think that will get us in under his command.

To Gunild, January 24, 1862
[Van Doren Mss.]

Camp Randall, Madison. I think we have got matters fixed so that we are sure to get into Jim Lanes Brigade. I saw the old fellow down in Chicago and I know he wants us. *Postscripts to Hilda and Edmund.*[5] *To Edmund:* I was glad to get your letter, and I am glad to hear that you see to my store. You must be pa pas bussiness Man, bye and bye. If you are good, I will have you all come down and see me when I get down into Kansas.

To Gunild, January 26, 1862

HEAD-QUARTERS, 15TH REG. W.A.M.
CAMP RANDALL, MADISON, WIS.

Jan. 26th 1862.

DEAR GUNILD

I could not go home last week because I have to go to Waupun to morrow to meet the State Prison Committee.

I think I can get through in Waupun by Wednesday, and if you will have Hans Wood meet me in Milwaukee with the

[4] James Henry Lane of Kansas had been made a brigadier-general by Lincoln in the summer of 1861 and had organized the "Kansas brigade." In the winter of 1861–62 he was planning an ambitious expedition into the Southwest, but for various reasons it did not materialize. *Dictionary of American Biography*, 10: 576–577.

[5] Hilda Heg became Mrs. Charles N. Fowler. Her husband, a graduate of Yale University in 1876, served for many years as a congressman from New Jersey. The boy Edmund apparently was James E. Heg, who was for a long time the editor of the *Lake Geneva Herald*, became president of the Wisconsin Press Association, was for a time a member of the Wisconsin state board of control, and died on April 6, 1914, at Waukegan, Illinois. He was buried at Lake

Team Wednesday Evening or Thursday morning, I will try to be on hand.

I want you to get ready to come up here with me, and stay a week or two. I have found a place to stay for us.

My love to all of you.

Yours

HANS

To Gunild, January 27, 1862
[Van Doren Mss.]

MADISON Jan 27th 1862.

DEAR GUNILD.

I wrote a letter with Doctor Newell [6] yesterday, saying that I would be in Milwaukee Wednesday or Thursday. It has snowed so much I do not think it is certain that I shall be there by that time. I have agreed that I shall come back here from Waupun, and I will go home on Saturday.

Let Hans Wood meet us at Eagle Prairie on Saturday. You can go up to Captain Pierce and stay there while Hans Wood goes up to Eagle after us. The cars get to Eagle about 2 °clock, or after. We will try and be at Eagle sure on Saturday afternoon.

I am just in the Depot waiting for the train, it is 2 hours behind time. I shall get to Waupun to night, the Committee is along.

My love to all of you, and especially to little Elmer.

Your own

HANS

Geneva. Elmer Ellsworth Heg, who was named in honor of the noted Zouave commander, was born at Waupun on February 23, 1861. He was educated at Beloit College and the Bellevue Hospital Medical College of New York. In 1888 he removed to Seattle, Washington, where he became a prominent physician. He was at one time state commissioner of health for Washington; he was a major in the Spanish-American War; and after 1909 he was medical director of the Pulmonary Hospital of Seattle. He died in 1922. One child of Colonel Heg died in infancy and is buried in the Norway churchyard near Waterford. A brief biography of E. E. Heg is included in *Who's Who in America*, 10:1246.

[6] G. F. Newell of Waterford was second assistant surgeon of the regiment. *Roster*, 1:804.

To Gunild, February 4, 1862
[Van Doren Mss.]

Madison. Heg has received a letter from Washington say-ing that we will not be ordered to Kansas. We will most likely be called to Kentucky. He adds, We will not leave here till some time in March. An undated fragment that perhaps accompanied this letter contains conventional greet-ings to Hilda and James Edmund.

To Gunild, February 11, 1862

HEAD-QUARTER'S, 15TH REG. W. A. M.
CAMP RANDALL, MADISON, WIS.

Febry 11th 1862.

DEAR GUNILD.

I must write you again to day. I wrote you a letter Sun-day but it did not get away till yesterday.

I am well and getting along first rate, the men are doing well, and they all seem to think a great deal of their Col. One man died yesterday, he belonged to the Waterford Com-pany, his name is Arne, he was a sailor, and a drunkard. We have not many sick.

The Companies are numbered as follows, and we know them only by their letters

Chicago Company is Co.	" A "
Wergeland Guards. Capt. Johnson —	" B "
Bear Hunters Capt Berg	" C "
Waupun Company is Co.	" D "
Odins Rifles. Capt. Ingmanson Co.	" E "
K. K.^s Protectors " Gustafson "	" F "
Rock River Rangers Capt Gordon "	" G "
Knud Simes Company. "	" H "

This Company is Called Hegs Rifles.

Waupacca Co. Capt Gasman. Co.   " I "
Clausons Guards, is Company   " K " [7]

We have in all 810 privates and about 40 officers, our Regiment is now full to the 850 men and I shall probably be mustered into United states service.

I go to Waupun on Friday and shall return on Saturday, as I said in my letter before, if the weather is fine I would like to have you and the Children come up to Madison, by having Hans Wood take you up to Eagle in time for the train. You can meet me at Milton Junction. But you must suit yourself. If the children are not well, or if the weather is not good, I would not come. I will come down after, if you dont come, just as soon as I can get away from here. Jones will have to go by the board I think. All the officers of the Regiment have sent a pettition to the Governor asking him to muster him out of the service. It will be done — he has gone home now.[8] Write to me yourself as often as you can.

Your own

HANS

[7] The first captain of Company A was Andrew Torkildsen of Chicago, who was succeeded by John M. Johnson of Madison in the fall of 1862. Captain Ole C. Johnson of Company B rose to be successively major, lieutenant colonel, and — after his escape from Libby Prison — colonel. Captain John Ingmundsen of Neshonoc, Iowa, was the first officer of the regiment to be killed. He was shot at Murfreesboro on December 30, 1862. Captain Charles Gustaveson of Manitowoc was a Swede who came to America in 1846 and served as a volunteer in the Mexican War. Fredrick R. Berg of Milwaukee served as captain of Company C only until June 12, 1862, when he resigned his commission and was succeeded by Hans Hansen of Norway, Racine County. John A. Gordon of Beloit served as captain of Company G until early in 1865. August Gasman of Waupun was captain of Company I until April, 1863. The captain of Company K was Mons Grinager of Freeborn County, Minnesota. "Clausens Guards" were named in honor of Claus L. Clausen, the first chaplain of the Fifteenth Wisconsin. See *post,* p. 69, n. 21. Biographical sketches of the officers of the Fifteenth Wisconsin are included in Johnson, *Det Skandinaviske Regiments Historie,* 103–134.

[8] Kiler K. Jones of Quincy, Illinois, had aided Andrew Torkildsen in the recruiting of Company A, chiefly in Chicago and other parts of Illinois, and he was made the first lieutenant colonel of the regiment. The precise reasons for his unpopularity are not made clear in Heg's letters. Jones was mustered out of service in March and replaced by David McKee of Lancaster, Wisconsin, a captain in the Second Wisconsin. Buslett, *Det Femtende Regiment Wisconsin Frivillige,* 317–318.

Little Hilda.

I am going to write you again, but I have not time to write to Edmund. I will write to him next time.

I want you to be a good girl, and before I go to war, I will buy you something nice.

My love to Edmund, Elmer and yourself — also to Hans Wood.

from your   PA PA

To Gunild, February 12, 1862

[Van Doren Mss.]

HEAD-QUARTER'S, 15TH REG. W. A. M.
CAMP RANDALL, MADISON, WIS. Febry 12 1862.

DEAR GUNILD

I got a letter from you to day, or rather from Hilda, Edmund and Hans Wood.

I thank you all very much for the Dressing Gown and the pictures. The Gown fits exactly. The pictures are really nice, and I will keep them a long time.

I sent you my Portrait in my last letter. I will let you have a big one that I have here when you come up here, or if you dont come up I will bring it with me when I come down.

I am going to Waupun on Friday morning, and I will come back on Saturday. If you intend to visit me while I am in Camp you must come up here on Saturday, if the weather is good I shall look for you at Milton Junction, and stay with me a few days, so I can show you how good a *Colonel* I am. The war will soon be over now, and we must be called away soon, or we will not get any chance to do anything.

Your Own HANS.

Write yourself. I can read your letters first rate. I had almost forgot to tell you that John Evenson was here to day.

I had hardly any time to talk with him.   I was very bussy.
He is in town to night.

HANS.

DEAR EDMUND —
   I have got you and Turk in my drawer — I was very glad
to get it.   I was very glad to get the Dressing Gown too.
   You must see to my bussiness, down there.   I expect you
and Hans Wood to take care of my affairs.   You must go up
and see how the sheep are getting along on the Farm.   I
expect you to meet me at Milton Junction on Saturday when
I come from Waupun.

Your Pa Pa send[s] his
Love to you

DEAR HILDA.
   I think you can beat Edmund writing and I will try and
buy you a gold Pen soon.   I was glad to get yours and Sin's
Picture.   I will keep it till I get back from the War.   Tell
Elmer I will spank him because he does not write to me.
Good Night

Your PA PA

DEAR HANS.
   I have so little time to write that you may think I am
forgetting you.
   I shall owe you much for the kind care you show my
family.   I feel perfectly safe as long as I know you attend
to their wants.   I hope the place is pleasant to you.
   If I can get my pay from the State before I go away I
shall want to build some up on my farm during the summer,
and shall leave it with you to attend, if you will stay with
us.   I need a Barn there very much.
   Write to me as often as possible.

Your friend
HANS C HEG

To Gunild, February 18, 1862

[Van Doren Mss.]

Camp Randall, Madison. The regiment has its marching orders and will leave about March 1. He invites his wife to come and see him and to plan to go with him to Chicago and perhaps to Cairo. I came from Waupun last night, found my sword, which is one of the handsomest you ever saw. It cost 125 Dollars.

To Gunild, February 20, 1862

[Van Doren Mss.]

Camp Randall, Madison. Edmund and Hilda arrived the preceding evening. He is greatly disappointed that Gunild did not come. The children report that Elmer is sick. Jones has come back, and is just about the same fellow as ever. Colonel Heg believes that the war will soon be over.

To Gunild, March 4, 1862

STEAMER CONTINENTAL
ST LOUIS March 4th 1862

DEAR WIFE

I have but very little time to write. I have only time [to] say that I am all well, and the boys are the same. We are ordered to Birds Point, instead of stopping here. We shall see service before long. I am feeling first rate and I hope you do the same: give you no consern about me. I am going to come out all right.

My love to you all.

I have all I can attend to and more too. Jones is still with us.

HANS C. HEG

To Gunild, March 7, 1862

[Van Doren Mss.]

HEAD QUARTERS BIRDS POINT Mo.[9]

March 7th 1862.

DEAR WIFE

We came here yesterday morning on board the steamboat Continental, and landed our men at this place, got them all into good comfortable quarters, and I am now in command of this place.

I live in the house occupied and owned by *Bird*. I have him now in my charge as a prisoner of War. Also 3 of his sons. Besides our own Regiment, there is one Illinois Regiment, the 22d and one Artillery Company with a few fragments of companies that are left here sick. I have probably in all about twenty five Hundred men under my command.

The boys are feeling good and enjoying themselves first rate. Mathews [10] is sick to day. Dr Himoe did not leave Madison till Monday and came here today.

Ole and Nanna lives upstairs in this house, and they keep house for me.[11] I have got me a negro that does all my hard work. He is about 16 years old, says his master died in St Louis some time ago as prisoner. He used to live on a farm up in Missouri, he seems to be a good Nigger. I got him a pair of pants and he struts around as big as a Monkey. I find that I have a great deal to do — more than I had at Madison.

Col. Jones took command of the Regiment, but to day the papers came mustering him out of the services, and I told

[9] Bird's Point, Missouri, was opposite Cairo, Illinois, and the mouth of the Ohio.

[10] Selah Mathews of Waupun succeeded Ole Heg as quartermaster on June 6, 1862. *Roster*, 1:804.

[11] Ole Heg, a younger brother of Colonel Heg, served as quartermaster of the regiment until his resignation on June 6, 1862. He was born in Norway on June 21, 1831, and came to America with his father's family in 1840. His first wife, Emilie Christenson, Danish by birth, died in 1856, and on January 27, 1861, Ole Heg married her sister Nanna. He died at Burlington, Wisconsin, in 1911, and his widow died some years thereafter.

Reese[12] to take charge. Jones has come back again to night, and still claims to be Lt. Col. To morrow I am going over to Cairo to see Genl. Pain and have the matter decided. I am very well pleased with my place now and should like to stay here all the time. It is just the kind of bussiness I like.

I am living very cheap and if I am allowed to stay here I can make money. I met W. P. Lyon of Racine to day and had a long talk with him.[13]   I was as glad to see him as he was to see me.

We had a great time comming down the River, the boys suffered a good deal, and there are quite a number of them sick to day. If I should stay here any lenght of time I could have you come down here, but I suppose we will not be here long.

Dr Himoe paid me One Hundred Dollars on the note I had against him.

You may lend out your money if you can find a good chance to do it after you have paid the insurance on my life.

If you can not lend them where it is safe, then send them to the Farmers & Millers Bank Milwaukee, and make a special deposite of them for Three Months, and they will pay you interest at 6 per cent for it. After this I shall send you what money I can save, and tell you what to do with it.

You need not feel uneasy for me. I am enjoying myself, first rate, the only difficulty is with Jones, when that matter is settled then we shall all feel easier.

There is not much chance for any fighting, at least not where we are now, and I believe the fighting is nearly over — but soldiers will be wanted for a long time yet. If I

[12] Major Charles M. Reese of Madison was a Dane by birth but had played a part in the development of the pioneer Norwegian-American press. From 1852 to 1854 he was editor of *Emigranten* and later in the fifties he was connected with *Den Norske Amerikaner* and *Nordstjernen*. He resigned his commission in the Fifteenth on June 8, 1862, and George Wilson, captain of Company H, was appointed to his place. *Cf.* Blegen, "The Early Norwegian Press in America," in *Minnesota History Bulletin*, 3:506–518 (November, 1920).

[13] Lyon, a captain in the Eighth Wisconsin, was commissioned colonel of the Thirteenth Wisconsin in the late summer of 1862. He later rose to be chief justice of the supreme court in Wisconsin. Clara Lyon Hayes, *William Penn Lyon* (Madison, State Historical Society of Wisconsin, 1926).

get a permanent location anywhere I will have you come down and stay with me.

I have written you a good long letter, and how soon I can be able to write you so much again, I dont know. My best love to all of you — write yourself.

Your own HANS

To Gunild, March 9, 1862

BIRDS POINT March 9th 1862
Sunday Evening.

DEAR GUNILD.

I have time to write again to night and I will do so. We are still here and we expect to stay here some time. They are fighting about 40 miles south of here, and we have heard the cannon boom all day. One Regiment that is laying here is ordered to leave to morrow at 8 oclock. The Boat is just up from Madrid where they are fighting and it is said we have won another victory. As to myself, you must not give yourself any uneasiness. I am very comfortable. I have a good big house to live in, with a very fine office. Ole and Nanna is living up stairs and I am boarding with them. I can not take charge of the Regiments as I am commander of this Post, and the Regiment is under Joneses charge. He has been mustered out of the service, but I have got nothing yet to show that he is out. As soon as I get the papers the gentleman must walk.

I have 20 or 25 Secesh prisoners under my charge. One of them is the owner of the house I live in and two of his sons — old Bird — who owns Birds Point. They say he is worth a million of money. He had 48 negroes and they are all loose now, most of them are around here, washing for the Soldiers, and working around in different places. They all seem to feel very good because they are free — and they say old Bird will never get hold of them again. My Board is about so so — nothing to brag of. My cook chest came very handy. Ole and Nanna has nothing with them at all — neither Bed clothes nor any thing els. You see I have still been lucky, there is no Wisconsin Col. that has got promoted as fast as I have, having been made commander of a Post imidiately, but I can asure you the honor is small and the work plenty.

My Negro works good — Blacks my Boots, makes my bed and does chores for Nanna, he is a good boy, but he has one poor hand — it has been crippled. He says he will go with me where ever I go. He is very anxious to learn to read, — a very funny fellow I can assure you. I am so bussy all the time that I have never felt homesick. There will be a time when this war will be over, and we can all live well together again. I see a great many wemen along with the soldiers, and even small children, but the poor things suffer awfully. Mrs. Gasman is homsick, & would like very much to be back again. Nanna is not so. Mrs. Hanson runs around like [a] sick hen.

I have a Guard out side of my office night and day. The office is crowded from morning to evening, and I have a great many things to do that I have never known anything about before, but I shall get out of it well enough.

It is raining like fun to night. It has been warm all day, just such weather as we have in May or April in Wisconsin. There is no grass here, but the trees begin to sprout.

We lost 3 men comming from Chicago. Two of them we have heard of — but one they think has either been killed or lost, as he was very drunk. We had hard work to keep the boys together in Chicago. Many of them got awfull drunk, but I soon ordered all the whiskey poured out.

Dr Himoe has told me that Rolfson could not get my furniture. I have written to Madison about it and I guess it will be all made right. Hans Wood must try and sell my ponies if he can — or get them traded of[f] where the money will come in some time safe. You must learn to do bussiness now, while I am away.   Cant you lend some one a Hundred or two Dollars, and sell the Horses with it?   If you can sell them for a Hundred and Seventy five Dols. then let them go.

I shall try and get permission to go home in April or May, to settle up my affairs that I had to leave unsettled.

If any thing happens to you or the children you must let me know imidiately.   I can get home when I want to.

Write to me yourself, and tell Hans Wood to write at least once every week.

Kiss the children for me.

Yours   HANS

I forgot to tell you that there is one Col. in this house who has been wounded.   He has lost one leg.   He was a prisoner for some time.   His wife is here with him now, and he is getting along well.   His name is Col Dougherty — of Ill.

To Gunild, March 11, 1862

[Van Doren Mss.]

Bird's Point, Missouri.   Heg is still perturbed about Jones and writes that he sticks to us like death to a negro.   Otherwise everything goes well.   He adds brief notes of greeting to Hilda and Edmund.

To Gunild, March 18, 1862

[Van Doren Mss.]

STEAMER GRAHAM, NEAR ISLAND N° 10. MISS. R.

March 18th 1862.

MY DEAR WIFE —

I have not written to you for some time for the reason that I have had no opportunity to do so.   I was ordered away from Birds Point on Friday last week, the 14th, and came down the river with this expidition with 570 men —

expecting to have a fight.   We have laid here since Saturday,
and the Gun Boats have been firing at the enemy all the
time since we came here.   We have had a splendid chance
to see every shot fired — but there is not much chance for us
to get into the fight, we shall probably land, after the Gun
Boats have taken the fortifications.

Doctor Himoe is making a sketch of the river and the batteries for me that I will enclose in this letter for you to see
how we are located.[14]   Ole and his wife are left at Birds
Point, but I expect them here every minute as I have sent
for all our baggage and men that are left there.   The boys
are nearly all well, everybody well pleased.   They got hold
of a Secesh, yesterday, and took all his Pigs, Hens, a great
lot of Pork and Mollasses.   You must not give yourself any
uneasiness about me.   I shall take as good care of myself as I
can, and you must trust to Providence for the rest.   I have
a strong faith that I shall come out unharmed — and if I
should not — it will be no more than thousands of others
have suffered for a good cause.   Take good care of yourself
and the children — and there will soon be a time when we
shall meet again, and live happily together.   I have hard
work, and poor fare just now, but as soon as we get down a
little farther — we shall live better.   I shall try and get permission to go home next month.   I will write oftener after
this, as long as we lay here I will send you a letter every
time a Steam Boat goes up.

We are located about 30 miles, within 8 miles of a place
called Madrid, which you can find on the map.   If we take
this place, then we will probably go right down to Memphis,
and perhaps New Orleans.   The Cannon is booming all the
time.   We have only had about 10 or 15 men wounded and
killed on the Gun Boats, how many the Rebels have lost can
not be known of course.

[14] A sketch such as Heg here describes was found among the papers of Heg
presented to the Wisconsin Historical Society and is reproduced here as an illus-
tration.

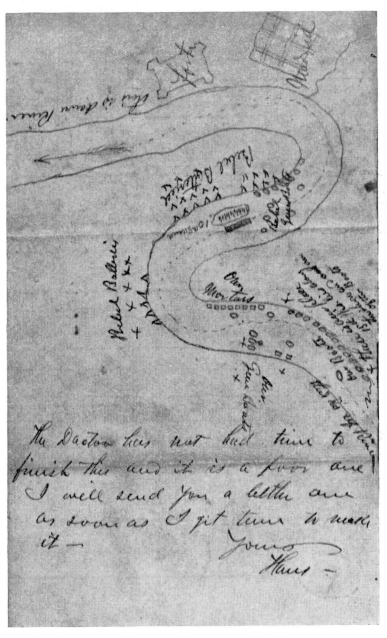

ISLAND No. 10: A SKETCH BY DR. HIMOE

Kiss the children — for me — and here is one for your-
self —   Good Bye — Your own
                                                    HANS
I will write again to morrow if
I have chance to send it.

To Gunild, March 19, 1862

STEAMER GRAHAM ISL. N° 10.
March 19th 1862.

DEAR WIFE.

The first thing I have heard from home since I left Madison was a letter from you Hans Wood and the children
sent to Birds Point.   I wrote you yesterday and have nothing new to day.   I was out with two companies yesterday
afternoon, when the Cannon Balls flew around some.   Some
of them falling near enough to some of the boys to spatter
mud and Water over them.

I have been in no dangerous place yet, and may not get
into any.   It is all running first rate.   We can not do any
thing with our men — the fight is all with cannon.   If we
have to go ashore we may have some fighting to do — otherwise we will not.   This expidi[tion] is going down the river
perhaps to New Orleans.   We may stop before we get there
to garrison some post.   But this is uncertain.   Ole is not
with us — he cant leave his wife.   Doc Hansen the same —
he got sick.   The track is getting fresh — and cowards get
sick.   If you ever become a widdow, you shall never be the
widdow of a coward.   You can rely on that.[15]

---

[15] This reference by Colonel Heg seems to be unwarrantedly severe.   The allusion is to Dr. Søren J. Hansen, who is characterized by Dr. Knut Gjerset and
Dr. Ludvig Hektoen as " possibly the ablest and best educated physician who
came to the early Norwegian settlements" in America.   Of his work at Island
No. 10 they write, " In that marshy and unhealthful region the efficient hospital
service organized by the medical staff of the regiment aided greatly in preserving
the health of the soldiers."   Dr. Hansen's wife accompanied him as a war nurse.
Because of illness he was obliged to resign from the service on October 20, 1862.
Gjerset and Hektoen, " Health Conditions and the Practice of Medicine among
the Early Norwegian Settlers, 1825–1865," in Norwegian-American Historical
Association, *Studies and Records*, 1:50–51.

My love to you all.

You will hear from me when ever I have an opportunity.

Your Own

HANS

To Gunild, March 20, 1862

STEAMER GRAHAM NEAR ISLAND N° 10
MISSISSIPPI RIVER March 20th 1862.

DEAR WIFE.

I wrote you a letter yesterday, and should have done so this morning before the mail left, had I had the time. I am going to try and send you a letter every day, after this and give you a full account of what happens, and if you will take care of the letters, they may be interesting hereafter.

I have nothing particularly new, to write about. Early this morning I ordered the Boat to move up the river in order to get a better place for the landing as the river is rising very fast, and the place we laid at was nearly over flowed. The Gun Boats have been firing their guns as usual, none have been hurt on our side. Yesterday Co. B & Co. G. was out on duty and had several shots fired at them, some of them falling near enough to throw mud and water over the boys.

The mail came in yesterday and I got the first letter I have had from you since I left. I was glad to hear from you, and especially for Hilda and Edmund, and your own letters. Our goods, or the most of them came down from Birds Point yesterday but Ole did not send me my trunk, or anything except my over coat, which I do not need at all. There is not much chance for us to get into any fight, but we have got the enemy sorounded here and cut off so that they will have to give up before many days for want of provissions. Col. Buford came on board of our Boat this evening and stays with us to night. I have got to be quite a pet of the old man, and I have had to promise him that I shall send my Photograph to his wife who lives at Rock Island Ill. He says I have got the best soldiers he has seen, and I think he will have us with him where ever he goes if the Goverment will allow him.[16]

You know I am generally lucky in making friends where ever I go, and I shall succeed here just as well as I have done before.

There is no Wisconsin Regiment that has got along any faster than the 15th. We came right out of camp — took command at Birds Point — from there was ordered right into one of the most important expiditions started since the war commenced.

I have written to the Govornor, asking him to appoint W[m] P. Lyon of Racine in Joneses place. If I can get him it will be a great relief to me. He is a good man & quite a millitary man. I hope he will get the appointment soon, as I need some help.[17]

I wrote to Ole to day telling him to send his wife home, and come down here him self and I told him to send up by her one Hundred Dollars that I left with him.

I could not get time to subscribe for the Chicago Tribune when I was at Chicago. Get Russell to send down and subscribe for the daily Tribune for one year. I want you should do that by all means, do not wait for me to do it for you as I have no chance to. I owe Mr. English of Racine 65 Dollars for my saddle. When you get this money by Nana I wish you would pay that for me. I send you the Bill in this letter. This is a splendid Boat we are on — and while I am sitting here and writing the boys are laying all over the cabin floor, snoring and sleeping. Some are still sitting up writing letters to their friends. The upper deck is full of soldiers, and so is the lower. Mathis Kroshus was very sick at St.

[16] Napoleon B. Buford of the Twenty-seventh Illinois Volunteers participated in the campaign at Island No. 10 and "commanded the garrison after its capitulation," according to the *Dictionary of American Biography*, 3:244.

[17] That Heg showed good judgment in asking the governor to make this appointment may be inferred from the later career of Lyon. See *ante*, p. 58, n. 13.

Louis and was left there at the Hospital.[18] I have not heard from him since. I will write to you as often as I can get time, at least every other day.

My love to you all.

Your own HANS

10 oclock at night)

To Gunild, March 23, 1862

CAMP SOLBERG. Sunday March 23[d] 1862.

DEAR GUNILD.

I was very glad yesterday to get another letter from you. I hope you will keep on writing yourself. You are learning very fast. You see I have dated this Camp Solberg. Our Boat, the Graham is lying alongside the shore and our boys have thrown up their tents on land close by. Solberg is with us, and as a complement to him I have called the Camp — "Camp Solberg" very much to his satisfaction.[19] Day before yesterday, I went out with Col Buford to the Gun Boats and was introduced to Commodor Foot.[20] The Col paid me a very high complement, by saying that I had the best disciplined Regiment he had seen in the service. Com. Foot is a real fine old gentleman, very sociable, and appearantly a very brisk, smart man, and from his looks I should judge him to be a man of courage.

The river is rising very fast, and yesterday I ordered the Boat to go up the river about 1½ miles, to a place where we found a good dry landing. There is a man living right here,

[18] The name " Mathis Kroshus " does not appear in the roster of the Fifteenth. Probably, however, he may be identified with Mathias Mathiasen, a private in Company C who was killed at Murfreesboro on December 31, 1862.

[19] Carl Fredrik Solberg, the editor of *Emigranten*, accompanied the regiment when it left Madison for St. Louis and served during the campaign at Island No. 10 as a correspondent for his own paper. His " Reminiscences of a Pioneer Editor," edited by Albert O. Barton, appear in *Studies and Records*, 1:134–144. Some of Solberg's contemporary letters appear in *Emigranten*, March 17, 24, 31, April 14, 21, 1862.

[20] Commodore Andrew Hull Foote was commander of naval operations on the upper Mississippi. *Dictionary of American Biography*, 6:499.

who has over 40 negroes. The man who owns this plantation lives near Madrid where he owns another plantation
and lots of negroes. He is a secesh, and his negroes will
probably be allowed to go where they have a mind to before
long. I have protected his property so far, and not allowed
the soldiers to destroy any thing, but if I can be assured he
is a rebel — I can assure you I shall not give him much pro-
tection to his negro property. Yesterday Col. Buford sent
a Boat up to Hickman with troops, and the Captain of the
boat took the Boat 8 miles above — saying that he made a
mistake — it was in the night. The Capt. is undoubtedly a
traitor, and he was imidiately arrested when they came back.
There is not any firing this morning. Everything is quiet.
The Enemy is very strongly fortified on Island N° 10 and we
can not land for high water.

One of my soldiers came down from Madison yesterday.
He says, they got everything belonging to me, and sent it to
Eagle — or some other place. If you write to J. A. Johnson
at Madison he will give you a full account of what has become of it. Ole was down here yesterday, and went back
to send his wife home. I sent $100 — with her, and my
scabbard. As soon as I get a Lt. Col. I will get permission
to come home — and stay a week or two. I think that Island N° 10 will be taken sometime this week & then we will
probably be quartered there or sent back with prisoners.

DEAR HILDA.

I was very glad for your letter. You write such nice letters. You must write again. Elmers letter is a nice one.
You can tell the little rat that if he is a naughty boy I will
spank him when I come home. I am glad to hear that you
are a good girl.

Good Bye from your PA PA

DEAR EDMUND —

I got your letter too, and was very glad of it. I hope you
will see to my things up there till I come back. You can tell

Hans Wood to fix the ponies up as well as he can, and try to sell them. Mr. Moe is a good hand to sell Horses. If he can not do any better, he may send them up on the farm, and let Ole Luraas use them, and you may raise a colt from the mare. You must learn to ride horseback on the mare — and I will let you keep her for your pony.

I have not time to write any more now. Tell Hans Wood I will write to him soon.

Your Father

H. C. Heg.

be a good Boy

To Gunild, March 26, 1862

[Van Doren Mss.]

Steamer G. W. Graham, near Island No. 10. There has been no firing for sometime, the river is too high for landing any where, and we are waiting for Gen¹ Pope to come in back of them and clean them out from the rear. *One of Heg's men has been shot by pickets and another is dead at St. Louis Hospital. He criticizes his brother Ole. He predicts that Island No. 10 will soon be taken.* If I can find a nice Secesh girl I will keep her for Hans Wood.

To Gunild, March 29, 1862

Sᵗʳ GRAHAM.   NEAR ISL. N° 10.

March 29ᵗʰ 1862

MY DEAR GUNILD —

We are still in the same place, and doing nothing. The river has raised so that all the country around here except where the rebels are, is overflowed. I can tell you nothing new. The Boat moves around from one place to another to find dry land, but there is not hardly any to be found.

Major Reese, Capt. Berg and Ole are still at Birds Point. I am trying very hard to get the Regiment together again, but I have not succeeded yet. I think that there will soon

be a change here — and we will go down and take Island
Nº 10.   I do not think there will [be] much fighting for us.
It is mostly done by the Gun Boats.   I hope you are living
comfortable and well.   You must not have any hessitation
about getting such things as will make you so.   Keep all the
help you want.   You have got money enough, and I will send
you more whenever you want it.   I am not spending any
money here, but saving my sallary — and as fast as I am
paid off, I will send it to you.   I am waiting every day to
hear from the Govornor about who is to be our Lt. Col.   As
soon as we get one, and it is possible for me to get away, I
will come home and spend a couple of weeks, to settle up my
affairs, and see you.   This war is fast being closed up and by
next winter will probably be ended.   At all events I will by
that time get to a place where I can have you and the children with me.   I find that Clauson is a great help to me, he
is a real good man for me.[21]   Borchsenius is also a good officer,[22] in fact they are all different from what they used to be,
as they get no liquor.   Dr. Himoe & myself are together
most of the time.   Time passes very pleasant and very fast.
It is almost a month since we left Madison & it hardly seems
like a week.   We have a good many men who are sick, but,
I have been a good deal healthier here than I was at Waupun, I have much better apetite.   One of Company D. died
in St. Louis about a week ago — and one new recruit was
shot at Birds Point.   This is all we have lost yet.   Elias
Windlake has been quite sick, but is better.   Lt. Rice has

[21] C. L. Clausen was a prominent pioneer Lutheran minister, Danish by birth but identified with the Norwegians in the West, who served as the first chaplain of the Fifteenth Wisconsin. He was the outstanding leader of the anti-slavery cause in Norwegian church circles. See Svein Strand, "Pastor C. L. Clausen," in *Symra*, 9:204–223 (1913); Margreth Jorgensen, "Claus L. Clausen, Pioneer Pastor and Settlement Promoter, 1843–1868," a manuscript master of arts thesis, University of Minnesota, 1930; and J. M. Rohne, "Claus Lauritz Clausen," in *Dictionary of American Biography*, 4:166–167. Clausen himself tells about moral and religious conditions in the regiment in Johnson, *Det Skandinaviske Regiments Historie*, 92–94.

[22] Hans Borchsenius, the regiment's adjutant, was a Dane who migrated to America in 1856. He was the publisher of *Nordstjernen* from 1858 to 1860 and was a Democrat. Johnson, *Det Skandinaviske Regiments Historie*, 112–113.

also been sick.[23]   Gasman is sick at Birds Point.   I have
written again to Madison about the Furniture & I hope you
have got it by this time.   If you have not, you better let
Hans Wood go up to Madison and see after it.   Albert Skofstad I think will soon be Captain of his Co. as Campbell has
resigned and is only waiting for his papers to go home.   I
think I shall try and get Andrew Clement in his place.   I
have written to the Gov to day about it.[24]

I must close again this time with my best wishes for all
of you, and I hope to hear that Hilda and [*blank in Ms.*]
have been good children when I hear from home.

My thanks to Hans Wood for his promptness in sending
me letters.   I hope Ole will soon be up there & see to our
bussiness.

Your own

HANS

I had a letter from John Jacobson.   He says his boy has
been very sick.

To Gunild, April 1, 1862

STEAMER GRAHAM, NEAR ILS. N° 10.

April 1ˢᵗ 1862.

MY DEAR WIFE.

I have again a chance to write to you, and this time I have
some thing of importance.   I told you in a letter sometime
ago that I had got to be quite a friend of Col. Buford who
commands this expidition.   On Sunday morning he came on
my Boat, and asked me if I would go with him on an expidition to Union City, a small place east of Hickman Ky. where
there was said to be a larg number of rebels encamped.   I
was glad of the chance you may believe, and I got ready 425

---

[23] John Rice of Waterford, originally a second lieutenant, became captain of
Company C.   *Roster*, 1:810.
[24] See *ante*, p. 49, n. 2; and on Clement, *post*, p. 98, n. 4.

men, with one days ration and went to Hickman by Boat.[25]
From there we started about 1 °clock P. M. in all, about 1200
men. Union City is 15 miles from Hickman — and as we
marched along the dusty road — singing and playing — I can
assure you I felt good. It was very warm — and the boys
soon began to get tired. By 5 oclock there was not much
singing. I being on my splendid black Horse got along first
rate. We marched on till about 8 o'clock when we got on
one side of the road, and laid down, as quietly as possible
sleeping on our guns, ready at any moment to jump up and
have a brush. I did not sleep a wink — but the boys all
slept like logs. We could have no fire and made no noice,
as we did not want to be discovered. About day light Col.
Buford came to me and said he expected a bloody day, and
gave his best advise and encouragement, & my orders what
position to take &c. We were then within 2½ miles of
Union City, the rebel camp. We started about 6 o'clock in
the morning, and after traveling about one houre we began
to hear our pickets commence firing. It is no use for me to
give you any describtion of how the men felt. I will do [so]
when I come home. It is enough to say that in a few minutes afterwards Col. Buford rode up to me and told me to
advance my Regiment, and take up a position on the left of
his Regiment the 27th Ill. We were in the thick woods, with
timber laying in all directions, but the regiment formed and
came up in a stile that Col. Buford afterwards said, he had
never seen better — cannon booming — smoke & fire — had
no effect on any of the men with me. I was myself as cool
as if I had been eating my dinner, except when I had to swear
a little to the men. I will give you a better account when I
come home, & I suppose the newspapers will also give you an
account of it. The Enemy run — leaving their tents, trunks,
Horses, Waggons and all their property. Our Regiment cap-

[25] A detailed account of the expedition to Union City, Tennessee, is given by
Solberg in a letter of March 31 published in *Emigranten* for April 21, 1862.
Cf. Johnson, *Det Skandinaviske Regiments Historie*, 19 ff. An official report
by Colonel Buford is in *War of the Rebellion*, series 1, vol. 8, p. 116–118.

tured 31 mules, 15 or 16 Horses — besides a great many small
articles of value which the boys have got. Most every one
has something, some have uniforms some this and some that.
Albert Skofstad is going around to day with a very fine Secesh uniform, even nice embroydered slippers. Many of them
have some fine articles, belonging to officers — things sent
them from home, a great many *Degauretypes,* Love letters
&c. I will send you a letter in this. This paper is Secesh —
the envelope the same. I have got a Flag that was taken
by one of the Soldiers that I would not take Five Hundred
Dollars for. It is a small cavalry silk flag on which is inscribed, "Victory or Death," and the letters C.S. for Confederate states and the letters H.C. for Hills Cavalry. I
learn from one of the Prisoners that it was a Flag presented
to this Captain Hills Company by the Sisters of Charity of
Memphis. Besides this Flag, I have a fine Rifle — or what
is called Sharps Rifle — a splendid pr of Saddle Bags, a large
good shawl — & several small things which I will bring home
for you as soon as I can get away. I have 10 or 15 Saddles
some elegant ones — enough about this. We left after burning everything on the ground, Tents, Barracks &c — provissions & Powder — and started for Hickman again about 10
o'clock, with what mules, Horses & waggons we had, loaded
with plunder. We did not stay, for the enemy had 20 Thousand men at a place called Humbolt, 25 miles south on the
railroad, and which they could bring in, in a very few hours,
and we were obliged to hurry back, as fast as possible. We
got back to Hickman about 4 o clock where our Boat waited
for us and came down here again last night. Although this
was no fight, as only a very few Rebels were killed, and they
ran away before hardly firing a shot, still it was a splendid
victory, as the Rebels lost at least 40 or 50 Thousand Dollars worth of property, and lost a good many men by being
taken prisoners & killed.

While I was sitting and writing this letter, the mail came
which brought a letter from Hans Wood, Edmund and Hilda.

I have not had any for a long time, & I tell you I felt glad to
get it. I have read it through and I shall try and get time
to write a letter to Hilda and Edmund both to morrow or
next day. I send you a letter from [a] Woman to her Husband. I have quite a number of her letters to him and some
of the boys has got her likeness and her Boys. If I can get
it I will do so, and bring it home to you.

It almost makes me sory to see these letters. It sounds
so much like hearing from you. I think you would say just
as she does, and feel about the same about me as she does for
him. How these poor people are fooled to go into an unholy
war, a war that will certainly use them up entirely.

I want you to have no fears on my account. I have a
strong faith, that I shall get through this war unharmed.

I have already now gained much credit for what I have
done. You have reason to feel as prowd of your husband as
the Lady who wrote the enclosed letter. I have a flag in my
possession that no Regiment from Wisconsin can yet beat.
If I could only have you and the children with me it would
be pleasant, but as I am so bussy all the time, it is not so
hard for me, as it must be for you, who are at home alone.
One Capt McKee has been appointed Lt. Col. of our Reg^t
and as soon as he comes here I shall apply for permission to
visit Wisconsin. I may not get permission, but I think I
shall. I want to be here all the time now, for the boys would
be entirly demorelised if I was not present. Everybody says
this Regiment would not be worth anything under any body
els[e]. Maybe you think I am bragging but that is not so.

We have smelled powder now — and I have never felt so
prowd of the soldiers as I have since we came from Union
City yesterday.

I shall save myself a good horse & saddle and one for Dr
Himoe.

The Horses and mules belong to Goverment, but they
can be had by the officers for a fair price.

I have written you a long fine letter this time & will quit

now, hoping soon to hear from you again. There is no prospect of any fight where we are now. The fighting will be done by the Gun Boats and when the Rebels give up we will have a chance to go and take care of the place & the prisoners, if we take any. The boys are all writing to day, about the *battle* and as Solberg was along with us, you will see a full account of it in the Emigranten. I have heard that *Nana* is sick at Birds Point. I want you to buy you a *Map* of *the war* — or *war Map* as it is called. Get Russell to get you a good one, and you can always tell where I am.

God Bless you my Dear wife.

HANS HEG.

To Gunild, April 3, 1862

STR. G W. GRAHAM, NEAR ISLAND N° 10
April 3ᵈ 1862.

MY DEAR GUNILD

I have got a chance to send you a few lines again to day, as the mail is going up at 3 o'clock this afternoon. I trust you have got my last letter in which I gave you a full account of our expidition to Union City where we gained such a nice little victory. Besides what I mentioned as having got in my last letter, I have a fine Robe and a larg Mans Shawl that I send up to Birds Point to be sent up to you by Nanna who goes home in a few days. You will also find a *towell* which has undoubtedly belonged to some rich officer. You will see that they fit out their husbands finely. Some of our boys have got a great many very elegant things. I have got me one Horse and two extra Saddles.

The whole number of Horses taken by our Regiment was 20 — and 45 Mules, 8 or 10 Waggons and some Harnesses. I got wind of another place this morning where there was said to be 250 Mules kept on a plantation for the Southern Army, and I started out with this Boat and two companies,

Viz. Co. B & Co E. but we went up a few miles and satisfied ourselves they could not [be] got at for Water, and returned to this, the old place. I call this the old place, because we have stayed longer here than in any other since we came down the river. Our tents are pitched but I sleep on board of the Steamboat together with the most of the officers. I have a fine State room, and good board in the cabin with the Captain and the rest of the officers of the Boat. This is one of the largest Boats on the river, and the best officers I ever met. When the war is over I am going to take you and the children over on the Mississippi and take a trip to New Orleans and other places. I have had invitations from several Steam Boat Captains to just come and stay with them as long as I have a mind to, and I shall remember it when the time comes. We will soon have Island N° 10, and bye and bye you will hear of us down at Memphis or near New Orleans. I do hope I may get to some place where I can send for you, and where I can keep you comfortable, how well I should feel. Ole has sent me his resignation and I think he will go home about the 1st of May. Nanna has been sick I understand but she is better now. I have got 7 companies here at present. 3 companies are at Birds Point Co D. C. and K — with Major Reese in command.

I have not time to write any more. I must write several letters to other persons before the mail goes and I must drop you. Keep the towell as a Trophy from Secesh — the Robe and Shawl you can take care of till I come home. Hoping you are all well — I close this with my heart full of love for you and the children. God Bless You.

> Hans C.
> Col. 15th Wis.

To Gunild, April 6, 1862

[Van Doren Mss.]

Steamer G. W. Graham, near Island No. 10. A Sunday morning. Heg is sending his wife the flag captured at Union

City and asks her to give it to Governor Harvey of Wisconsin. Tells of dining with Buford. Asks for various articles of clothing to be sent down and suggests also that she send him ten or twelve bottles of currant wine. There are postscripts to Edmund and Hilda, to both of whom he is sending gifts — a saddle to Edmund and a wolfskin robe to Hilda. He also sends a towel for Elmer and a shawl for Gunild.

To Gunild, April 9, 1862

ISLAND N° 10 April 9ᵗʰ 1862

DEAR GUNILD

Island N° 10 is ours, and your humble servant was one of the first to raise the American Flag over the fortifications.

On Monday afternoon I was informed by Genˡ Buford that it was supposed that we might get the Island that night, and that I must hold my Regiment in readiness to go on shore and take possession.

3 oclock Tuesday Morning, I ordered the men on board of the Boat, and the boat got ready to leave by day light. When I came down about 4 miles I saw that Genˡ Bufords Boat lay at the Island, and my Boat dropped alongside of his. He then ordered me to go over on the main shore and take charge there. Here was the biggest fortifications and I raised the first flag on them. We took something like 400 Prisoners, Buford had already 300, or 400 before.

The Rebels had left during the night, except those that did not want to go, or were unabble to go. Their Camp was scattered over 5 miles in length, tents standing, and most of their trunks and Baggage was scattered all over.

I can[not] give you a full account of all we got, but, I tell you we got a big lot, large quantity of Sugar, Beef, Pork, Rice, Corn, Poweder, Amunition of all kinds, about 100 Guns, Quartermasters Stores of every discription, though not very valuable.

My Boys captured 4 Secesh Flags of very elegant silk, and

very large on one of them is inscribed, " Mississippi Devils " —
presented by the Ladies."

I send you enclosed herewith a small Secesh Flag.   Keep
it as a trophy.

I have a good many fine trophies, worth a good deal, besides the Flags spoken of.   I send my trunk home by a man
from Chicago, and have instructed him to send it to you
from Chicago by express to " Burlington Wisconsin."

In my last letter I stated that Ole was going home, and
that I sent home some stuff with him for you and the children.   I can not send it now, as he left all those things up at
Cairo.

I have put everythink in my trunk that I can spare.   I do
not want a trunk, because I can get along much better with a
small valice or carpet sack.   I have a good saddle for Edmund and some other things that [I] can not now send you.

I can not tell where we go from here, but it is very probable
that I may stay here a few weeks — to keep command of the
place.   Gen¹ Buford likes my Regt very well, and I shall go
with his Brigade if we move from here.

I am healthy and well, and the boys are pretty good.   One
died to day.

I am very bussy and will write some more by and by.

Good By for the present.   My love to you all

Your HANS

HANS C. HEG.

I have written all in a hurry.
This Flag was captured by myself at Island N° 10.

To Gunild, April 11, 1862

ISLAND N° 10. April 11ᵗʰ 1862

MY DEAR WIFE.

I wrote you a very hasty letter yesterday, and I suppose
from my last two letters you hardly know what [to] think of

not receiving what I have been promising to send. At first I expected, Ole would go home with his wife, and I sent up a few things for him to bring up to you. He came down here day before yesterday, and told me that he could not get permission to go home with Nanna, and that she was so sick that she could not bring anything with her. I then fixed up my trunk in order to send it home with a man from Chicago, but he left in such a hurry yesterday that I did not get time to deliver him the trunk, so I have sent nothing yet.

I will try now and give you a little detailed discription of what we have done for the last few days. My Boat, the Steamer G. W. Graham, with the 7 of my companies aboard that have been with me since I left Birds Point, was the first to land on the main land, where the largest fortifications are — where I imidiately took Three companies ashore, and posted them all along the rebel camp, which had been deserted the night before we landed. I picked up however, about 300 prisoners, among which were 8 or 10 Officers none higher in rank than Captains. The camp of the Rebels is some 4 miles in lenght, and I could not protect all with my sentinels, but I guarded the most of it. Their camp tents all stood as they had left them, most of their trunks and baggage was there, but torn in all direction[s]. A great many Waggons — Clothing, Guns, and all sorts of goods was to be found every where. I have got a good many very fine trophies, the most valuable one is a splendid Masonic Apron, worn by one of the Generals.

Since that time all my men have been kept bussy taking charge of the spoils. I have used the mules we took at Union City every day hawling in Poweder — and Guns. I can not give you any idea of the amount of property we have captured but it must be immence, the most of it is on this side. I will give you one small item that I found. I gathered up about ($2000⁰⁰) two thousand Dollars worth of rice — and roled [it] on board of our Boat. After working here Tuesday, Wednesday and Thursday, I got orders last night.

to assume command, and I am therefor now commander of the place. I can assure you I have got my hands full. This morning I took three companies over on the Island, Comp. A. H. and F. The rest I have here. My own regiment is the only forces I have here yet, but there will probably be more here before long.

The people around here are flocking in to see me, and to try and make friendship with us. Wemen come in with their children begging to get their Husbands released. My sympathy has been worked upon in many cases, and I have released them upon their taking the Oath of alejians, in cases where they have come in voluntarily and given themselves up — but their greatest trouble is their negroes. They seem to be more anxious about the safety of them, than anything els. It is not much comfort they will get from me on that score. Where the negroes have been willing to return to their masters, I have allowed them to do so, but not otherwise.

I will write to you again in a few days if I get a little more time. I have worked so hard for a few days that I am entirely used up — and have very little inclination to write. Ole is here now — and attending to his bussiness. He does not think so much about resigning now. I have got a good house to live in — and plenty of negroes to wait on me. The Steamboat I have been on is gone down to New Madrid to day, but is expected back again to night or to morrow morning. Besides that Boat, I have several others under my controle, that have been taken from the rebels, but they need to be fixed up.

I am going out in the country to morrow to visit some men that I have got aquainted with, and if I should go and see some of the *fine, handsome* Grass Widdows, you must not wonder at it. I will have to give you permission to do the same. I have no doubt I shall become very popular amongst them, if I will only help them to take care of their negroes.

I am not very handsome for I have got to be quite care-

less about my dress, and I do not know but I ought to get
me one of these wemen to take care of me if I can not get
you down here.

I must go to bed, so good bye, and sleep sound. My best
love to all of you.

Your own

HANS C.

I forgot to tell you that we have lost two men since we came
down here. One of them, I think died from drinking too
much rebel whiskey, that he found in the camp.

To Gunild, April 15, 1862
[Van Doren Mss.]

*Island No. 10. His regiment is together again. Tells of his
command at the island.* We are now building fortifications
on the Island, and my soldiers are to work for extra pay.
He again voices his belief in an early peace. We have captured 3 more Secesh Flags here. One has the following inscription "Mississippi Devils" "presented by the Ladies."

To Gunild, April 18, 1862

Island No. 10. He is making friends very fast. I have invitations to come and take dinner with some one every day.
Lieutenant-colonel McKee has come down and Heg is very
much pleased with him.

To Gunild, April 20, 1862
[Van Doren Mss.]

*Island No. 10. Is sending home a trunk with various
trophies and gifts. Needs various articles of clothing.*
Send me a good Box of Cigars if you can. *As to prisoners:*
Capt Johnson is gone to Madison with 250 Prisoners of war
taken by us at this place. I have 125 more on hand and taking more every day.

To Gunild, April 21, 1862
[Van Doren Mss.]

Island No. 10. Characterizes the people of the surrounding region as strong <u>Secesh</u>. *The rich* live in large ellegant Houses, have plenty [of] fine furniture, and live well, are ve[ry] aristocratic. But the poor are the most misserable looking thing[s] you ever saw, a great deal worse off than the negroes, ragged, and dirty, and they live in little Misserable Huts, on Corn Bread, and Pork. *Heg describes the habit of dipping, as practiced by some women in the community.* They have a small brush, which they dip in snuff, and suck — is not that nice? *The manuscript of this letter is badly torn.*

To Gunild, April 25, 1862
[Van Doren Mss.]

Island No. 10. Has been sick, but is better. Reports receipt of news of Governor Harvey's death. That is an awfull thing for Wisconsin. I had a long letter from him a day or two before he left home. *There are brief postscripts to Edmund and Hilda.*

To Gunild, April 26, 1862
[Van Doren Mss.]

Island No. 10. Attempts to cheer up his wife. Regrets to learn that Elmer and Hilda have measles. Comments on suffering that he is witnessing. This whole country is full of destitute families, wemen sitting at home and the soldiers all around them, breaking into their houses and taking their property.

To Gunild, May 2, 1862
[Van Doren Mss.]

Island No. 10. He has heard from Commodore Foote that enemy gunboats may get up the river and so for three days has been busy mounting Guns on the Island. *As soon as all is safe on the river, will have Gunild come down.*

To Gunild, May 5, 1862

HEAD QUARTERS ISLAND 10
May 5th 1862.

DEAR GUNILD —

Ole came down to day, with your letter, and the other things you sent me. I am much obliged — for the Pantaloons, & Coat, and particularly the *Soldiers wife*, as they call the needle Books — down here.

I am not yet prepared to go home, but I shall go now in a few days since Ole came back. I am getting better every day, but I will have to get a certificate from the Doctor before I can get leave of absence.

I believe I told you in my last letter that Comador Foot sent me a Dispatch, warning me to be prepared to meet the gun Boats, should they try to get up the river. He was afraid that they might get by his fleet and if they did we would have to stop them at Island N° 10. We have worked night and day getting cannon in a shape to enable us to give them a warm reception.

I do not wish to go away from here untill I am certain that we are perfectly safe. It would be wrong for me to be away should there be any fight here.

The people down here are still strong *Secesh* — particularly the wemen. They seem to be perfectly crazy on this war. We have got New Orleans — and we are fast getting every important place. This war will soon be over. When this war is over I am going to own a good Farm down here somewhere. It is some of the richest country in the world and if such a man as Ole Luraas could be down here and work a Farm, he could get rich in a very short time. They are all lazy, and do not want to work dow[n] here. If it was not for their negroes they would starve to death.

I am in command of this place now, and acting *Brigadier General*. Borchs[enius — *Ms. torn*], my adjutant, is *acting assistant adjutant General* — all of which sounds very big,

but means very little.   It is getting late, and I must close.
Maybe I will come home, before I write another letter.   I
can not tell.

My love to all of you.   When I come home I want to see
Edmund ride on his new saddle, and his pony.

Your Own

HANS

To Gunild, May 10, 1862

CAIRO May 10, 1862.

DEAR GUNILD

I left Island N° 10 day before yesterday, expecting to go
home, but I can not get away for a week yet.   The Gen.
who is in command, was very anxious I should not go away
for a few days, and you must make up your mind to be disappointed again.   If nothing hapens to prevent me, I shall
start for home the latter part of next week.   This is Saturday, and I am going to try and get home by a week from to
night.

We all expect a big Battle up at Corinth, and I expect I
had not ought to go away untill after that Battle is fought.
If I should come and stay while that fight goes on, I suppose
people up there would say that [I] had come home to get out
of the way.   Although we do not expect where we are to
have anything to do with the Battle up at Corinth, yet if we
should happen to get beat up there, we may also have something to do.

A Battle must be fought within a very few days, and perhaps, already has been — but we have no information of it.
If the rebels are whipped there, the war will soon end — we
will have no more big Battles, but there will be need of soldiers for a long time yet.

I should have been very glad to have gone home to day,
but as I am nearly well again, and have plenty to attend to,
I do not feel as much anxiety about it except on your account.

I know you are very anxious to see me.

If I could only know the day I would be in Chicago I would have you meet me there but everything is so uncertain about the *army.*

I have neglected to write because I expected to go home. My best love to all of you.

Your Own

HANS

To Gunild, May 12, 1862
[Van Doren Mss.]

Island No. 10.   Is waiting only to hear from Corinth, before going home on leave.

To Gunild, June 4, 1862

CAIRO ILL. June 4, 1862.

MY DEAR—

I have got so far on my way back to the Regiment, and shall go down to the Island this afternoon.   I have heard from there that everything is nearly right.   They have lost several men while I have been away, among the rest old Benjamin, who you remember Doctor Newell spoke about.   He died of decease of the heart I hear.

I am feeling first rate, and perfectly well.   I hear the boys are all anxious to see me back.

I met Jones in Chicago, and had quite a talk with him, so much that had he not been a coward he would not have taken what I told him without showing fight.[26]   He has tried to raise a Norwegian Company for the 3 months service in Chicago, but I think he has given that up too.

There is sent down a large number of Troops to Columbus, on the Mississippi River, to repair the rail road from there down into Dixie, and it may be we will get an opportunity to

---

[26] Heg had visited Chicago and his home in Wisconsin in May during a leave of absence.   He alludes to his trip in a letter of June 27.   Lars O. Dokken in a letter of June 4, 1862, mentions the return of the colonel from a visit to Madison.   Ager, *Oberst Heg og Hans Gutter,* 106.

take Memphis by that rout. I shall be glad to get a chance
to do something, and I think we will if this expidition goes
on, but it will take a good while to repair the rail road.

Christopher Sögaarden spoke to me about getting the use
of one or both of the Horses for a while, and take them into
pasture & work them. I told him he might talk with you
and Hans Wood about it: but I guess if you can get pasture
for them at any place in the neighborhood, you need not let
them go. I met him just as I was going away & did not talk
much with him. Mr Moe will sell them I think pretty soon.

I have time for no more. I wrote this because I do not
know how soon I can send a letter again. The daily boat
has been taken off and it is uncertain how often we will be
able to send or recieve mail.

You must write often, and w[r]ite long letters. I know
you can when you have a mind to.

from Your Own

HANS

To Gunild, June 6, 1862
[Van Doren Mss.]

*Island No. 10. Came down on Thursday. All well, save
that* there was a good deal of strife and trouble going on
amongst the men. *Is angry about a rumor that he is going
to resign.* Our Boys have got new Uniforms and they look
first rate.

To Gunild, June 10, 1862
[Van Doren Mss.]

Island No. 10. We are off again — I have just received
orders to pack up and take my whole command except two
companies, and go on Steamer to Hickman — and from there
to Union City. *Captains Gordon and Gasman are to remain
with their companies to guard the port. Heg is* almost sory
to leave, but he is glad on the other hand to get out in the
field and a little more activity and work.

II. IN CAMP AND ON THE MARCH

To Gunild, June 14, 1862

HEAD Q^r UNION CITY
June 14th 1862

MY DEAREST —

I came here yesterday from Island N° 10, and I have not had a chance to write back home since, before now.   I have nothing particularly to write about, except, that all is O. K. I am living in my tent now, and getting along very well, although I do not live as well as I did at our old Quarters, Island N° 10.

There are plenty of Wisconsin Soldiers here, the 12 & 13th are both near by us.

This is a fine healthy country, and I believe it will be better for us than to have stayed long at Island N° 10.   I made a good many friends at Island N° 10, and shall never feel ashamed to go back there again.   When I came away, some of the ladies sent me several nice things, Flowers, Cakes &c, and plenty of invitations to come out and say goodbye. The plan is for us to march down through the country to Memphis, along the Rail Road, and to fix it up as we go along.   There is very little prospect of meeting any Rebels where we are now, as Gen. Halleck is down below us with his whole army.

Our Camp here is right on the same spot where we stopped when at Union City last Sp[r]ing.

We are in Gen. Michels [*Robert B. Mitchell*] Brigade, and still under Gen. Quinbys command.   Mitchell I have been aquainted with since last winter.   I must close by sending you my best love.

God Bless You

Yours, HANS

DEAR EDMUND

You must let me know how the store runs, and how it is with the ponies.

I know you will be a good boy and do what your mother tells you. *Good Bye.*

DEAR HILDA —

How is the Piano? Has your little fingers learned to play on it yet? When I come back next time I expect to have you play *Old John Brown* for me.

Give my love to Hans Wood and all others and Write to me often. Address it Union City Ky. [*Tenn.*] via Columbus Ky.

from Your *own* father —

HANS C. HEG

To Gunild, June 15, 1862

[Van Doren Mss.]

HEAD QUARTERS 15th WIS VOL.

June 15th 1862. UNION CITY KY. [*Tenn.*]

MY DEAR GUNILD.

This is Sunday morning and one of the prettiest mornings I ever saw in my life. We are camped in the woods, and it is very pleasant. Ole has got his resignation and will be at home in a few days. I have sent a man down to Island N° 10 to let him know that he may go home. I am very glad of it on account of the store in Waterford. He will make it pay — and Edmund will have to be in my place.

The pay master has not been here yet, and the boys do not want he should come now till after the 1st of July, so that we can get 4 months pay at once.

I hope you are enjoying yourself well — and not troubeling yourself too much about me for I am getting along well enough. I am healthier than I ever was at home and time goes off very fast. We are having our regular Battallion

Drill every day, and the ballance of the time I am riding around the Country on my nice black Horse. I have got the best Horse in the army, and I have already been offered 300 Dollars for him — but he is not for sale, for any money. If Secesh does not kill him for me, he is going to be my wifes riding horse when I get home — so you must commence to practice riding, I believe you can ride some.

I am not going to trouble myself any with my bussiness afairs up in Wisconsin now. I got everything pretty well arranged when I was there last, and what is to be done must be done by you, and *Edmund* — I think I have two good agents in you and him.

I have not heard a word from home since I left, but I hope we shall soon have our regular mail. Dr Himoe has not come back again yet. The soldiers are getting very healthy, and doing better than I supposed they would. I have just 500 with me here — besides one Battery of Artillery which is under my Command. We will soon start towards Memphis, I expect.

You must give my respects to all. The boys from near Waterford are all well except Jacob Nyhuus — who is sick at Island N° 10. He seems to be nearly crazy. Major Reese is gone home sick.

Borchsenius is getting well again, but has been very sick.

How does the sheep get along? and how have you disposed of the wool?

Write to me as often as you can — and write long letters, tell all that is going on and if there is anything wrong with you, or the children or any body els, let me know it. You know I can get home, should anything be wrong with you any time. Goodbye my Dear —

Yours HANS

To Gunild, June 17, 1862

UNION CITY, TENNESSEE
June 17th 1862.

MY DEAR WIFE

I do not get any letters from you yet, still I will try and keep you posted as often as I can how, and what I am doing. I wrote you on Sunday and sent it yesterday. I am still here, and I have quite a large command under me now. Besides the 15th Wis. I have the 22d Mo, the 7th Wis. Battery and the 2d Ill. Battery. I shall move the whole force from here in a few days to a place called Trenton 30 miles farther south. I am acting Brig. Gen — is not that big? But it is only honor, much work and no pay. I have my head quarters in a good house about one mile from the regiment. I ride up to get my meals 3 times a day. I swore in over 60 Secesh yesterday, and I tell you we swear them strong, and if they do not live up to thier Oath they are to be shot.

I have found a good many Union men in this place — more than at Island N° 10. Col McKee is commanding the Regiment. Capt Berg has resigned, and will go home in a few days. I shall appoint Hans Hanson Capt in his place. John Rice will take Hansons place. S. O. Himoe has not come back. I am very anxious to see him back.

The house is full of *Secesh* and Matthews is swearing the devils in, and letting them go. They are all a lot of ignorant people. Many of them have never known what they have done when they went in for the confederate goverment. A large majority of them do not know how to spell their own name.

I have been so bussy yesterday and to day that I have had no time to go out into the country. I have had many invitations to do so.

Gen. Halleck is moving down in the same direction where we are, and we will soon meet his forces on this rail road.

I am fixing up the Rail Road south of here, and the one run-
ing west to Hickman.

I am in hopes Ole will come up from Island N° 10 to day
and bring us the mail. We have had none since we left that
place. I never was healthier in my life than now. I hope
you are the same. If there is anything a matter with you
let me hear it. I will burn your letters as I promised.

My best love to you all and particularly to you. I wish
I could see you just for a few days — but there is no chance
till we get permanently located somewhere, when I will try
and make you a visit again. The paymaster is expected
here in a day or two.

Good by — Your Own

HANS

To Gunild, June 18, 1862

[Van Doren Mss.]

Headquarters, U. S. forces, Tennessee. Almost the entire
population has come in and taken the oath of alligeance.
Last night Gen. Quinby came down here and stayed with
me. I shall leave here to morrow or next day for Trenton
in this State, a place about 30 miles south of here, where I
expect we will stay for awhile to help put the rail road in
running order. *Heg hopes that the war will soon end.*
Beauregards army is entirely used up. I have sworn in over
25 deserters from his soldiers the two days I have been here.
The paymaster is soon expected. I shall get 450 Dollars —
and I shall send home 400.

To Gunild, June 19, 1862

[Van Doren Mss.]

*Union City, Tennessee. Has acted as post commandant
since preceding Monday.* Capt. Berg has resigned, and I
have recommended Hans Hanson Grinda for Captaincy of

MRS. HANS C. HEG

[From a photograph supplied by Mrs. Sophia Jacobson Sanderson
of Harmony, Minnesota.]

GUNILD AND HANS HEG

[From tintypes in the possession of Mrs. Sophia Jacobson Sanderson
of Harmony, Minnesota.]

THE HEG HOMESTEAD AT MUSKEGO

[From a print in the possession of Mr. Albert O. Barton, Madison, Wisconsin.]

the Company, and John Rice for 1ˢᵗ Lieut.[1] *He sends home
a picture of Lieutenant Henry S. Lee of the Seventh Wisconsin Battery, who is his adjutant at the post.*

To Gunild, June 22, 1862
[Van Doren Mss.]

Camp Ethridge, Tennessee. We left Union City on Friday,
and got here this morning. This is Sunday. I have had a
big command and plenty to attend to. We will probably
leave here on Tuesday or Wednesday for Humbolt, a place
30 miles south of here, and on the rail road from Columbus
to New Orleans. *He acknowledges a letter, postage stamps,
and a newspaper, and reports the return of Dr. Himoe.
Sharp criticism of his brother Ole.*

To Gunild, June 24, 1862

CAMP NEAR TRENTON TENN.
June 24ᵗʰ 1862.

MY DEAR.
I have just camped here at this place with my command,
and shall stay here at least till to morrow morning. I have
more time to write now than when I wrote you my last letter
from Camp Ethridge. We found all our mail here at this
place, and amongst the letters I got, was yours of June 8ᵗʰ.
I am glad to hear from you, and very glad indeed to hear
that you are having a pleasant time at home. That is all I
care for. I am all right myself and I hope you will not
trouble yourself about me too much.

We go from here to Humbolt, a place 11 miles south of
here on the rail road, and where we will probably stay for a

[1] Hans Hanson of Norway, first lieutenant of Company C, was made captain
on June 12, 1862; *Roster*, 1:810. In the same letter Heg observes that the
"boys" want him to make Christian Heyer second lieutenant. Heyer was
sergeant of the company. *Roster*, 1:811.

while.   It took us two days to get from Camp Ethridge to this place.   We traveled only a part of each day.   I have not had command of the Regiment since we left Union City, as I have been in command of the expidition.   I have had the 15th Wisc., the 8th and 7th Wis. Battery, the 22^d Missouri and a Signal Chorps under my charge.   Mathews and Henry Lee has been my *aids*.[2]   There is to be a Union meeting here to morrow, and we may stay over to attend it.   If we do I may have to make a speech.   There is many Union people here, but the most are Secesh.   I do not think it is any warmer down here than up in Wisconsin.   I have not felt it much yet, there is no musketoes, the night[s] are quite cool.   I was very glad to see from your letter that the Piano is good company to you.   I thought it would be, and I hope Hilda will learn to play on it.   Edmund I know will learn very fast.

There is not any prospect of any fighting down here — we may have some skirmishes but we will have no big fights. The only place the Rebels can do anything after this, is at Richmond.   They are perfectly used up here in the valley of the Mississippi.   Nobody knows where they are.   The most of them are comming home, and are glad of getting away. They are leaving by thousands.   I know it, for I have sworn in several Hundred myself — amongst them several officers. I am in hopes it will not last long, or at least if I am to stay in the army much longer I shall get to a place where I can have you with me.   The paymaster will pay us off in a very few days, and I will try some way to send my money home. I shall have a good deal to spare.   I will write a few lines to Hans Wood and send it in this letter.   If you think best to get along without him — you may let him have just as much money as he wants and let him give his note for it, and I will settle with him when I get home about his pay.   You may read what I write to him, and fix it up amongst you — but I

---

[2] The two aids were Selah Mathews of the Fifteenth Wisconsin and Lieutenant Henry S. Lee of the Seventh Wisconsin Battery.

still think you had better have some one to stay with you. I will leave it all to yourself however.

I have felt so mad at Oles crazyness in running home the way he did, that I have not got over it yet. By his foolishness he has made me a great deal of trouble.

I hope now that he has got it his own way he will stay at home — and never leave again till he gets old enough not to be homesick. Good By my Dear — take good care of yourself — and we will yet have happy times together.

Next time I will write to Edmund and Hilda. God Bless you all.

Yours, HANS

To Gunild, June 26, 1862
[Van Doren Mss.]

Camp near Humboldt, Tennessee. My tent is under the Shade of a large fine apple tree. We have the prettiest Camp we have ever had, plenty of good Spring Water, and on high and dry ground. *Writes of expected visit from paymaster.* I hope you will go out on the farm once in a while, and go amongst your aquaintances and visit, for it will help you much about passing off the time. *Postscripts to Edmund and Hilda.*

To Gunild, June 27, 1862

CAMP HUMBOLT TENN June 27 — 1862.

DEAR GUNILD

I have very little to do to day. We are laying idly in our apple orchard doing nothing but eat and drink. I have promised to write to you as often as possible and I will do so as long as your Postage stamps hold out for me, but you will have to send me some more before a great while. Do not send but a few at a time by mail, I may not get the letters.

I have heard from Island No 10 that Ole has come back, and I expect him here every day. The two companies that are left there will be here in a short time I think. Where we will go to from here, nobody knows. We may lay here a month, and we may not lay a week.

I send you a copy of the "Jay hawkers Dixie." They are camped right by [the] side of us. They came up and sere-naded me last night, and sang Dixie & John Brown, and I had to make a speech to the boys.[3] The Jay Hawkers and Skandinaves, are the best friends in the world. The Jay Hawkers came up to some of our boys yesterday and pro-posed to go in partnership with them, for they said we could beat them steal[ing] honey. Our boys found a place where there was 5 or 6 Bee hives, and the Jay Hawkers were watch-ing the hives till it should get dark so the Bees would be in, but some of the Skandinaves pitched right in, and never cared for the Bees, and took all the honey. The Jay hawk-ers are noted for stealing niggers, and for troubeling the rebels, more than anybody els. Doc Himoe has found many of his Kansas friends down here.

The soldiers are having exelent times. They have plenty of honey, apples, Blackberries and almost every thing els in the shape of eatables. Thier health was never better. Chickins, Sheep, lambs & Pigs, belonging to rebels, suffer awfully. I do not think we have any prospect for a fight, unless we should be moved towards Washington. Our Regi-ment stands very high now in the estimation of the General officers in command at present. I am next in command to Gen¹ Mitchell, and in his absence I am the commander of the Brigade.

He is very unpopular with the most of the Regiments, and will have a good deal of trouble with some of them. Mit-

---

[3] The "Jayhawkers" referred to by Colonel Heg probably were soldiers of the Seventh Kansas Cavalry, commanded by Colonel A. L. Lee. On the name and its association with violence and pillage in the free soil conflicts in the Kansas and Missouri border country, see Kansas State Historical Society, *Col-lections*, 14:203–207.

chell is pro-slavery, and wants to see niggers returned to their masters, as much as possible.

We expect a mail to day, and I hope to hear from you. I will write every time I have an opportunity to send letters. It is now nearly a month since I was at home. It does not seem that much to me. Time has passed off very fast, faster even than it used to do at Waupun. I heard from Island 10 to day. One of the officers of the artillery co. down there found 3 *Sece[s]h* flags in the cushion of a chair. He had learned it from some body, and he went and cut the cushion open, and found them. One is a large one said to be worth $150⁰⁰. Most every body is Secesh around here. They are very ignorant. The wemen sit in the hall and chew tobacco and eat snuff all day, while the niggers do thier work for them. This is a very fine country, if the people were not so lazy, this would be a great State. I will write again soon. Good bye my Dear.

Your own HANS

It has just comme[n]ced raining, but my tent keeps me dry & nice.

"JAY HAWKERS DIXIE"

1

Since Brown was hung in fifty nine
What times b[e]yond Masons and Dixons line
    Look away, Look away, Look away, Dixie line
There tar and feathers and Kansas agressions
Have all turned out in a mighty secession
    Look away, Look away, Look away Dixie line

Chorus

Then I wish I was in Dixie, away, away,
Over Masons and Dixons line I am g'wine
To fight or die for my country
    Away, away, away down south in Dixie
    Away, away, away down south in Dixie

2

When Abram Lincoln was elected
The southern states were all dejected
    Look away &c.
So South Carolina just seceeded
And went to the Devil where she was needed
    Look away &c.

Chorus

3

There's good old Mary in ages past
And out of her seven Devils the[y] cast
    Look away &c.
But Uncle Sams case is turned about
From him eleven Devils cast themselves out
    Look away &c.

Chorus

4

Gen¹ Butler said he would put down slaves
But they came to his camp and he found them Braves
    Look away &c.
So he caught an elephant I suppose
What to do with it old Abe hardly knows
    Look away &c.

Chorus

5

There's Jefferson Davis and rabbed Toom[b]s
Who think old Wemen can whip us with Brooms
    Look away &c
But we've a Broom of Northern steel
to Brush them down from head to heel
    Look away &c

Chorus

6

The south stole our money and shot our men
Want to borrow our guns and do it again
    Look away &c
They stole our Forts and they stole our cannon
I wish to God they^d stole Buchannan
    Look away &c

Chorus

7

Well if they dont come back, they^ll not be forgotten
And get nothing to eat but powder and cotton
    Look away &c
For old John Brown made them all turn pale
And old Abe is after them with a rail.
    Look away, &c

Chorus

To Gunild, June 28, 1862

CAMP HUMBOLT TENN.
June 28th 1862.

MY DEAR GUNILD.

I got your letter of the 23^d to day. I am much obliged. Hans wrote me quite a letter too.

I have just received orders to take command of the Post here, and to stay here with my Regiment, the 22^d M°, the 8th Wis. Battery and 2^d Ill Battery. I have already sent Co. "F" out to guard a Bridge on the Rail Road 3 miles from here. I am still ½ mile from the village, but shall probably move down to morrow, and take up my quarters. I have appointed Mathews Quarter Master of the Regiment instead of Ole, and I tell you he feels good. He has been very homesick &c, but he has brightened up wonderfully since he got the appointment. I shall probably also make Clemeson a

Leiutenant soon.[4]   Everything is going on first rate.   The boys are all getting well, and feeling good.   They are glad to stay here.   This is such a fine place and very healthy.

Gen. Mitchell goes to *Corrinth* with the most of his force, leaving with me what I have had command of ever since I left Union City.

The man that was shot, which I spoke about in my last letter is from Co. "B."   He was shot by *Luse Johannes* I learn.   The Lieutenant where he is says he was shot by a man in Co. "C." by the name of John Johnson, and he must be the One.   The man who is shot will be apt to die.   He was shot in the breast, going right through his lungs, but was alive two days ago.   I sent a carriage after him to day. Borchsenius has sent in his resignation also, and will go home soon.

Ole will be up here in a day or two.   No paymaster has been here yet.   We are getting short of funds very fast.

I have nothing more to write than to let you know that I am well and hearty as usual.   It is some warm but not too warm, to lay still.   Hans Wood promised to fill my Haver Sack with Sour Crout if I will send it up next fall.   I am afraid he is counting his chickins before they are hatched, and besides that I am no deuchman.

My kindest regards for all.   Write as often as possible.

Your Own HANS

To Gunild, July 2 and 3, 1862

HEAD QUARTERS HUMBOLT TENN.
July 2ᵈ 1862.

MY DEAR GUNILD:

I have neglected to write to you for a couple of days, because I did not know whether we were to stay here or not, and I do not yet for certain but I have been ordered in com-

---

[4] The reference is probably to Andrew Clement, who was made first lieutenant of Company K on October 10, 1862. *Roster*, 1:826.

mand of the Post, and have been so since yesterday morning. I am occupying a fine large Parlor with a piano in it, and as I am writing the boys are playing Dixie, John Brow[n] & other *national* tunes. I am boarding at the Hotel which by the way is kept by a rabid Secesh. I have a good room and Bed, but the board is nothing to brag of. He is charging 50 ^{cts} per meal. I have just notified him that he may have his choice, furnish us meals at 25 ^{cts} or shut up his shop. I shall make him do this if I am left to command at this place. I have it very pleasant here — a daily train of cars each way, a telegraph officer in the building, and I can telegraph to you any time I please. The operator just came down to let me know that Vicksburg is taken, and there is a general Hurah amongst the boys. I said that I do not know whether I am to stay here or not. I think I shall know it before I finish this letter, as I am only waiting for the train to come in with dispatches. Mathews is Quartermaster for the Regiment, and he is now also acting Post Quarter Master. He was appoint[e]d for that by Gen Mitchell. John Rice is in the office with me, but I shall soon have Hauff come down here if I stay.[5] I had orders yesterday to stay here with my Regiment and 4 companies of the Kansas Jay Hawkers, but Gen. Mitchell has had orders to come back here, as I expect to go on south. He telegraphed to me yesterday that he was comming back, as he had started for Union City. I have just issued orders for the celebration of the 4th of July — Firing of guns, reading the Declaration of Independence &c. The Secesh has burned a great deal of cotton around here — and I am sory to say there are a good many of the troops here that are behaving very badly, stealing and robbing the Houses nights. I have arrested a few.

We have had no mail for several days, but expect to get one by the train now comming in. Ole has not been up here.

[5] Henry N. Hauff, an immigrant of 1857, was originally first lieutenant in Company G. He later served as adjutant and then as captain of Company E. Johnson, *Det Skandinaviske Regiments Historie*, 123; *Roster*, 1:804, 814.

I am expecting him every day. Holmen came here yesterday. He is to go in partnership with Allen as Sutler. I will lay this letter aside and finish it as soon as the cars have come in.

July 3ᵈ 1862.

The cars came in about 3 o'clock yesterday afternoon and with them came orders for us to move. We go from here to Corinth and start to day sometime. I am sory to have to go away from here. We had such a nice place, but so it is, we must obey orders.

I shall take care of myself wherever I may be and I hope you will do the same. Before long this misserable war will close, and we shall yet have a chance to enjoy life together. I do not know how soon I shall have an opportunity to write again. If you should not get another letter for a week, you must not feel uneasy. I am not sure yet whether we go by foot or by car. It is 80 miles from here to Corinth, and by foot it would take us a week. By cars we can go in 6 or 8 hours. I hope to be able to get a chance to go by Rail Road. Ole has acted badly by not comming on and bringing up the rest of our Quarter Master Stores.

The Paymaster has not paid us yet. I hear he is sick at Trenton. We have very little sickness in the Regiment. I suppose from what little I have been able to hear by Telegraph that we have had a big Battle at Richmond. I hope we have come out all right. If we have, it will undoubtedly soon put a stop to the war. If we are whiped then it will prolong it for sometime. There is not much prospect of fighting down here. The rebels are all scattered in every direction. Tennessee, is becomming loyal.

I must close. I shall watch every chance to send you a letter. You must write me often. I would like very much to spend the 4ᵗʰ of July with you, but I expect to have to march instead of celebrate. I am in exelent health, and doing finely. I hope Edmund and Hilda are good children.

If they are I will soon come home and see them. My best love to all of you.

From Your own Dear husband,

HANS.

To Gunild, July 4, 1862
[Van Doren Mss.]

Humboldt, Tennessee. Is sending seven hundred dollars to Gunild by Ole. Ole has bought Colonel Heg's interest in the store and given him a note for two thousand dollars. Advises Gunild on how to bank and invest her money. An undated fragment repeats much of this and contains postscripts to Hilda and Edmund. To Edmund: I have sold to Ole my part in the store, but I want you to attend the store and learn to be a good clerk, so that when I come back I can have you tend store for me.

To Gunild, July 6, 1862

CAMP NEAR CORINTH MISS
July 6th 1862.

MY DEAR WIFE.

I am again able to write you. This is a beautifull Sunday morning, and it would be pleasant to be at home with you such a day as this. We left Humbolt on Friday the 4th of July on the cars, after haveing celebrated the 4th very pleasantly. A very pretty spot was selected in a grove, where our Regiment was drawn up, and Three companies of a Minnesota Cavalry Regt. Govornor Ramsey of Minnesota delivered an address after the Declaration of Independence had been read. Our Band played very fine. A good many citizens with thier wives & Ladies were present. Several Toast[s] were given and speeches made. I must brag a little on my own speech. I felt better — and more in a humor to speak than I ever did in my life. Col. McKee made a speech, but run into politics too much. He is very ultra, in his political v[i]ews, too much so to ever become a pleasant speaker. He lacks policy. I will not bother you any more about this but go on and let you know something about our present prospects. From Humbolt to Corinth is 80 miles. The cars are not run in the night for fear of an attack from the Rebels, so we laid over at Jackson till yesterday morning, and reached Corinth about noon. There is no good camp ground at Corinth so we were ordered to move 4 miles farther down along the rail road, where we are now. The 8th Wis. Regt. is here close by us. I visited Capt Lyon, and Col Murphy [6] yesterday, and had a very pleasant time with them, drinking wine, Beer &c till nearly night. They were very glad to meet us, and I tell you it is pleasant to find such men as Capt Lyon & the Col. We are attached to Jeff. C Davis[es] Divission now, not the Rebel Jeff. Davis, but one of the best generals in our army, who unfortunately has nearly a simmilar name to the traitor Jeff. Davis. We are only waiting here for our waggons and teams to come up, by the road, when we will move 9 miles farther down the rail road to a place called Rienzi. We are then nearly in the front ranks of the army. I do not know how letters from you will reach me, but I send you an envelope with directions, which I have no doubt will reach me — of course letters directed to me . . . .

To Gunild, July 8, 1862

CAMP NEAR CORINTH.   JULY 8th 1862.

MY DEAR GUNILD.

I wrote to you on Sunday, but the letter has not been sent yet. It will be sent to day. I also sent an addressed envelope inside — but We shall probably not go down to the place we were ordered to then, and so I wish you would not

---

[6] Robert C. Murphy of St. Croix Falls, Wisconsin, was colonel of the Eighth Wisconsin. *Roster*, 1:577.

use that envelope. My address will be Corinth I think, at
least for a while. Address your letter — " Col. H. C. Heg,
15ᵗʰ Wis vols. in Robt. B. Mitchells Brigade, near Corinth
Miss."

We have moved our camp three miles since last Sunday,
and have a very fine healthy place — and plenty of good
spring water — but the *flies* are so awfull thick, that if it was
not for my musquito Bar they would eat me up. The latest
papers we have here are of July 4ᵗʰ. It seems from them
that we have got whipped at Richmond. If we have — I
am afraid it will lenghten out the prospects of peace — for
sometime. I do not think there is much prospect of any
more big fights down this way. The fighting will be done
down at or near Richmond. All the reports in the news-
pepers about fights and skirmishes down here are mostly
fals. There was a small fight at a place called Boonville a
few days ago, but It was all cavalry on both sides. Boonville is 20 miles south of here. I believe it is the object of
Gen. Halleck to keep us near this place untill the weather
gets a little cooler, before he sends us any farther south.
There are any quantity of camps around here — the whole
country is covered with tents, but a great many of the Regiments have not more than three or four Hundred men — the
16ᵗʰ Wis. has not more than 300 men fit for duty — the 18ᵗʰ
is still worse — the 17ᵗʰ which has not been in any fights
either, has only about 300 men on duty. In the 8 companies
I have with me, I have 500 men for duty. My Regiment is
one of [the] biggest now in the service. I see that three Hundred Thousand more men are called for. This will be apt
to clean out a good many more people from Wisc. I am
glad I went in as early as I did. It may become necessary
yet to send all the able bodied men we have in the north.
We have had no mail for over 10 days, & I have not heard
from you for a very long time. I am quite anxious to hear
how you are getting along. It is quite warm and uncom-

fortable, but not any warmer than I expected to find it down here at this season. Everything is very dear, but we can buy any thing we wish at the Sutler shops. I will write again soon — and therefor stop this time. Ole can tell you all about how we live. I suppose he is at home by this time.

My Dearest, Gunild, how glad I should be to have you with me. It will be a pleasant time when I can come and live with you once more. Good Bye —   HANS

To Gunild, July 9, 1862

HEAD Q^{rs} KANSAS & WIS BRIGADE.
NEAR CORINTH MISS.
July 9th 1862.

MY DEAR GUNILD —

Mathews brought us up a large mail last night, and amongst the rest was your letter of July 3^d. It is so pleasant to hear from home, and especially to hear that you are all doing well and that you are enjoying yourself. I am glad that you do not trouble yourself too much about me. I am as usual doing well and in good health. Gen. Mitchell is sick, and yesterday was put under arrest. I do not know for what. I am now commanding his entire Brigade. I am now in a new bussiness again — how I shall get through this, I do not know. I trust in Providence, and my usual good luck. If I make mistakes — it will be because I do not know my bussiness. It is very easy for a man to get himself into difficulty here. This large army is commanded by strick army officers & require matters attended to punctually. Mathews saw in the papers that he is appointed Quarter Master, and he feels good. Matters in the Regiment are in good order. The boys have plenty of money and are sending a good deal of it home. There are but very few sick. It is hot during the day, but in the night we have nice cool weather. We will not move to Rienzi, at present — but in all probability stay where we are for a few weeks. It is a very pleasant camp ground — but the worst trouble we have is the flies. There are some Secesh 20 or 30 miles from here — but not any great number of them. Not much prospect of fighting. They are all staking their chances on Richmond now. When Richmond falls, the confederacy is played out. It may not be possible for me to get home for sometime, but if I ever get permanently settled at any station I shall certainly send for you if I can make you comfortable, no matter what it costs. When the fighting is all over, the troops will be kept to garrison posts &c and keep the people loyal to the United States.

Willard has just come up from Island N° 10 with some of our goods.[7] He is not very well. I shall make him commissary Sergeant if he gets well enough. He looks poorer than when he left home. Furgeson is acting as my orderly.[8] When this war is over I shall have some good friends amongst the boys in this Regiment. I have made them what they are. I have also some that are not so much my friends. These men that have been compelled to resign, do not love me more than the law compels them. I trust Ole has come home all safe. He left with a good deal of money — for different persons. Tell Hilda to go down to the Store and buy her a new pair of shoes — and it will make her Toe well again. You must not be too sparing with your funds now — but live as well as you can. I am not suffering. We have plenty of good stuff to eat, and I often visit some of the Wisconsin Regiments and officers. Amongst the rest I see Lyon — and Col Murphy.

Give my Respects to all. My love to yourself and the children. Tell Andrea to write to me or let me know how she gets along.

Good By my Dearest

Yours — HANS C. HEG

[7] Probably DuBartus Willard of Racine, a private in Company C. *Roster,* 1:812.
[8] Perhaps "Furgeson" was Fergus Ferguson, a corporal in Company D. *Roster,* 1:813.

To Gunild, July 11, 1862

HEAD QUARTERS MITCHELLS BRIGADE
NEAR CORINTH
MISS: July 11ᵗʰ 1862.

MY DEAR.

Last night I got your letter of June 28ᵗʰ. I had already
got your letter, a day or two ago — of July 3ᵈ. I am glad to
see that you get my letters regularly. There is very good
mail arrangements here, so the mail comes here daily. We
get the daily papers, and they are generally about two days
old. The last news we have had from Richmond is not so
bad as we first heard. I think we will soon have Richmond.
The Army will do everything that is possible to be done to
take it now.

I have not much news to write you. I will tell you what
little I have. Clauson is going up to Cairo to morrow with
about 8000 Dollars to send home by Express for the Soldiers.[9] We were paid for two months and have still two
months due us. I think we will soon be paid again. Yesterday a big fine looking Negro *boy* came into my head
Quarters and after talking with him a little while I began to
suspect that it was a woman dressed in boys clothing. I
asked him what his name was, and after stopping a while he
said very modestly that it was *Mary Ann*. She had traveled
with one of the Batteries all the way from Humbolt, in
mens cloths. She looked very sory, and expected I would
send her back, but seemed very glad when she found out
I was not going to do it. I sent her down to Doc. Himoe
to attend on him. She is washing to day, and I see the Doc
has got her into Petticoats again. She works for the Hospital.

I still keep a finding some of my old friends again, to day
I met Gen. Buford, and had an invitation to come over to a

---

[9] " By common consent," writes Miss Jorgensen, Clausen " was appointed
custodian of such funds as the soldiers sent home." " Claus L. Clausen," 134.

place where he was to be presented with a fine sword and trappings. The Gen. took hold of me like an old friend. The tears fairly rolled down the old mans cheeks.

Gen. Hamilton of Wisconsin is camped right by our side.[10] Hamilton is Alberts old Colonel.[11] We live well here — have not much to do — plenty to eat and drink. If it was not for being away from all of you I should feel as well as I ever did.

But it would be nice to be with you again. I do not want you to understand that I would feel well to leave the service at the present time. No. When the war is over — when I have done my duty, Then I shall feel happy to go home and live with those I love. I will not say what I will do then, but I know we can enjoy ourselves.

I am waiting to hear from you again to day, but maybe I am expecting too much, to expect letters so often. What stories there is told about me by any body, does not trouble me at all. I hope you are not foolish enough to allow such things to trouble you. You said that certain persons told stories about me.

I have hardly time to write to any body but you. I wrote to Mitchell yesterday, which is the only letter I have written to any one except you for a long time. If you have the money on hand yet, get Ole to help you — and loan it out on a good Mortgage for about 10 per cent. If you cant do that send it to Holtons Bank for Deposit as you did the 400 Dollars when I was at home.

Next letter I will write Hilda and Edmund. I hope to hear that you will always be good children.

I am going to Bed. Good night. I trust you will sleep well.

Good night my Dear.

Your — HANS

[10] General Charles S. Hamilton organized the Third Wisconsin Volunteers. *Dictionary of American Biography*, 8:183.
[11] Albert Skofstad served as a private in the Third Wisconsin for several months before he became an officer of the Fifteenth. *Roster*, 1:402, 812.

To Gunild, July 14, 1862

H^d Qu^{rs} 3^d Brigade 3^d Division
Army of the Miss.   July 14th 1862

My Dear Gunild.

I will drop you a few lines again to day — haveing nothing particularly to do before 9 °clock this morning, when I have to report up at the Head Quarters of Gen. Rosecranse.[12]

Yesterday I visited the 16th and 17th Regiment. They are both in very bad condition. The 16th has not more than 300 men fit for duty. The 17th burried a great many last week. I understand as many as 9 in one day, but they have still more men than the 16th. The 14th and 18th are just as bad off. The 18th I understand have not more than 200 men for duty. We have the largest Regiment from the State at present, and besides that, our men are nearly all well and feeling in good condition. I am really proud of their appearance. I see that Wisconsin has to rais five more Regiments, besides filling up the old ones. They can not rais that many with out drafting. I want to see them draft. We will make some of these fellows come out who have laid at home sucking their thumb.

I think you may feel glad now that I went the time I did. It will be some credit to a man to have gone early. There will not be much credit for a man to enlist, or go in when he is obliged to do so — besides I have now already been of some service to the country. I have some experience now, that entittles me to a position &c. The best thing I ever did was, to go into this war when I did. If the service does not suit me I have a claim now, and I can resign whenever I please without being considered a coward or be looked upon with disgrace. I have done my duty — and can leave the service when I see fit. You must not flatter your self however that I am going to do so. I intend to stick it out, if I can — if my services are of any account. The country has a

[12] Major General William S. Rosecrans.

right to them in these times—and as long as you and the children live well and enjoy yourselves I must stay where I am. I am in hopes however, that this war will not last as long as it looks—and after being in the field a while, I may get a situation where I can have you with me. For that reason I sold out my store to Ole—and I have got my affairs in such a condition now that I can leave them with out any danger or injury. I am writing as usual, with my tent full of people, and every little while I am obliged to answer questions & sign papers. There is no time to be lonesom or homesick.

The time is comming when I can be with you again. Have good courage.

My Deares[t] wife—Good Bye— HANS

To Gunild, July 15, 1862
[Van Doren Mss.]

Camp near Corinth, Mississippi. Predicts that the crucial fighting of the war will be done near Richmond. Declares that the war would have been closed before now if politicians had not had the running of it. *Adds,* We have been fighting for Slavery so far, long enough.

To Gunild, July 17, 1862
[Van Doren Mss.]

Camp near Corinth. Every thing is just as quiet here as usual—the troops are all lying still doing nothing. Gen. Halleck has been ordered to Washington, and Gen. Grant takes his place here. Gen. Mitchell has been released from arrest, and of course my Brigadier Generalship is played out, he has taken command of the Brigade again. *Tells about food in camp.* It is Bread and Ham and Coffee three times a day. *Comment on sutlers:* Some of the Sutlers bring in a few things, but they charge enormously for what they have to sell.

To Gunild, July 19, 1862

CAMP NEAR CORINTH MISS.
July 19th 1862.

DEAR GUNILD.

Once more I have the pleasure of writing to you. This is about the only pleasure I have too, as I have no time to write to anybody els, if I wished to.

Our mail is still very unregular, and I have not any letter from you since the one that was dated the 10th July. I am still as healthy and in as good spirits as I ever was. Col. McKee is not very well and there are several of the soldiers unwell at present, but not a great many however.

There is some prospects of my getting a Brigade of my own to command. Gen. Hamilton of Wisconsin, in whos Divission we now are, is a good friend of mine. I visited him last night and had a couple of glasses of wine with him. He is a fine man, and very anxious that my Regiment should go in his Divission. It makes but little difference whether I am in command of a Brigade, or only my own Regiment, unless I could gain the tittle of *Brigadier General*.

Two of my officers have resigned this morning because I reported them for the Board of Examination, Lt. Tjentland, Co. E. and Irgins of Co K. both good for nothing.[13]

The news we get are mostly bad — both from Richmond and other places. It can not be otherwise. When the Goverment learn[s] to put in Generals that are true and loyal, and men that are not afraid to hurt slavery or the Rebels, then we will begin to see the end of this war. There will be a new policy adopted after this. The war will be carried on in a different way from what it has been.

You must keep up good courage, do not trouble yourself too much about me. I shall take good care of myself, and I have faith that I shall come out all right. It would not

---

[13] First Lieutenant Iver William Tjentland of Moscow, Wisconsin, and Second Lieutenant John E. Irgens of St. Ansgar, Iowa, resigned officially, according to the roster, on September 3, 1862. *Roster*, 1:814, 826.

have been possible for me to have stayed at home now anyway, and it is worth thousands to me that I went into the
service at the time I did.   I am now far ahead — and if my
health holds out, and the Goverment will do me justice —
you will not have occation to be ashamed of your *husband*.

You can hold up your head anywhere.   If I do have a
hard time now and then, I am well paid for my trouble when
I remember that I have a family at home who can feel proud
of the course I have taken.   Keep yourself cheerfull, and
trust to my management, and you will find that I shall come
out all right, and when the happy time comes that I can
come home and stay with you it will be real pleasure.

There is no use in fretting for it only makes you feel worse.
As long as you are all well — there is no trouble.   If any of
you should get seriously sick, I will get a leave of absence
when I ask for it.   I must close.   My Dear Good By —
write often.

Your own HANS

To Gunild, July 21, 1862

CAMP NEAR CORINTH MISS.
July 21ˢᵗ 1862.

MY DEAR GUNILD.

I do not get any letters from you, still I must not forget
to let you know how we are getting along.   The mails are
very unregular, and I suppose many of our letters still go to
Island Nᵒ 10.   We shall move again to morrow morning,
about 10 miles, where I expect we will stay quite a while.
The place we have here is very good, but it is right in the
woods where there is not a house to be seen any where.

The troops are moving in several directions to day.   There
is probably over One Hundred Thousand men here, but they
will soon be scattered in several directions.   This place is of
no account to hold, and the Rebels will never come here to
fight us.   We are attached to the 4ᵗʰ Division, commanded

by Jefferson C. Davis. His Head Quarters is at a place called Jacinto about 10 miles south from here. My address, now will be as I have marked it on the paper enclosed. I also send you a Picture of Adjt: Hauff — please keep it.[14] I will send you the pictures of the boys as fast as I can get them. I shall take mine as soon as I have time to do so, and send you, so that you may see how I look down here. I am about the toughest and healthiest man there is here. Col. McKee is not very well.

I am in good spirits, and very glad to move away from here. There is too many troops here to be very comfortable, besides a good many of our men are getting sick from being too still. There may be such a thing as my comming home before long. I have made an application. I dont want to hold out any hope to you, for fear I may not succeed.

I have very little time to write and my tent is full all the time.

You must excuse this poor *letter*. I will write you a good long one when we get down to our new place.

Good Bye My Dear Wife.

Your Own

HANS

To Gunild, July 23, 1862

CAMP NEAR JACINTO,
July 23^d — 1862.

MY DEAR GUNILD.

Again we have moved about 10 Miles. We are now near the County Seat of Tishomingo County, a little place called Jacinto. We are in the 2^d Brigade 4th Divission, the Brigade is commanded by an Illinois Col. by the name of Carlan.[15] The Divission is commanded by General Jefferson C. Davis.

---

[14] Hauff was not officially made adjutant until October 1, 1862. *Roster,* 1: 819.

[15] William P. Carlin, colonel of the Thirty-eighth Illinois, was from Carrollton, Illinois. He was promoted brigadier general May 7, 1863. *Report of the Adjutant General of the State of Illinois,* 3:74 (Springfield, 1901).

We are imidiately in the front now — and if there is any
chance to do anything we will have a chance. I hope you
will feel no uneasiness on that account. The fact that I
have got a position in the front shows that we are appreciated. There is no signs of any enemy here now. A force
of 6 or 800 is said to be located 20 or 30 miles south of us,
but they are very carefull not to come very near us. I said
in my last letter that there might be such a thing as my comming home sometime during the summer. I want to try
and rais another Regiment.[16] General Rosecranse and General Hamilton are both very anxious that I should do so, and
they have both written to the War Department asking for
leave of absence for me to do so. I do not care to have anything said about this, untill I see whether I get the leave or
not. It is generally expected that there will not be much to
do down here for a month or two, and if I can rais one more
Regiment, I can get me a permanent Brigade.

We have an excellent camp ground here — and have laid
it off in good stile. It rained very hard last night, and a
good many of the soldiers got wet, as they had not had time
to get up their tents last evening after they came in, but I
had my tent up, and the Doctor and myself had it as comfortable as could be. It is true we have it pretty hard sometimes, but we are all right as a general thing. I am just now
setting by my table in my tent, which is cool and shaded,
and my cook, a man by the name of Solberg, just brought
me in a nice cup of coffee, after Dinner. I have good white
sugar, sent me by the Doctor, and Jacob takes care of my
horse, makes up my bed, brushes my cloths &c. If it was
not for being away from home, and not seeing you around
me, I could feel happier here than anywhere els I have been.
The Regiment got a big mail on Monday, but not any letter
for me from you. I was disappointed. Ole has not written
either although he wrote to another man in the Regt.

[16] Heg's letter of July 30 to Reymert in reference to " one more Scandinavian
Regiment " is discussed ante, p. 33.

We still get the daily papers quite regularly, and it is a great help to us. The Chicago Tribune comes here about 2 or 3 days old. You must take that paper — all the time. I hope to have the War Department agree to my project of raising one more Regiment, and I will come up and see you, and take you around recruiting with me. I got well aquainted with the Govornor of Minnesota, and got permission to raise recruits in his state for this Regiment. If I can get two Scandinavian Regiments in the field I will claim to command them. Tell me in your letter how the crops look up on the farm — what they say about Ole comming back, and all the news you think of. Anything is interesting. I am well and hearty as usual — never was better. Good By my Dear — remember that when I come home I expect to find you cheerfull & happy & not troubling yourself too much about me.

Your own

HANS.

To Gunild, July 26, 1862
[Van Doren Mss.]

Camp Erickson near Jacinto, Mississippi. We get Newspapers very regularly, to day I got the 23^d, but our letters go poorly. *Tells of camp conditions.* I took dinner yesterday with the officers of Company A. and dined on Green Corn, Potatoes, Chicken Soup, Wine and Coffee. *Discusses the business of the sutler:* Holmen is doing a big business, he sells frequently for One Hundred and Fifty Dollars a day. *Tells of the people and the country:* The wemen down here are a great deal worse than the worst Norwegian or Deuch wemen you ever saw. They are dirty and ragged, and chew tobacco & spit tobacco juice as expertly as any Dandee, but few of them can read, and most of them never saw a Newspaper in thier life. The Country is very poor, heavy timber, and full of Bluffs, it looks very much like the California Gold

Mines. *Hopes for vigorous army movement and declares that few in South are loyal. Believes that his regiment has liberated more Negroes than any other regiment in that part of the army. Praises Companies A and C as* the best and healthiest *in the regiment, but condemns Company K.* They never can do anything except read thier Norwegian prayer Books and hang out a long face. *Asks for a keg of currant wine. Postscripts to Edmund and Hilda.*

To Gunild, July 29, 1862
[Van Doren Mss.]

Camp Erickson. We are right in the front now, there are no Union Troops south of us, but we have had Scouts out far enough to know that there are no Rebels near by. *He meets the captains and lieutenants twice a day, an hour each time, to give them instruction. The companies drill one hour a day.* How is Turk? Do you think he remembers me? I almost wish I had him here. *The war will not last always.* The people begin to sing "old John Brown" now, that is the best sign I have seen.

To Gunild, August 1, 1862
[Van Doren Mss.]

Camp Erickson. I am just now going up to Corinth to see Gen. Rosecranse, about my getting leave of absence to go to Wisconsin to fill up my Regiment, and to start another.

To Gunild, August 3, 1862
[Van Doren Mss.]

Camp Erickson. I got back from Corinth last night. *Tells of meeting Grant:* I got aquainted with Gen. Grant, and had quite a long talk with him about going home to raise another Regiment. They are all anxious that I shall, and Grant said I ought, to go up with the recruiting party that I am authorised to send by law, but I am waiting to hear from the war Department, and I hate to go up in the recruiting party because people would say that I picked myself out to go because I wanted to go home. *Speaks of his sons:* I want to give the <u>boys</u> a good education, but no money — let them work for it <u>as</u> you and [I] have done.

To Gunild, August 5, 1862

CAMP ERICKSON, MISS.
Tuesday morning Aug. 5th 1862

MY DEAR GUNILD.

The Regiment got a big mail yesterday but not any letter for me from home. I do not know as I could expect any, for I got a very good letter from you only a short time ago. I have just made out an application for the appointment of Captain Ingmanson — and Lt. James Larson as recruiting agents for the Regiment. I shall send 4 Privates more with them. They will probably start from here in about a week from now. I will have some of them come up and see you. I have heard nothing from the War Dept. yet, in answer to my application to go home and raise one more Regiment. I am expecting it daily though.

I have no great anxiety about going home at present. I have not been out long enough to have any right to go home on a visit, and if I am permitted to go home recruiting I will not be able to spend much time at home anyway. They are issuing some stringent orders to officers that are absent from their commands now. I am glad to see it. There are lots of these fellows spouting all over the Country. Just as well as they ever will be that ought to be with their Regiment and Companies.

I have not any news to write about at all to day. Everything is quiet. Some of our troops are moving from one place to another — but most of them are laying still. A good many of our men are not quite well — but none are very sick. I dreamt last night that I saw you. I thought

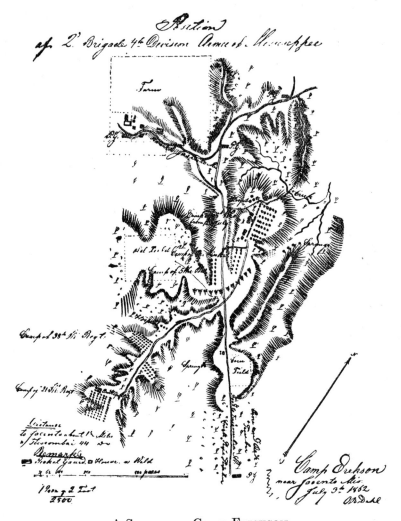

A SKETCH OF CAMP ERICKSON

[From original map that accompanied Colonel Heg's letter of August 5, 1862.]

you had come down to see me — but I waked up and found myself — alone in my tent. I had a visit from some old Wisconsin friends yesterday, and had a good jolly time of it.

Lt. Col. McKee is getting very anxious to go home — but I do not suppose there is any chance for him.

I think you ought to feel glad that I went into the war at the time I did now that almost everybody will have to go. I could not have stayed at home now any way — without being looked upon as a coward. I tell you my Dear — I would not have missed taking the course I did for all I am worth. I have done more for the goverment than any man that has gone from Wisconsin. You will say I am bragging. Well you know I can afford to brag to you — you are used to hear my brags.

I want to get this Regiment full — and if possible get one more of the same kind — and then I know but few will have done more to fight this Rebellion than I have. And even if I should stay in the army my full three years — I believe I can stand it. I shall be able to have you with me before long — and I could stand [it] ever so long if I was only stationed where I could have you along.

I send you in this letter a map of our camp, drawn by a man by the name of Dahl — it is very correct.

I get the Madison Papers every time the mail comes. It is very interesting to hear from Wisconsin. I suppose the people up there are harvesting now — and I see from the papers that the crops are very good. Ole Luraas I hope will raise enough for you on the farm, — and I would advise you to have your part of the wheat brought down to Palmer and Moes mill — and put in there and draw it out in Flour as you need it. The Oats you must not thresh, but feed it to the sheep — in the Bundle. Potatoes and such things you know what to do with. You ought to get you a good cow as soon as the one you have quits giving milk. Do not be too *stingy* — live well — no matter what it cost. I will get you all the money you want. I want you to keep healthy

and well—so that when the war is over I can have some
pleasure in spending my time with you and the children.
We will take a trip to Norway &C—what do you say?

Well the paper is all gone, or I would keep on writing
more nonesense. Good By my Dear.

Your own—HANS

To Gunild, August 7, 1862
[Van Doren Mss.]

Camp Erickson. Slavery is already dead and gone. *A general view:* The United States Goverment must be sustained, or we may as well all die defending it—we have no other place to go. *Heg foresees success of North:* But do not you believe for a moment that there is any danger—but what this goverment will come out right—and you will see it sooner now than you expect. *Much of the letter is devoted to cheering up his wife.*

To Gunild, August 9, 1862

CAMP ERICSON, NEAR JACINTO MISS.
Aug 9ᵗʰ 1862.

MY DEAR GUNILD.

Yesterdays mail brought me a letter from you and one
from Hans Wood. I am very glad to hear from you and
especially when you are all well. I get letters from you
about as often as I expect. If you will write to me once a
week I shall feel very well. If any of you should be taken
sick you will of course write oftener. Hans Wood wrote me
a good long letter too. The crops are good I understand.
Hans Wood says he does not know but he may get drafted.
I want he should come right down here, and I will keep him
from getting drafted, and give him good employment. I
wish Hans Wood would come down. I can find plenty of
employment for him. I shall write to him today. You will
have to let him have some more money if he wants it.

I was General Officer of the day yesterday and in riding around the Camps I came to old General Bufords Quarters, and had to stop and take dinner with the old man. He thinks a great deal of me, and the soldiers of the 15th Wis. He says there are no soldiers equal to them. He always has plenty of wine, and I can never get away from him without emptying a Bottle or two at his table.

The newspapers of yesterday gives us the news of another call for troops and that they are to be drafted. I am very glad to see that. I wish I had the power to draft some persons that I know. The rebellion will soon find its end now. If they will only work in earnest in this matter, send us down one million of men — and let them go to work — not keep puffing them through the newspapers telling what they will do — and never do anything. We are all the time reading about the gallant officers, and gallant Regiments that are being got up in Wisconsin and other places — and that is the whole of it.

My application to Washington for leave to go home and raise another Regiment has not got back. I do not know why it does not come. I do not want you to expect me — if it does come now. I do not know how I could be [of] any service if they are going to draft — and I may not come home even if I should get leave. I have not any particular anxiety to go home, unless I can do more for the goverment there, than I can here and as long as you and the children are well I could not be of any service to you if I did come home to stay a day or two.

The paymaster is here to day, and I think our boys will be paid off again. If we are, then I will send you some more money. I am going to send home one man from each company to enlist for the Regiment and they will probably start from here in a day or two. Some of them are going right to Waterford & I will write with them to you. There are some things I want you to send me, when they come back. Should Hans Wood — or anybody els take a notion to come down here and join the Regiment, so you could get a chance to send anything safely — you may send me — say 10 or 20 pounds of good white lump sugar — a keg of nice Butter — a jar or two of preserves — and have them buy me a box of *Catawaha Wine* on their way at Chicago — a good nice chees — would be all right. I dont expect you to send all these things — but they would all be acceptable. You can have them packed in a Box — and marked for me — and nobody will have any trouble in bringin[g] them along. I have got as much clothing as I can take care of — unless it should be a few pocket Handkerchiefs.

I can get all the things I have mentioned down here except Butter — but it costs like sixty. I should like very much to have Hans Wood come down. There are plenty of places for him here without going to soldiering. Albert has written for Even Skofstad to come down. I wish they would draft some of those fellows and make them come.

I am as usual — in fine health and good-courage. When I am only satisfied that you are not troubeling yourself too much about me, I am all right — but I hate to think that you are worrying about me and making yourself unhappy for a thing that can not be helped.

The hot weather does not trouble me at all. I do not feel it as much as I did at home. The boys from Co C. are nearly all well — very few are sick. I see the boys write in the Emigranten that I am keeping them strict. They are glad of it now. We have got the name of being the best diciplined Regiment — in this vicinity — it is all because I have kept the boys strict. I cant help feeling very proud of the appearance of the Regiment. They look fine.

I have bought me another Horse. I have 3 Horses now. I had to buy Borchseniuses, because I had signed his note and he is not able to pay it. I have 3 exelent Horses. They are worth down here over 600 Dollars. I shall keep the Black one and the one I bought of Borchsenius to take home for carriage Horses. They are well matched.

I got Hildas letter too, yesterday. I am glad she has a new Dress. I will send her and Edmund a letter by the men that goes up to enlist.

The crops are good. I hope that Ole Luraas will do well — But he is too anxious to sow wheat, and now when help is scarce he will have trouble to harvest it.

I will stop now. I do not know as you can read my letter anyhow. I have a very poor Pen. Clauson has made me a present of a Gold Pen — but it is not good.

Tell Edmund to write to me. I forgot to say that I have got Postage stamps every time — and that I am much obliged. I will pay you — when I come back.

My Dear Good Bye. Your HANS

To Gunild, August 11, 1862
[Van Doren Mss.]

Camp Erickson. I have given up getting any permission from Washington to go to Wisconsin — as they will commence drafting, there will be no necessity for raising Volunteer Regiments. *Expresses regret.* I should have liked very much to raise another Norwegian Regiment; but it will not be necessary now. *Reports that he is* passing time off studying — the Col. commanding the Brigade, is a young fellow of about my age, and a Captain in the regular Army for some time. He has a school every day — and we study millitary matters together. It is very valuable to me to have got into his Company, as I am learning a great deal.

To Gunild, August 14, 1862

CAMP ERICKSON NEAR JACINTO MISS.
Aug 14th 1862.

MY DEAR GUNILD.

We are under orders to march once more. This time we shall move about 16 or 18 miles East, over on the Memphis and Charleston R. R. The place we are going to is called

Iuka. It is said to be a very handsome place and good camps. Gen. Mitchell is there — and is in command of the Division now. Gen. Davis has gone home sick. The Regiment is going to march around by a place called Bay Springs, and it will probably take us three or four days to get around to Iuka, but the baggage is going through direct.

We may have a little brush with Secesh down at Bay Springs. They have been down there for some time and every time any of our men have come towards the place they have run. I have no idea [where] they are to be found. The Brigade consists of three Regiments and two Batteries. One of the Batteries is a Wis. Battery.

The boys are very glad to move — it keeps them much healthier.

Iuka is on the Rail-Road — and near the Tennessee River — a much more lovely place than this is. This war is winding up now. You will see the worst of it over by three months. I am in condition to know something about it. The rebels are suffering awfully — and they will not be able to stand it much longer. You have no idea what they are suffering down below here.

I have not time to write much more. I must superintend the getting ready of the Regiment. I have lived up to my promise of writing every other day, since I came here. You may not get any letter from me for a few days now, as I shall not be where I can send any. I will write as soon as I get where there is a chance to mail letters.

We will probably get to Iuka by Monday or Tuesday — to day is Friday. My best love to all of you. Good Bye.

Your own
HANS

III. FROM IUKA TO PERRYVILLE

To Gunild, August 16, 1862
[Van Doren Mss.]

Camp near Iuka, Mississippi. Tells of march from Camp Erickson to Iuka. The village is very pretty — with some large country residences. It has been one of the southern fashionable watering places, and a good many of the rich merchants from Memphis had their summer houses here. *He adds,* But the place is very much gone up now, there are a few families living there, but the houses are mostly all used by the officers and Soldiers. *The commander of the division has taken a large house* and lives like a lord in the Secesh Pallace. *Asks Gunild not to look too much at the dark side of things. Boasts of the regiment and his own part.* When our Country is all right again — and our Goverment is safe — then is the time for us to come back and live happy at our homes.

To Gunild, August 18, 1862

CAMP NEAR IUKA MISS.
August 18th 1862.

MY DEAR GUNILD.

I received a very good letter from you yesterday, dated Aug. 9th also a good lot of News Papers. It is very pleasant to get a cheerfull letter from you — and I hope as you get used to getting along alone it will not be so hard for you. You may be disappointed at my not comming home as you expected. The war Department has not answered my application. It would not have been much satisfaction for you to have had me come home and stay a day or two and then go away again.

This place is the prettiest camp we have had since we left

124

Wisconsin. *I U Ka* is an Indian name. It is a small village with some very exelent Houses for summer residences and a fine Spring said to be healthy. The weather here is just as cool and nice as it is anywhere in Wisconsin. I do not think I have suffered as much from warm weather down here as you have up in Wisconsin. The nights are very cool, and I always have to sleep with a Blanket over me.

We shall move away from here in a few days on quite a long march. We are going East from here — it is said — through some very pretty country. I am just as comfortable on a march as when we lay still. My Black Horse — that you would like to get a Mortgage on — is just the finest riding Horse there is in the Army. When night comes, I hang my *Hammock* up between the trees, and roles myself up in my Blankets as comfortable as if I was at home. The only thing I miss is you. We have just got another Doctor in Newells place. His name is Whipple — a fine looking fellow.[1] One of the State Agents are also here, looking after the Wisconsin Soldiers.

As usual — I am in fine health. I do not believe, I have been as healthy as I am now for many years. If Bullets do not kill me, I am pretty sure I can stand it as well as anybody, and a good deal better than the most of those who are in the Army. I shall write to you again before we leave this place. You may direct your letters the same as you have done. They will come through all right. I see that they are enlisting very fast up in Wisconsin. I want to see them drive some of the Germans into the Army from around Waterford.

I have nothing more to write this time. I have got to muster the Regiment to day, and all who are absent, without leave, will be court martialled and punished. Major Reese will go by the Board. He is not here.

We have a fine lot of peaches down here. My Negro

---

[1] Alfred H. Whipple of Racine. He resigned on November 26, 1862. *Roster*, 1: 804.

brought me in over a Bushell last night.   They are very nice
and large ones too.   I intended to write a letter to Edmund
and Hilda in this, but I have not time.   I will send them one
to night if I get time to write it.   Good Bye my Dear Gunild.
Take good care of yourself and keep cheerfull.   Your own
                                                         HANS

Major *Crane* — of the 3ᵈ Wisconsin Regt. I see is killed.
You remember, *Crane* who visited us at Waupun.   The 3ᵈ
Wis. has had a hard fight.[2]

To Gunild, August 19, 1862
[Van Doren Mss.]

Iuka.   They say now it begins to be only fun to be soldiering.   The probabillity is that we shall have to march a good
deal hereafter.   I think we shall go from here into East Tennessee.   The place we go to from here is Decature Alabama.
It is a place on this Rail Road — the Memphis and Charleston — about 60 or 70 Miles east of here.

To Gunild, August 20, 1862
[Van Doren Mss.]

Iuka.   In your last letter you offered to lend me some money
if my Note was good, or if I would give you a Mortgage on
my Horse.   *He sends her five hundred dollars.*   To let you
know that I am not quite as hard up as you suppose, I just
enclose you a few Green Backs.   *Clausen, he reports, is going
north if he can get leave.*   He is a very fine man — and has
been a good deal of help and service to me.

To Gunild, August 22, 1862
[Van Doren Mss.]

Eastport, Mississippi.   We are going to East Tennessee, to
help Gen. Buel — who it is said is in a bad fix.   *Clausen has*

[2] Louis H. D. Crane of Ripon, a lieutenant colonel in the Third Wisconsin,
was killed in action on August 9, 1862, at Cedar Mountain. *Roster,* 1:385.

started for Wisconsin, but may get only as far as Cairo.
The boys feel good — and are very anxious to get off on this
march — and they hope to get a chance to fight before they
get through. We go through with a big force and ready to
meet any ordinary amount of Secesh.

To Gunild, August 25, 1862

FLORENCE ALABAMA
August 25th 1862

MY DEAR GUNILD.

I did not expect to get any chance to send letters from
here — or I should have written you a letter this morning,
but the Gen. just told me he should send the mail off to day.
Saturday we left East port about 4 in the afternoon. Even
Skofstad came just as we were ready to leave, and how glad
I was to get such a good long letter from you, and the other
things you sent me. Everything we get down here is rather
hard except we buy it from the sutlers, who ask about two
Dollars for such bottles of Jelly as those you sent me. Yesterday was Sunday. We started at 4 in the morning and
marched through some very fine country, well settled —
where we stopped for Dinner. I got a good glass of wine
and some nice Ham, Bread, Milk and preserves for my Dinner. She was a widdow woman — and was very anxious to
have some one stay and take care of her chickens, turkeys
and geese. I took as good care of her as I could — but the
boys got about all her geese, and turkeys anyhow. We
passed through some of the prettiest farming country I have
seen since we left Wisconsin but the men are in the rebel
army, and nothing but the wemen, and Negroes are at home.
Our living has been good now for a few days — plenty of
Peaches — chickins, turkeys, and sweet potatoes. Last night
we camped a mile outside of this town, and started again at
4 oclock this morning, but as we came up into town, we got

orders to leave all our extra baggage, and tents, except one
tent for myself, and fill our waggons up with provissions. So
we are still laying here getting our baggage handled over.
Whether we shall start off to night or not I can not tell, and
I can not tell where we are going. It is said, that Gen.
Bragg has a big force somewhere east of here — but where he
is I do not know. The soldiers begin to expect some fighting
now because they have been ordered to leave most of their
baggage — and they all seem to feel glad to get a chance.
I do not much believe we will get any chance — but I am
ready for anything. I shall try and do my duty if the time
comes.

I shall write to you just as often as I have any chance to
send letters, but you must not feel uneasy if you do not hear
from me as often as you have heretofore. I am glad you are
lending out your money. I hope you will have chance to
lend what Clauson took with him for you too. I rather
guess — the Soldiers widdows up in Wisconsin are the richest
people there is there now — from what I have seen sent home
to them.

I have a good deal of money with me yet, and shall probably let [you] have One Hundred Dollars more, and I have
some two months pay due me again. I am very happy to
hear that you are cheerfull, and taking things as I expected
you would. It helps nothing to fret about me now. I cant
come home honorably by resigning. You know that — for
you will see that all who have resigned without any good
reason will never hear the last of it. It will stick to them as
long as they live. I am glad to know that I have a wife —
not so chicken hearted as to get the consumption because I
can not be right along side of her all the time. It is good to
know that I have a good sensible woman at home to look
after my children and one who knows how to take care of her
self. You can think how a man in my place would feel if he
had a woman with no courage — and no idea of getting along
alone. In the first place — I do not think I should have

gone into the army at all. The greatest consolation a man
has, is to know that every thing is right at home.

I have no time to tell you anything how this place looks.
It is a fine village and plenty of people living here yet —
mostly niggers and wemen.

Good Bye my Dear Gunild. You will hear from me
again before long.

Your own
HANS.

Direct your letters as usual. I do not expect to get any mail
for a long time — for I dont know how it will find us. It
will be hard for the soldiers, should we have much rain, as
they have no tents. Our tents will be sent us by Rail Road.

To Gunild, August 31, 1862

CAMP NEAR FRANKLIN TENNESSEE
August 31st 1862.

MY DEAR GUNILD.

Once more I have an opportunity to write to you and in-
form you of my whereabouts. I wrote to you from Florence,
Alabama. If you got that letter, you know how we had got
along to that place. We left our tents and extra baggage
there and got orders to go to Nashville in this State as fast as
possible. It was supposed that a force of rebels was marching on that place. After marching through from Florence to
Franklin, we again got orders this morning to go to Murfrees-
borrow, and we are now within 15 miles from that place.

I have no doubt but that we are on a fools errand. I believe the force they expected to go towards Nashville, has
gone to Richmond. We have traveled through some of the
prettiest country I have seen in the South — and I do not
know but it is the prettiest I have seen anywhere — all settled by rich slave holders. Amongst other places, we passed
Gen. Pillows place — and Gen. Polks pallaces. I am well,
and as usual in good spirits. I shall expect to get som mail

at *Murfreesburro* if we stay there any time. I commenced writing with a very poor pen, but got me a better one to finish this letter with. I just saw Gen. Mitchell, and he told me that it is very probable that we will stay at Murfreesborro for some time. We will at least stay there a few days. I hope Clauson has been to see you and given you my present, that I sent by him. If he came that way he no doubt told you all about how I get along. I have not heard from him since he left us at Iuka. You must address your letters as usual 2ᵈ Brigade 4ᵗʰ Division Army of the Mississippi. It will find me whereever I may be, provided the mails run. I may be able to give you better directions in my next, but I know no other now. I will write next time to the children.

After leaving Florence we have traveled altogether through the enemys country, and got a sight at some Gueirilla Cavalry. Some men of our Brigade had a shot or two exchanged, and we captured a few. I do not know how many. I know that I captured a pistol belonging to one of them, which I have still in my possession. Seven men from one of the Regiments in this Brigade, who stragled behind were taken up by them, and released upon parole.

This march has been hard on the boys. They have had to get up at 2 oclock in the morning and march at 3 and 4, generally making about 20 miles a day. Their feet are terrible sore. Many of these officers who have had nice times, little or nothing to do and getting from a Hundred, to a Hundred and Fifty a month have earned their pay the last 10 days. As to myself — I have got along well enough. My Black horse, is a[s] fine as a fiddle, and very easy to ride on. We get plenty of Peaches and Watermellons. Your Jelly came just in time for this march. Your stuff that you sent me has made our mess good natured several times, and I have still some of it left. After I get into camp at night I have had one of the bottles of Jelly, some crackers, a cup of coffee and a little white sugar with it, and I tell you it has tasted good. I also bought me a Box of wine before I left Eastport, and it has been very serviseable on this trip.

We have not seen a paper from the north for over a week, — but expect to find some at Murfreesborro to morrow. The report here is that there has been a great Battle, on the old Bull Run battle ground, and that the Rebels had been badly whipped.

There is where the fighting has to be done. There will not be much of it here in the south, if the Rebels are only whipped at Richmond. Even Skofstad is with us. He has got him a Mule and is riding along with the train. He seems to enjoy the fun first rate.

They will get some goods soon I suppose and commence selling. I shall write to you now again as often as the mail arrangements will permit me. Do not fret too much for me — take good care of yourself and trust me to my luck.

Good Bye my ever Dear Wife.

Your own
HANS.

To Gunild, September 2, 1862

MURFREESBORRO TENNESSEE
Sept. 2^d 1862.

MY DEAR WIFE.

I am afraid you have been very uneasy in not hearing from me for such a long time. I have felt uneasy myself — not for not getting letters, for I did not expect to find any mail down here, but because I was not able to let you hear anything from me. I wrote to you last night, fearing that we might not stop long enough here to write, but it seems that we are going to stay here a short time. We are camped in a very fine grove, one mile from the village of Murfreesborro. If you have got you the map I asked you to buy, you can find the place on the Nashville and Chattanoga Rail Road, about 30 miles south of Nashville.

We have had a march of about 150 Miles since we left Jacinto — mostly through the enemys country. We have had no serious trouble although we have seen a few of the Guierillas and taken a few Prisoners. There is no [new]s to be had here, so we are entirely ignorant [of wha]t is going on — and but very little [infor]mation do we get of what is transpiring [aroun]d here — always all kinds of rumors — nothing reliable. I do of course get some information from Gen. Mitchell and what he gets is also limitted I should judge. There is a continual movement of troops from one place to another with no signs of any engagements. As I said in my former letters — it is still my opinion that there is no plan of the enemy to bring on any heavy force to this section of the country. Richmond, and the vicinity of Washington will witness the settlement of this struggle as far as great Battles are concerned, untill the Rebels are driven away from Richmond. They may then, if they have sufficient strenght pitch in to attempt to reopen the Mississippi River.

We get Nashville papers here, which give some accounts of a Battle in Virginia on the Old Bull Run Battle field, and that we shipped them.

This is now Buels command [3] and I suppose we are cut off from getting suppleis, or have been for a short time. Still you need not have any fears for our suffering. We live as well now as we [ever] did. The country is full of Corn — W[heat] and Beef, besides lots of Fruit — and vegitables. The Regiment has got [more] healthy since we commenced marching. There is hardly a sick man amongst them.

At Florence we received orders to leave all our extra Baggage and tents, but we managed to bring two tents for each company. I brought mine, and the Lt. Col brought his one — so I am as comfortable as usual. By the way, I have got a good negro woman for cook. The Lt. Col., Adjutant Hauff, Mathews and myself Mess together. We have never had any good cooks, but I found a woman two or three days

[3] General D. C. Buell. The reader of Heg's letters may find it profitable to consult Henry M. Cist, *The Army of the Cumberland* (New York, 1882).

ago that is doing first rate. She seems to be a real good cook and the prospect is now that we will live better than we have done. Nearly all the officers messes have provided themselves with wemen cooks lately, as there is very few good men cooks to be found.

If we stay here any lenght of time, we will no doubt get our Mail sent us, but we shall have to be patient for some time I expect.

Time passes off very rapidly. It is [now] nearly one year since I got my com[mis]sion as Col. I hope you will be [brav]e enough to keep up good courage — [an]d not to fret too much for me, if you do not hear from me as often as you have heretofore. I shall write just as often as I have a chance to send by the mail, but it is not altogether certain that the letters will get through hereafter — as there is a great many Guierellas back of us robbing mail trains and burning Rail Road Bridges.

I should like to see you, and I am still looking for a time pretty soon that I can either come home to you, or send for you to come down here.

This fall will settle the worst of the troubles, if matters are drove as they should be.

It is getting late, and I am quite tired. I want some rest after the march and I must go to bed.

Good night my Dear. Do not feel bad because I can not write as often as usual. I know you are getting used to live alone — and when you can hear that I am safe and wel I know you will not feel uneasy.

Kiss little Elmer and tell Edmu[nd and] Hilda to be good children.

Your own
HANS

Address your letters To Col. Hans C Heg, 15th Wis. vols 2^d Brigade, 4th Diviss.[4]

[4] This sentence has been crossed out in the original.

To Gunild, September 5, 1862

NASHVILLE TENNESSEE.
Sept 5th 1862.

MY DEAREST GUNILD.

I am afraid you are getting uneasy for not hearing from me. I write this hoping it may reach you, but according to present appearances, it is quite doubtfull. The Rail Road between this place and Louisville is cut to pieces by Bridges being burned. The only means of getting letters through is by stages which are run through by individuals.

I wrote to you from Murfreesborro, and from Florence Allabama, but they may both have gone to Dixie for what I know. I do not know when to expect anything from you. I do not at least expect to get any mail till we have cleaned the rebels out behind us. I do hope you will not fret too much on account of not hearing from me. We will come out all right soon.

The accounts we get look blue — but I never loose courage — it will soon brighten up again. Our cause is bound to succeed — but we have a great many bad generals, & poor officers, and it will have to be a good many changes made before we succeed.

I commenced writing this letter while I had no candle and, I commenced it at the bottom of the sheet. *I am not tight* for the very good reason that there has hardly been anything to be had for a long time. Since we left camp Erickson, we have marched 200 miles at forced marches — and it has put the boys right through. We have marched about 20 miles a day — but they have stood it well, and are healthier to day than when they left.

We are now laying here, and I have had a trip through the City of Nashville. It is a large city, and it is being well fortified. I would like to stay here a while, but I do not think we shall stay here more than a day or two. Bragg and Smith are moving up through Kentucky, and I expect we will be ordered to march to some point where we can interfere with their arrangements some way.

I am bussy all the time and dont feel lonesome or tired, but I am afraid you are feeling so uneasy about me. I have all confidence of getting through all right. I could tell you the reason of my confidence, but it is not necessary. This war will end in due time. Slavery will be cleaned out, the goverment reestablished, stronger than it has ever been, and our goverment will not be curssed with so many reckless dishonest politicians, for they are mostly in the army as officers and will be killed off. Remember now that I do not count myself as a *dishonest* politician. I am going to come through and the 15th will show a good hand. We have a better reputation now than any regiment in the Brigade for dicipline, and I think the boys will stand up well in a fight.

If we could be stationed here, I would send for you to come down and see me. The 10th Wis. is comming here to morrow. Col Chapin has his wife here — but she is rather bad off now, as there is no way of getting back home.[5] The 1st Wis. was here and left last night. I can not tell where they went to, as that would be contraband.

My Dear I know you are courageous enough to get along in my absence — let me see and hear that you are no coward. I am not a coward and I know you are not either, when it comes to the scratch. I am occupying a position that you need not feel ashamed of. You have plenty to eat, & drink and money enough to spend. I will look out for myself. When the war is over, we will make up for this seperation. You say that there will be many widdows made in this war, and that you always expect to be one of them. I hope you will not make up your mind *too soon* that you are a widdow. It is time enough when the time comes. You might have been a widdow even if I had stayed at home, — sooner than where I am.

[5] Alfred R. Chapin of Milwaukee was colonel of the Third Wisconsin. *Roster*, 1:644.

I wish you was as cheerfull as I am.   Many of the boys in the Regiment, especially the officers, feel homesick and dull — but, I generally have to cheer them up.   When any of them gets the blues they generally come to me and get cured.

I have rambeled over this paper a good deal of stuff, and if Secesh get it they are wellcome to it.   It will be no more than fair play.   I have caught many of theirs.

I can not tell you where we go to from here, for it is contraband.   We are not going South just now.   Good Bye my Dearest.   You shall hear from me again soon.   Good night my Dear.

Your own

HANS

To Gunild, September 9, 1862

[Van Doren Mss.]

Nashville.   We are at present stationed within a Mile of the City of Nashville, and I think there is some prospect of stopping here a while.   Most of the troops have gone up into Kentucky.   We have also been expecting to go, but it does not look like it now.   There is some fears of Gen. Bragg, attacking this City, and they are making strong fortifications to defend it.   *He has no news to report.*   We are just about as usual, only healthier.   I am as fine as a fiddle, the only thing that troubles me, is in not hearing from home.   *He has had no colds during the summer, although he has slept in the open air, most of the time without tents.   He speculates about the possibility of Gunild coming to Nashville.*   Nearly as large as Milwaukee, and is a beautifull place.

To Gunild, September 11, 1862

[Van Doren Mss.]

Nashville.   The Rail Road communication is still broken, and the only means of getting any information from Louisville, is by stages, and they are very often captured by the Rebel Geiurillas. *Laments the number of poor and inefficient officers in the army.* Let me tell you, I am getting tired of the loose dicipline that is carried on by the American officers. *As to suffering that he has witnessed among the Union people:* I have seen thousands of men wemen and little children, traveling along in the dust and hot sun, following the Army, their houses having been burned, thier property taken away from them, many of thier relatives hung or shot. *The Sioux Outbreak:* I see the Indians are playing awfully with the white people of Minnesota, and that many Norwegians have been killed. *He adds,* I am glad you are in a safe place. I should not feel happy if I knew that you and the children were in danger.

To Gunild, September 26, 1862

SEPTEMBER 26th 1862.
10 Miles from Louisville Ky.

MY DEAR GUNILD.

I hardly know what to write, it is so long since I have been able to send you any letters. We have been cut off from all comunication so entirely that we have heard nothing from home, nor been able to send any letters.

The best thing I can let you know is that I am still alive and as well and healthy as ever — can I send you any better news? I trust I shall be able to hear the same from you whenever I get a mail. I will not try to give you any discription of what we have gone through on this terrible march — of over 400 miles of forced marches — night and day — but I have stood it better than any one in the crowd — and here I am as tough and strong as ever. We have followed up the Rebels very close, but as yet we have been in no Battle — the Armys now are in a situation that a Battle may be fought any day near this place. Gen. Bragg is within a few miles of

Louisville and is expected to attack the city. We have very poor chance for any information. One thing is certain some fighting will have to be done in Kentucky before a long time — and as soon as Bragg is cleaned out of this State — we will have rest — and you can either expect me home or expect to have me send for you to come down here. I wish you would be ready to come right away to Louisville, as soon as you get a Tellegraph Dispatch. We are now where we can reach you either by Mail or Tellegraph. Should I send a Dispatch for you to come to Louisville — you will go to Chicago and there buy a ticket direct for Louisville and stop at such a place as I will state. If I can not come home and see you — I shall certainly send for you — and I want you all to come, and take a girl along to help you take care of the children.

I have got one of the prettiest Trophies of the war for Edmund. I have got a *Pony* about as big again as Turk — the nicest little thing you ever saw. He is just as gentle as a pet lamb — and about 8 or 9 years old — and I bought it on the 22^d of September — Edmunds Birth day. The Saddle, Bridle and Pony cost me about 40 Dollars. He was taken or bought down in Allabama by some of the troops. The first chance I have I will send him up to you. I intend if we should move away from here before I get a chance to send him — to leave him at some Farmers place to be taken care of till I get an opportunity to send him.

I have troubled myself a good deal about you for the time I have not been able to write to you, but I told you in all the letters I have written since I left Jacinto that we might get where we could not send any letters and I have hoped all the time that you would not be so foolish as to fret yourself sick till you could hear from me again. I have seen some hard times — and have been where we have been called out to get ready for a fight, both at night and day times — but still we have been in none yet. A good many Rebels have been killed and taken Prisoners by us on this march — but no general engagement has been had with the enemy except at Green River, where they captured over Four Thousand men that was stationed there — most all new troops. Our men however killed over one thousand of them, and lost only 30 by death & wounds. It has looked black for some time, and how soon this war will end, it is hard to tell — but it can not last very long. It must come to a close soon. How pleasant it will be to come home once more. Do not think however that I am either homesick or discouraged. I am happy, you do not know how happy I am to know that you are in a safe and comfortable place. Let the war rage as it may — you are all right, and safe. I am going to see the end of the struggle if possible. I will not resign as long as I am as healthy and well as I am at present, and have been since the war began.

I have seen no Paper from Wisconsin or from Chicago since we left *Iuka*. I saw a paper yesterday. It seems that matters around Washington looks brighter. I trust it is so.

Doc Himoe is all right. I would have been lonesome often, had it not been for his company. I hope you will do the best you can to make his family comfortable. You must remember she has no home up in Wisconsin.

We have orders to march in two hours from now. Where we go I do not know — but I do not think it will be very far, perhaps up to the city. Gen. Mitchell still commands our Division. I generally get as much information from him as he has. He is a good fellow — and I think a fine General.

Direct your letters as follows — Col. H C. Heg 15ᵗʰ Wis. 2ᵈ Brigade, 4ᵗʰ Divission Army of the Miss. via Louisville. I wrote to you several times on the march, but expect the letters were lost. My best love to you my Dear. Kiss the children for me. Good Bye. Your own

HANS

To Gunild, September 26, 1862

Galt House.
(Enlarged 1859.)
Corner Main and Second Streets,
Silas F. Miller & Co., Lessees.

[Printed letterhead]

LOUISVILLE, KY., Sept 26 1862

MY OWN DEAR WIFE.

I wrote you a letter this morning not knowing whether I should be able to get into town to write. We marched through the city to day, as dusty and ragged as any one could be — but the cheers and hurrahs they gave us showed that we were not thought any less of for being dirty. The girls came out and distributed water, cakes and other articles to the boys all along the streets. My Regiment went through, singing Norwegian Songs, and attracted more attention than any other Rgt. that passed. The Doctor and Col. McKey [*McKee*] are down taking a Bath, and I have just come up after having a good wash. I am as fine as a Fiddle — but very tired. Just as we left Iuka Rosecranse had a fight with Price, and whipped him. It does not seem that we are made to see much fighting. We have had a terrible long march, and seen the enemy, and been drawn up in line of Battle several times, but every time they have fled. I will write every day as long as I am here in town.

I have one of the prettiest little Ponies you ever saw, that I bought on Edmunds Birthday. I have been offered a Hundred Dollars for him, from Officers that want to send him home to some boy. I am sure Edmund will have the prettiest Birth day present anybody ever got. I shall try to morrow to get him sent by express to Burlington. If it does not cost altogether too much, I shall send him by express, otherwise I will send him with Borchsenius who will probably go home in a few days. I have not had time to look or en-

quire for mail.   There must be a large mail here — and by to
morrow I expect to hear from you.   It is stirring times in
Kentucky just now — and will be for some weeks, till Bragg
and Smith is whipped.   By next fall I hope to be able to
send for you.   Should I stay here a week or two, then I will
send for you anyway.   I must go to bed.   Good night my
Dear Gunild.

Your own
HANS.

Address as before — only add via Louisville

To Gunild, September 28, 1862
[Van Doren Mss.]

Louisville, Kentucky.   The Rebels are very thick about 30
or 40 Miles from town, and we will no doubt move out to see
them as soon as the boys are clothed up some.   *Since he will
not be permitted to carry a trunk in the campaign, he has
packed various items, including some papers and books, and
is sending them home.*   There is one Norwegian Book, that
you must read.   It is one of the old Histories of Norway,
and it will interest you very much, take care of it.   *Later in
the letter he writes,* All is excitement here now, and if I should
send for you, I might be 50 Miles away from here, and you
would not be allowed to come any farther than this place.
*He expects important fighting within the next two months,
but adds,* The Rebels are in an awfull condition — mostly
without clothing, and but very little to Eat.   *He closes with
the usual admonition,* Do not fret for me, trust to my good
luck — you will see me again before a great while.

To Gunild, September 29, 1862
[Van Doren Mss.]

*Louisville.   Much about sending his trunk home and about
pony, saddle, and bridle for Edmund.*   I shall get my Photograph taken to day if we stay here long enough and send it to

you — that you may see if I have changed any. I am heavier than I was while at Waupun, and considerable fleshier. *Speaks of the feeling in the army against Buell. Tirade against officers resigning.*

To Gunild, September 30, 1862
[Van Doren Mss.]

Louisville. Up at 3:00 A.M. with orders to move at once. Much about the pony for Edmund. We are now designated as the 9ᵗʰ Divission 31ˢᵗ Brigade Army of the Ohio. *As to the promised photograph:* I went up to take my Picture yesterday but, did not get a good one — and to day we are off — so you will have to wait till some other time.

To Gunild, October 1, 1862
[Van Doren Mss.]

Louisville. We did not leave yesterday, it was a false alarm. This morning we march at 6. o clock. *Colonel Heg believes that the purpose of the move is* to attack Bragg and Kirby Smith who are not very far off.

To Gunild, October 3, 1862
[Van Doren Mss.]

Headquarters, Fifteenth Wisconsin, Camp near Mt. Washington, Kentucky. We left Louisville day before yesterday and traveled out about 9 miles. Yesterday we started again at 8 °clock and traveled very slow, and camped again at 4 in the afternoon comming about 6 miles. Soon after Camping we heard pretty sharp Canonading, but we have had a very quiet night, and have not learned yet what the Canonading meant. *As to food,* Heyer is running a Boarding house waggon, and the officers are all boarding with him at three Dollars a week. *As to the enemy,* Bragg and Kirby Smith are still in this State, and I hope they will stay long enough to allow our slow generals to get up to him. *Postscripts to Edmund and Hilda.*

To Gunild, October 7, 1862

CAMP NEAR SPRINGFIELD Ky.
October 7th 1862.

MY DEAR WIFE

I have just got time to drop you a few lines, hoping to find an opportunity to mail it. We are near the enemy, but he is running ahead of us. We are capturing a good many of their men that fall back. Gen Bragg is imidiately ahead of us. Gen. Smith is also near by with a large lot of troops. The prospect is that they will fight before a great while. We must undoubtedly have one big Battle here in Kentucky. I do not see how the Rebels can avoid it.

I am well — in good spirits and going first rate. Many of my men are getting sick, from sleeping out doors.

Clauson is at Louisville.

We are to move imidiatly and I must close. Good Bye my Dear. I will write again as soon as possible.

Yours &c
HANS

To Gunild, October 10, 1862

[Van Doren Mss.]

NEAR PERRYSVILLE KY.
Oct 10th 1862.

MY DEAR WIFE

I have not much time to write. Today is Friday. Day before yesterday we fought a big Battle. I have been through it and am unhurt, and still better, not a man of my Regiment is wounded — although we chased them two Miles — through showers of Bullets and Cannon Shot.

We are fast using up Braggs Army — and he will soon have but few men left him.

My Regiment will fight and stand up as long as any in the service.

As soon as Bragg is whipped — I shall make application to go home and get my Regiment filled.

Do not bother yourself for me, trust to my good fortune. I am standing the hardships and trials of this war, better than almost any one in the service.

I am well and healthy. Doc Himoe is the same. Mathews got thrown from his horse, and got very badly hurt. He knocked out all his teeth — and is badly bruised. Erick Erickson Scheise — was left on our March from Louisville to Bardstown — very sick. I knew nothing of it for a day after wards — I am afraid he is gone up.

The rest of Co. C. Boys are well except Toms Brother who is quite sick — but he is with us, riding in the Ambulance.

Tell Jim Gibson that his boy is all right. John Rice is all right. Clauson has not come up to us yet.

Good Bye My Dear Gunild — take care of yourself and the children — good bye.

Your Own HANS.

To Gunild, October 13 and 15, 1862

IN CAMP NEAR DANVILLE Ky.
October 13th 1862.

MY DEAR GUNILD.

This is the first time I have had to write you a full letter since the great Battle of last Wednesday.[6] I sent you a few lines Thursday Morning, and wrote a letter to Ole at the same time. You know what time we left Louisville, well from that day (Oct 1st) we kept on marching as fast as possible, and finally caught up with Braggs Army on last Monday Oct 6th near Bardstown. On that day we were behind,

---

[6] The battle of Perryville, October 8, 1862. On this battle see Cist, *Army of the Cumberland,* ch. 6, and Thomas B. Van Horne, *History of the Army of the Cumberland,* 1:ch. 15 (Cincinnati, 1875).

and could only hear the canonading in front as the United States troops drove them on. The only sign we could see, was a few dead Horses, and one dead rebel. On Tuesday our Divission was in front and my Regiment the 2ᵈ so that if there was any enemy we expected to see them. The cavalry, being still in front of us, kept them so far a head that we had no chance to fight untill 2 o'clock in the afternoon, when we were ordered to form line of Battle. Pretty soon canonading commenced very lively, but we remained quietly in line of Battle during the afternoon and night. Early in the morning canonading commenced again and we started of[f] at 7 oclock but did not go more than 1/2 mile when we laid down again. Here we laid till 2 °clock in the afternoon, listening to the very heavy canonading and firing, about 3 miles ahead of us. The order finally came for us to advance. I called the men together, gave them such advise as I thought proper, and spoke to them a few minutes. Everybody was anxious to go ahead, and with much earnestness promised to do their best. Forward then we started. Mitchell commands three Brigades. One of them turned to the left, and ours and the other to the right, through the woods. On top of a hill we formed in line. From here I could see the whole Battle field at a time when it was raging the hardest. It was a sight I shall never forget. During the time we waited there, the enemy were having the advantage, and were gaining ground on our men. The smoke and dust filled the air a great deal — and a constant rattle of cannon and muskets, and now and then came a ball whistling by me so near that I would sometimes bow my head down without hardly knowing it myself. While standing and looking on — Col. Carlin rode up and ordered me to advance. The balls were then flying around us thick. He said, *advance, and if you meet the enemy, overpower him.* We started towards an open field from where the firing seemed to come — and soon was out of the woods. Here we came very near up to the enemy, but all at once, as they saw us come out of the wood they turned and run. Their cannon was in a corn field nearly half a mile in front of us, with that, they peppered away at us but their shots all flew over. The country was broken, and as we advanced — we would go at a keen run as we crossed the hills. While passing these high places we were much exposed to the shot and shell. As soon as we got out of the woods I spoke of we began to find dead and wounded rebels quite thick, as well as every thing els naturally left on Battlefields such as Knapsacks, Coats, Guns &c — but we went on. Their cannon soon wheeled around and off it went with the rest of their men. After having run about one mile through a heavy fire from their cannon we reached a high hill. From this we could see the village of Perryville and betwen us and the village were the rebels *skedadeling*. Soon their Battery stopped, and again opened upon us. We stayed here about 5 minutes, or less. (When I say we — I do not mean the whole Brigade, for by this time the 15th Wis. and 21st Ill. had out run the rest, so that we saw nothing of them.)   Up again and after giving one big shout we again started after the rebels. This time we kept on till we reached the village. Here the rebels halted their Battery and commenced firing very fast. Soon our Battery, which came up after us, & opened on the enemys. We in the mean time laying down in line of Battle the shot flying over us both from the enemys Canon and our own, shells would burst right over our heads, and pieces fly in all directions, often comming very near the men, but not one of us were hit. One shell burst, a little to the right of where I stood, and wounded 4 men of the 21st *Ill.* We laid here nearly two hours, till it got too dark for the Canon to fire. While we laid here the ballance of the Brigade came up, and laid down by our side. Here we began to capture prisoners, and soon we had a big crowd. Finally, along came a train of Waggons, who had mistaken us for their own men, thus we captured 13 waggons loaded with amunition, one ambulance, two *Caisons* and some over one hundred Prisoners. Then the orders came to go back about one mile and stay during the [night]. The next morning we started after them again, but they had left.

During the day we moved over to the right, where the heaviest fighting had been, and on Friday we laid still. I went all over the Battle field along with Doc. Himoe but there is hardly any use in me trying to discribe how it looked. It was awfull. I think the Rebels must have lost nearly one third more than we did — and I think we must have had 12 or 15 Hundred killed. The Rebels left all their dead, except officers and also nearly one Thousand wounded.

I commenced writing this letter the day it is dated, but did not get time to finish before we left. I will complete it now.

CAMP NEAR CRABB ORCHARD, Ky.
Oct. 15th 1862

Last night we again had a little skirmish with the enemy — but none of us were hurt. I find that the 1st, 10th, 21st and 24th Wis Regiments were all in the fight on the 8th and that they were mostly all badly cut up. The Papers will tell you more about it than I can. I shall send a report to the Governor on what my Rg^t did during the fight.[7] It is admitted that our exploit was the best during the fight, so much so that Col. Carlin will be made a Brigadier General on account of it.

Bragg is now retreating towards Cumberland Gap — and we are very closely on his heels. I suppose we shall have to follow him up. We are having hard times, no army has had it any harder; still I am all right. I am standing it first rate, but I shall certainly ask for a leave of absence as soon as we have cleaned Bragg out of Kentucky. I know I have done my share — and will be entittled to a short rest. I am writing and it [is] so dark I can not see anything. If the lines are crooked you must not lay it to my being tight.

[7] Heg wrote a brief report to Governor Edward Salomon on October 18. It was published in the *Wisconsin State Journal* for November 8.

I hope Edmund has his pony now.   I am waiting to hear from him.

I would be very glad to write you every day, but there is no chances to write now.   You have no Idea how much the people down here are suffering.   It is awfull.   Wemen and children, left homeless, and fatherless by thousands.   I can see no more.

Good night.   God Bless you all.

Your own
HANS

To Gunild, October 16, 1862

[Van Doren Mss.]

Camp near Crab Orchard, Kentucky.   His troops are standing their hard service well, none of them better than himself. Bragg is hurrying out of this State very fast, going to Cumberland Gap.

To Gunild, October 18, 1862

[Van Doren Mss.]

Crab Orchard, Kentucky.   Compliments Gunild on her management of her affairs — you have sold the Ponies first rate, and done well.   You will make a good bussiness man if I stay away long enough.   *On conditions in Wisconsin:* I see the crops have been poor.   It will be quite hard for the farmers in Wisconsin to pay thier heavy taxes with poor crops.   *On the recent fighting:* The part we have taken in the Battle of the 8th and the skirmish at Lancaster, has done our men much good.   They feel much more confidence in themselves and in me.   *He comments on the soldiers' belief in his good luck for the regiment* — you know the Norwegians are superstitious.

IV. THE BATTLE OF MURFREESBORO

To Gunild, October 23, 1862

CAMP NEAR LEBANON KY
October 23ᵈ 1862

MY DEAR GUNILD.

I wrote several letters to you by Mathews and others, from Crabb Orchard, the most of which I suppose you have not recieved. Mathews started for Louisville on last Sunday, and has been taken Prisoner by Morgan.[1] He was paroled and I understand has since been sent to Camp Chase Ohio — so I suppose Mr. Morgan has had a chance to read the letters intended for you. I am sory now that I have not written in Norwegian, and no one down here could have got anything out of it. But the best Joke is on the Quarter Master. The day of the Battle of Perryville — he lost all his *teeth* by being thrown from his Horse and he was very anxious to go to Louisville to get a little rest, as he was quite unwell after the fall he had. Well, I suppose he will get some rest now. It is very probable he will get permission to go home a short time. Since we left Crabb Orchard we have marched 3 days, to get to this place. The March is very hard as it is so very dusty. I am as well as usual, and am enjoying myself first rate.

Clauson has returned, and I got all your good letters — and wrote you several in answer to them that I suppose you will not get. I am very glad to know that you have disposed of the Ponies and the Sheep so well.

Dʳ Himoe, Clauson, McKee and myself are boarding together. We have just commenced a mess together and we are living first rate. The longer we are in the Army the better we learn to take care of ourselves.

[1] General John H. Morgan, Confederate cavalry raider. For a critical account of this figure see Howard Swiggett, *The Rebel Raider* (Indianapolis, 1934).

149

I was up to Lebanon to day, and there I met Dr Walcott of Milwaukee, and several others from Wisconsin going out to Perryville to see our sick and wounded Soldiers.

We are looking anxiously for some mail, but we get it very slow.

I should like very much to take a trip home, and stay long enough to get my Regiment filled up — and long enough to see you all, and especially to see that little rat *Elmer* that you write so much about. I have not time to write more now. I want to go to bed. Good night my Dear. I will write again to morrow if we stay here.

Your own
HANS

To Gunild, October 26, 1862
[Van Doren Mss.]

Headquarters, Fifteenth Wisconsin, near Lebanon, Kentucky. Moved to new camp yesterday. Necessary to get our men clothed up — our Horses shoed &co — we may stay here a week or more. *Tells of rain and snow:* As the men have no tents I ordered them to build rail huts, and cover them well up with straw. *Reports removal of Buell and elevation of Rosecrans. Opinion of Rosecrans:* He is the best general in the service — and he knows me and my Regiment also.

To Gunild, October 31, 1862

ADDRESS MY LETTERS [*Ms. mutilated*]
BOWLING GREEN KY Oct 31st 1862.

MY DEAR WIFE.

Last Sunday I wrote you a letter from near Lebanon Ky. I had hardly got my letter sealed up before I got orders to march in the morning. I had no time to write again, and have had no opportunity to write since. I have not been well for a few days, and yesterday we came to a place called Cave City where the cars pass through, and I got Clauson with me and went on the cars to this place, got me a good room at this Hotell, The Morgan House — where I am now staying waiting for the Regiment to come up. It will probably be here to morrow some time. We left it 30 miles from here. I am not sick, but I have hurt myself riding, so that I can not ride Horseback. I am getting better though, and in a couple of days, I shall be all right again I think. I hurt myself first on the day of the Battle at Perryville, but did not pay any attention to it. I have since caught cold and it has laid me up.

I am very comfortably situated here, but miss you very much. It is lonesome to be obliged to lay still, but I have had plenty to read to day, and have passed the time off first rate. We are going on to Nashville, and the Regiment may stay here a day or two to get some shoes, and clothing and be paid off.

There is a good many of my men here — who were left when we passed up towards Louisville, and some have come up from Louisville yesterday and to day. Bart. Willard I have understood is here, but I have not seen him. A good many of my men have been up here to see me to day.

The weather is very fine here now, and we are all feeling first rate at the prospect of being put once more under command of Gen. Rosecranse. We will be away from Buell, as soon as we get to Nashville. There will no doubt be very important work done before New Year down here, and I hope the same will be the case on the Potomac. The war ought to be closed up by the 1st of April anyway, and can be if the Generals in command do their duty.

I have seen pretty thoroughly what it is to be on duty in the field, and I am prepared to stand anything most. All I am anxious for, is to get well enough to get on my black Horse again.

I have had only two letters from you since we left Louisville. We have had no mail for many days. I hope and trust you are all well. I know you can be comfortable if you

are well. I can not hold out any hopes for you that I am
comming home. If I should, I will try and let you know before hand. Kiss the children for me. I will write again to
morrow. Good bye. Sleep good tonight. Your own

HANS.

To Gunild, November 2, 1862
[Van Doren Mss.]

Morgan House, Bowling Green, Kentucky. I am still stopping at the Hotel where I have a good comfortable room, and
live tollerable well. *Predicts peace by spring.* If we can
defeat the rebels in Virginia, the whole rebellion is gone up.
Information about family finances.

To Gunild, undated fragment

From Bowling Green.[2] I have just been up to Rosecranses
Head Quarters, and had a shake of the old fellows hand. He
always calls me Heck. You do not know how pleased everybody is at the change of Buell for him. *Has had no mail
since letter brought by Clausen.*[3] *Refers to Erick Erickson
Scheise.* I have not been able to hear from him yet. I am
afraid he was taken Prisoner, or that he is left sick at some
house. We missed two men from Company C. at the same
time — Erick, and a German boy that we have not found
yet.[4] *As to a picture:* If I can get a chance to morrow I will
have my picture taken and send you in my next letter.

[2] This letter was appended to a partial draft of a letter to the editors of the
Racine Advocate, in which Colonel Heg began a report on the participation of
Wisconsin regiments in the battle of Perryville. The report seems not to have
been printed in the *Advocate,* but as has been noted, the *Wisconsin State Journal* of November 8 contains Heg's report to Governor Salomon.
[3] Clausen had been north on leave. It should be noted that because of ill
health he resigned his position as chaplain and left the regiment on November
27. A soldier of the Fifteenth wrote to *Emigranten* that the chaplain " in his
unassuming manner " had " certainly done much good," and that " it is with
sorrow that we see him leave." *Emigranten,* December 8, 1862, and Jorgensen,
" Claus L. Clausen," 139.
[4] In the Wisconsin roster " Erick Erickson " is recorded as having been discharged on February 7, 1863, because of disability. *Roster,* 1:810.

To Gunild, November 5, 1862
[Van Doren Mss.]

Morgan House, Bowling Green. The Regt. left yesterday for Nashville. I have been quite sick and unable to travle. I am better now — but will not be able to join the Regiment for several days. *About twenty of his men are in hospitals in Bowling Green. Refers to fight at Perryville and speaks of the important part played by his brigade.*

To Gunild, December 5, 1862
[Van Doren Mss.]

Louisville Hotel, Louisville, Kentucky. The letter is mis-dated November 5.[5] *Came in afternoon and will leave at eight the next morning for Nashville.* I learned before I left Milwaukee, by Dr Himoes letters to Andrea that the Regiment has started from Nashville and was going south slowly. *He left Milwaukee at two o'clock on the preceding day and arrived at Louisville twenty-four hours later. Discusses property in Waupun.*

To Gunild, December 8, 1862
[Van Doren Mss.]

Camp five miles south of Nashville. Heg arrived Saturday and was welcomed right heartily by the boys. *Gifts for*

---

[5] Heg was returning from a leave of absence of thirty days. The *Racine Advocate* for Wednesday, November 12, 1862, announced that Colonel Heg had visited its office on the preceding Tuesday. He had suffered an injury when his horse fell with him in the battle of Perryville and his leave was granted him " to come home and recover his health." " Colonel Heg," wrote the *Advocate,* " gives a glowing account of the change produced in the army by the removal of Buell and the appointment of Rosecrans." The notice concludes with the statement that Heg would remain at Waterford, Racine County, " during the next ten or fifteen days." Lars O. Dokken in a letter of December 12, 1862, reports the return of Colonel Heg to his regiment on December 7. Heg brought with him, he says, a mass of gifts of shoes, overshoes, and socks for soldiers in Company C. Ager, *Oberst Heg og Hans Gutter,* 116. It may be noted that General Rosecrans in a special order of November 24 gave honorable mention to the Fifteenth Wisconsin and the Thirty-eighth Illinois for the capture of forty-six prisoners and some equipment taken from guerillas. *Milwaukee Sentinel,* December 4, 1862.

soldiers: The packages for Company C's Boys, you can hardly suppose how gladly they recieved them. *Reports that Erick Scheise was last heard from at Bardstown Hospital.* I am glad I brought the Butter, it costs 75^{cts} a pound here. *Speaks of sale of house in Waupun and plans to buy new house for Gunild.*

To Gunild, December 11, 1862

[Van Doren Mss.]

CAMP NEAR NASHVILLE TENN
Dec 11th 1862.

MY DEAR GUNILD

I would have written to you yesterday being our *marriage day* — did you remember it?

Eleven years ago — in the old log house — it does not seem so very long to me — how many changes since then. I think we have spent those eleven years as happily as most people — 14 years more, and we can have our silver wedding. I hope we may. I find myself very well contented in my old tent once more, the officers and men are rejoiced to meet me. I have got me a cotton Mattrass, a Stove, and I have not much to do. The enemy is said to be close by us, but there is not any prospect of an imidiate Battle. We can not tell though, a Battle may occur any time. We are prepared for them. They will not find another such a lot of men as they found at Hartsville, where the rebels took a whole Brigade prisoners. You must not think that because I say that I am so well contented down with my Regiment, that I was not as much contented while at home. I did feel as happy as I ever did in my life and nothing in the world would have pleased me more than to have stayed with you all right along, but I felt ashamed when I got to Milwaukee and Madison and saw so many officers loafing around the streets. I felt as if it was a shame for an officer to be away from his command. As I sit here writing the report comes that Rich-

THE HEG MONUMENT AT MADISON, WISCONSIN
PAUL FJELDE, SCULPTOR

mond is taken.   It is too good to be true — but may it not
be.   I hope to God it is true for once.

My last letter was written to Edmund, and I ought to
have written to Hilda this time.   I can not now, but if I
have time I will write to her to morrow.

We have orders to give up our tents, and go into what is
called *Shelter tents.*   They are very small just big enough for
Three men to lay in.   I have a right to keep three big tents
for the Head Quarters, one for myself, one for the Major and
Lt. Col. and one for the Adjt. and Quarter Master.   I may
have Doctor Himoe with me in my tent — Though he is
Brigade Surgeon, and as soon as another Surgeon comes for
our Regiment, he may go up to Col. Carlins Head Quarters.

We moved our camp yesterday, we are now in a fine grove
about half way between the Franklin and Murfreesborro
Pike — about 5 Miles from Nashville.

The rebels are not very far off, as they are seen every day
by our Pickets.

To Morrow I am Field Officer of the day, and shall take a
ride along our lines and see what I can see.

Good bye again my Dear wife.

Your own HANS.

To Hilda, December 13, 1862
[Van Doren Mss.]

*Camp near Nashville.   Plans to send Hilda a saddle next
spring.   Asks her to commence taking music lessons again.
Assures her that every body likes Hilda Heg.   Postscript to
Gunild.   Speaks of the happiness of the soldiers in receiving
mittens and socks.*

To Gunild, December 15, 1862

CAMP NEAR NASHVILLE, Dec 15th 1862

MY DEAR GUNILD.

Yesterday was quite a long Sunday but I did not get time

to write any letter for the reason that I had considerable other writing to do. The wind has been blowing terribly from the south for several days, and shaken my tent so as to almost tear it down. The enemy is close by us in front, and we see them every day. Co. B. had quite a skirmish with some of the enemys cavalry yesterday, being sent out with a forage train. None of our men were hurt, while they claim that several of the rebels had to bite the dust. I got orders last night to keep the men up and under arms after 4 o'clock this morning, which was done, but nothing occurred. Every thing is now quiet. I hardly believe we will have any fight here. Rosecranse is evidently waiting for the enemy to attack him. If we can get them to pitch into us, we can give them a big threshing. Matters are looking better now than they have ever done — and the war can not be a very long one. I am feeling remarkably well. We have good living and plenty of it, for instance we had for supper last night — Roast Turkey, Roast Beef — Potatoes, Pickles, soft Bread — Peach Sauce, Apple Pie, and cake — with tea and coffee. I think that we are beating you just now, in the way we live. We bought us a small cooking stove, and we have got hold of one of the best and neatest cooks I ever saw. I bought me a Moss Mattrass for $7^{50}, also a stove for my tent for $5.^{00} so that, if I only had you with me, I could be as comfortable as any one in the world, but oh — how I miss you. Time passes off so fast, and I have so much to attend to that it is very easy for me. I remember you most — while alone on my cott, at night. I have been away so long that I trust you will not fret as much as you have done. If you will only have patience, it will be so pleasant when I can come back again for good, and stay with you all the time. It would not be pleasant for me to come back untill I have done my duty in this crisis. I would rather stay the entire Three years than return to have people point their fingers at me as a coward, who got too homesick to stay in the army.

Whatever you and I have to suffer now by being seperated

we will make up for sometime hereafter. I think we will make a short march to morrow to some place. I just rec^d orders to that effect.

I will close again. I may not get chance to write again for a few days.

Good Bye — my own.

Yours,
HANS.

I sent $400. by express to Farmers and Millers Bank — and ordered them to send you the certifficate.

To Hilda, December 19, 1862
[Van Doren Mss.]

Camp near Nashville. Next fall I am comming home to stay for good, and then we will have nice times, wont we? *Touches on many matters.* I want to hear that Hilda Heg is the best girl in Waterford. . . . When I get into Battle I might get shot, but if you are a good girl and Edmund is a good boy, God will take care of me for you.

To Gunild, December 22, 1862
[Van Doren Mss.]

Camp near Nashville. Yesterday his birthday. Received letters as presents. Description of routine of day. Wrote long letter to Holton of Milwaukee yesterday.

To Gunild, December 24, 1862

CAMP NEAR NASHVILLE. Dec 24th 1862

MY DEAR GUNILD.

For two days, I have not been able to write to you, as I have been on duty part of the time, and this morning at 5 oclock we were called up and ordered to march at daylight. We got up and was ready, but did not march till 2 oclock in the afternoon. When we started, we headed south, but went only two or three miles, and got orders to go back to camp. I have no idea what this march meant — it is kept entirely dark, but there is no doubt but that there will be lively times here pretty soon. We got back to camp a little before sun down, and got our tents up again in the same place and everything fixed in nice condition. This evening we were all invited by Heyer to take a Christmas supper with him. He is boarding the officers, and has his Hotel in a school House close by the camp. I have just returned from the party. We had a nice little time. The best fun was got up by me, getting one of the boys dressed up in wemens cloths, and comming into the house just as if I had a lady on my arm. Dr. Himoe also had the same kind of a woman with him, and we kept the house roaring for a good long time. The boys — including myself — have had a jolly *Christmas Eve*. It does not seem to make much difference, even if there is a prospect of fighting soon. The men are in good spirits — and as jolly as ever.

My comming back to the Regiment, has made a great change. It was a very good thing for me that I went away — the men, and the officers have learned something by my absence.

We have got orders to move again to morrow morning. Where we are going, no one knows I suppose, except old *Rosy*, as he is called.

It is 10 o'clock, and I have to get up at half past three — but I do not know how soon I will get a chance to write again, and I would not go to bed before I finished a letter to you.

I hope you will not feel uneasy for me if you do not hear from me for a few days. I shall write again as soon as we have an opportunity, — there is so much uncertainty about our movements, that we can not tell a half an hour before what is to happen — or where we are to go. We may not move at all to morrow. We have often had orders in the evening that were changed again in the morning. If we should not march to morrow, then I will write you again to morrow evening.   I have fully recovered, and I think I am just as well as I have ever been.   I am taking good care of myself — and if a Bullet should not hit me, I have not much fears about standing anything els that is to come.

The weather is splendid.   It is just as warm as May or June in Wisconsin.   The men are most all well — and feeling in good condition.   We have enough to eat, and I think our men are capable of standing more than anybody els in the service.

You may expect to hear that the rebels are soundly whipped down here, after we get hold of them.   I do not think there will be another such affair as at Fredricksburg.

I should like to fill my sheet — but I must have a little sleep and I must close.

It is Christmas to morrow.   I wish you all a merry Christmas — and a happy New Year — and I shall hope to spend the next Christmas with my Dear wife and little ones.

God bless you all.

Your own
HANS.

To Gunild, December 25, 1862

CAMP NEAR NASHVILLE Dec 25th 1862

DEAR GUNILD.

I wrote to you last night, and promised, if we did not march this morning I would write again to night.   As I expected, we did not go this morning, but I was ordered to take my Regiment out with a waggon train after forage — so I started out at 7 o'clock this morning, and I have spent Christmas out amongst the Secesh.   We met the enemy — and got a good chance to fire at them, but they run as usual without trying to fight.   They fired a few shots at us and put spurs to their horses.

We went out about 8 miles on the Franklin road.   They

say in camp that they have heard firing all day in the direction of Nolandsville, and I should not be surprised if there has been quite a fight out on the left of where I went out. We have orders to be ready to march at an early hour to morrow morning, but I think it is like the order we got last night. At all events we can not march very far, for the rebels are very strong not but a few miles from us. I am very tired, and can not write you a very long letter. I did not sleep much last night, and have been in the saddle since 7 o'clock till just now, and it is 8 o'clock now. I must stop again. I am feeling first rate. Good bye to you all. I send you a Christmas *Kiss*.

> Your Own
> HANS C.

To Gunild, December 26, 1862
[Van Doren Mss.]

Camp near Nashville. We shall move this morning, where to I am unable to tell. *Reports change in number of brigade and division* — it is now 2ᵈ Brigade — 1ˢᵗ Divission.

To Gunild, December 27, 1862

ON THE BATTLE FIELD NEAR NOLANDSVILLE
December 27ᵗʰ 1862.

MY DEAR WIFE.

I am still safe and sound. The 15ᵗʰ imortalised itself yesterday.[6] I charged with my Regiment up to a Battery and captured one Brass Cannon, 7 Horses, 3 Prisoners and one Caison — and what is the best of all — not one man wounded. We fought yesterday for 4 hours, after having marched during a heavy rain, through mud knee deep some places. We have driven them so far, and we are bound to do it all the time.

[6] The action here described took place on December 26 at Knob Gap, near Nolensville. See Cist, *The Army of the Cumberland*, 87–89, and Van Horne, *History of the Army of the Cumberland*, 1:220.

Several of my men were knocked down by shots, and pieces of shell but strange to say not one is scratched.   The Brigade has lost as far as heard from som 5 or 6 killed and 12 or 14 wounded.

We left camp yesterday at 7 A. M.   Marched till 12 o'clock through heavy rain, and fought the rest of the day till nearly dark.

The cannon captured by the 15th is the only one taken, that I know of — and belonged to the 14th Georgia Battery, and the Prisoners say it was captured from us at Shilo.[7] Give this to Ole & let him give us credit for what [we] have done — in the Sentinell.

Good bye my Dear.   Your own

HANS

To Gunild, December 28, 1862

IN CAMP NEAR NOLANDSVILLE
ABOUT 18 MILES FROM NASHVILLE
Dec 28th 1862.

MY DEAR —

I am afraid you are becomming anxious for me.   I know you have had no letter from me for some time.   I wrote yesterday with a Pencil stating that I was safe and sound, after a sharp Battle, in which we (the 15th) captured a Brass Cannon and Three Prisoners.   We have only moved two miles since day before yesterday and are laying quietly in camp drying up.   Dr. Himoe is well again.   The men never felt any better.   I was myself first at the Cannon and secured it, and the Prisoners.

Even is going home and will of course give you all the news.   I am as well as I ever was.   The rebels have no doubt left Murfreesboro — and we shall have no fight this side of Chattanooga.

Our Brigade lost in the fight three killed and 10 or 12 wounded.   The 15th lost none.

[7] Cist states that two guns were taken.   *The Army of the Cumberland*, 88.

We have won a reputation now, that will be hard to beat. It is very probable that letters will get through very unregular, and that we will not have chance to write as often as heretofore, but you must not get uneasy. I shall take as good care of myself as possible. You must do the same. The rail road between Louisville and Nashville has been torn open again I understand, and we will not of course get any mail for a few days.

I have given an account of our exploit, in capturing the Caisson, to the Govornor, and Fleischer, so you will see an account of it in the papers soon.[8] I have not time to write as much as I would like. I will do better next time.

I have now gone through several sharp fights, and I am getting quite well used to the music of war. Providence will yet lead me through this terrible struggle, and send me safe home to my nice little family.

I never fail in courage. You will not hear that I have ever played the coward.

My Dear wife — I hope you may always have occation to feel satisfied, and prowd of my behavior.

Once more good bye.

Your own
HANS.

To Gunild, January 4, 1863

BATTLE FIELD NEAR MURFREESBORRO
Jan. 4th 1863

MY DEAREST WIFE.

Thank God I am still able to let you know that I am safe and well. We have fought a terrible Battle, and lost a great

---

[8] K. J. Fleischer was on the staff of *Emigranten*. A letter from Colonel Heg to Governor Salomon appears in *Emigranten* for January 12, 1863, accompanied by one of Colonel Carlin, the brigade commander, praising the regiments of the brigade for their part in the action. *Emigranten* of the same date also publishes a very interesting letter of December 28, 1862, by one of the officers of the Fifteenth. Another detailed report written by a soldier of the regiment appears in *Emigranten* for February 2, 1863. It includes a warm tribute to Colonel Heg.

many men.[9] My noble Regiment is badly cut up. We were in Three heavy engagements, first on Tuesday evening, when I lost between 40 and 50 men killed & wounded. Amongst the killed was Capt. Ingmandson — and wounded, Capt. [Mons] Grinager, and Capt. [George] Wilson, the latter only slightly. I had my big Horse shot from under me. On the next day we fought twice. The 1st time Lt. Col. McKee was killed. Lt [Christian E.] Tanberg wounded & taken prisoner, also our new Lt. [John N.] Brown who belonged to Co I, but was on duty in Co E. I will give you the names of the killed, wounded and missing in Co. C for information to their friends. Killed — Mathis Krashus [10] — Gunder E. Hanson & Knud Finkelson. Wounded and supposed to be taken prisoners — Hans Jacobson Ronningen — Samuel Johnson — Knud Hanson — and Jacob Jordd [Jordahl]. There are some more missing in Co. C but not from Muskego. I can give no description of the Battle. I have lost one Horse and saddle, all my baggage except what I have on my body which is my old coat and Pants. Send by Even Skofstad one wollen under shirt and one over shirt also a pair of Drawers and a good pair of gloves.

My Dear — for your own sake as well as for my own I beg you not [to] feel uneasy for me. I have passed through thus far unhurt and Providence will yet bring me safely through the struggle. I have been in the thickest of the fight and led my men whereever they have fought. The official account of my action will be no disgrace to you or me. Lt. Col. McKee was shot through the head, but his body has not been recovered.

There is no use denying the fact we were badly whipped the first day — for the same reason as usual — an infernal fool of a General allowing himself to be surprised. Gen [R. W.] Johnson on our right was attacked while his men were

[9] On the battle of Stone River, or Murfreesboro, which Heg here describes, see the account and accompanying footnotes in the introductory sketch.
[10] See note on Mathias Mathiasen, *ante*, p. 66, n. 18.

in bed, and whipped.[11]   This being the case were outflanked, and we fought to no purpose.   The Rebels had it all their own way till about 12 °clock when old Rosy met them himself — and routed them terribly.   There has been two or three severe Battles since Wednesday in which the rebels have been badly whipped.   We have not got Murfreesborro yet, but they will be beaten out of there before many days. Thousands have been killed and wounded on both sides.   So far I think the rebels have suffered the most.   I have no means of writing any more.   D[r] Himoe is well.   I have had a hard time, but it is soon forgotten.   We are resting to day. Let Ole see this.   I have no time to write to anybody els. Maj. Johnson writes to Emigranten.[12]   M[a]y God bless you, and save me for your sake.   Your own

HANS.

To Gunild, January 6, 1863

CAMP NEAR MURFREESBORRO January 6th 1863.

MY DEAR

I am able at last to sit down and give you a full account of the tremendious Battle we have just fought.   On the 26th of Dec. we left our camp near Nashville, and sent all our teams back to the city.   On the same day, after marching 10 miles in a heavy rain we had an engagement with the enemy, drove them, and my Regiment captured one cannon without losing a man.   The next day it rained very heavy, and we advanced only about 2 miles and camped near Nolandsville.   The next day was Sunday and we remained quiet, the weather being good.   Monday morning we started

[11] An account of the Stone River campaign may be found in Van Horne, *History of the Army of the Cumberland*, 1:ch. 17.

[12] A long and interesting letter from Major Ole C. Johnson to his brother John A. Johnson, dated January 7, appears in *Emigranten* for January 17, 1863. "It is unnecessary," he writes at the close of this letter, "to say anything about Colonel Heg's part in the battle.   You are acquainted with him and you know that he would not swerve an inch from his duty.   He has always been at his post and has done everything in his power to ease the sufferings of his soldiers. The regiment has a devotion to him that increases daily."

again towards Murfreesborro, but met no enemy that day. In the evening we camped about 6 miles from Murfreesborro, so near the enemy that we were not allowed to have any fire. About 6 o'clock Tuesday morning we left our camp, in line of Battle, expecting to have a fight that day, and about noon, having come four Miles we met the enemys skirmishers in a heavy piece of woods. Lt Col. McKee was ahead with our skirmishers, Captain Ingmandsons Company, and they kept up firing till 2 oclock, when Capt Ingmanson was killed, and one more of his company badly wounded. My Regt. and the 21st Ill. was in advance, and was ordered to attack the enemy. This my Regiment did in fine style. Advancing clear up to where the enemy laid, under the heaviest fire I ever saw, both from Cannon and musketry, but the Regiment on my right gave away and run back. Nothing then was left for me but to fall back as well as I could. I fell back only one Hundred yards to a rail fence, giving the enemy two solid volleys as we retreated. In this engagement Capt Grinager was shot through the leg, but stayed with his company like a hero till he fainted from loss of Blood. Capt Wilson was slightly wounded, also Lt [Thor] Simonson of Co. F. In this charge fell also Gunder Hanson of Co C. son of the old man at Oles Store, and about 6 others killed and about 30 wounded. Our dead and wounded we got off to a House near by, and they were well taken care off. We had no fire during the night, and remained on the field where we fought. My Horse was shot through the head while I was on him, a ball evidently intended for me. After that time I remained on foot. Before daylight in the morning we were up and ready for an attack,— but the attack was made on our right, General Johnsons Division. He, it is reported was taken by surprise, his men being mostly in bed. His men off course run, but it was not known by our Brigade commander that Johnson had given away and we remained in our place till the enemy came upon us in force. After moving around a little I stationed my men behind a rail fence and waited till all the

other Regiments had given away and retreated past us, when
I ordered the men to fire.[13]   I gave commands to my men,
and kept up fire till the whole force of the rebels had almost
sorounded my little band of heroes, for they are nothing els.
Lt. Col. Mc.Kee fell here — shot through the Head — Lt.
Tanberg was wounded, Lt. Brown of Co E. also, and both
taken prisoners.   We now had to retreat through an open
field while the rebels poured into us an awfull volley of musket balls.   What men I had left, about 100 — I again rallied
on the other side of the field, and in company with what was
left of the Brigade, retreated towards the Murfreesborro
Turnpike where we knew old Rosy was stationed with the
center of the Army.   We made one more stand just before
we came up to the turnpike and gave the rebels another warm
time, but there was too many of them and we were again
forced to give away.   Here Mathis Krashus was killed.   As
we retreated, the Rebels came pouring along shouting like
Indians, through a cedar t[h]icket little dreaming what they
had to meet.   No sooner were they out of the cedars, than
old Rosy opened on them.   It is impossible for me to describe
the terrible slaughter they met.   All his Artillery and his best
Infantry were here massed and for the first time the victorious rebels found themselves checked.   During the rest of the
afternoon our Brigade remained quiet, and I rode up to witness the Battle as it raged.   Not satisfied with their first re-
puls, they again rallied three or four times, only to be routed
anew, with the most terrible slaughter.   When night came
we had beaten the enemy but they still held the ground that
our divission fought them on in the morning, and held the
Hospital we had established the evening before taking all the
wounded prisoners.   This was the last day of the Year 1862.
The longest day I have ever spent in my life and I hope
never again to see so gloomy a day.   The night came, but
we could off course have no fire.   It was a cold frosty night,

[13] Someone has drawn a line through the first six words of this sentence in the
original letter.

and as I walked along my little regiment, watching the men
sitting on the rocks and cold ground shivering from frost, I
could not help but think how little the people at home know
of the suffering of the soldier.[14]

The bright New Years morning came, and with it the same
rattle of cannon and musketry. We however remained quiet,
and built a strong fortification in front of us. All the fighting that day was done by the forces to our left, excepting a
skirmish, in which our skirmishers took part, where we captured over two Hundred Prisoners and never lost a man.
The fighting altogether was against the rebels. Another cold
night and no fire. A sharp engagement on Friday morning
where the rebels were again beaten. About 3 oclock in the
afternoon another terrible Battle commenced on our left, at
first the rebels drove our men a little but it soon changed.
The Rebels were put to flight, and old Rosy came galloping
down the Pike where we lay, the sweat pouring down his face,
and sent for Col. Carlin. He told Carlin the enemy was
routed and ordered him to advance with his Brigade to per-
sue them. His exact words to Carlin were — "I beg you for
the sake of the Country and for my own sake to go at them
with all your might. Go at them with a whoop and a Yell."
I had the honor of leading my little regiment in the advance.
The place belonged to the 21st Ill. but we had earned the
reputation of doing the best fighting on the Tuesday and
Wednesday before, and Carlin remarked to me as he ordered
me to lead — "I can rely on you all the time." We advanced
over two miles, driving the Rebels towards Murfreesborro in
a perfect rout. Again the Balls flew around us, but no attention was paid to that. We never fired a Gun but pressed on
capturing a great number of Prisoners. It soon got too dark
however, and we were compelled to give up the chase. This

[14] "The cold night fell," writes James K. Hosmer in his historical account of
the same event, "the winter heavens dimly lighting up the groups shivering by
the camp-fires and the dreadful field with its burden of mutilation and death."
The Appeal to Arms, 233 (*The American Nation: A History,* vol. 20 — New
York, 1907).

time the whole Rebel Army was routed, and two hours of
daylight would have enabled us to have captured and routed
the entire force. We did not halt till the moon was up, and
we were within one and a half miles of Murfreesborro. Now
came the most trying time of the whole Battle. It commenced raining, and again we were to spend another night
without tents or fire. The next morning we found ourselves
knee deep in mud, and the rain still pouring down. We were
now without any thing to eat, no coffee, and every man wet
to the skin, and the mud getting deeper and deeper. It was
no doubt Rosy⁸ intention to have attacked them during the
day, but the rain and mud prevented it. This was Saturday.
As night came on there was another heavy engagement on
our right, after dark — in which it is reported that the Rebels
lost heavyly and were defeated. About two oclock in the
night we got orders to leave our position and retire to the
rear. We then marched back to this place, and for the first
time for five days and nights were again where we could build
comfortable fires. Sunday morning, the sun came out bright,
and as we sat by our big fires rosting our pork and cooking
our coffee, the report came that the Rebels had left and that
old Rosy was persuing them with fresh troops. I am still
ignorant of what Rosecrance is doing. Yesterday we heard
heavy firing, and all sorts of reports are in circulation. One
thing is very certain, we have got Murfreesborro, and driven
the rebel army, what there is left of it, towards Chattanooga.
While we have lost a great many men, it is also certain that
the Rebels have lost much more. I have thus far given you
an account of what I know about the great Battle. Now I
will say a little about myself.

Although I have lost a splendid Horse & Saddle, my Blankets and Bedding, my sachell with all my cloths, and have
nothing left me except what I have on me, I am thankfull
that Providence led me through the terrible struggle safly.
Poor Mc.Kee, I believe he expected to be killed. He was
very gloomy the day before, and in the morning before the

fight began, he asked his hostler to take his horse — and
wanted him to take his watch, and also gave Dr Himoe most
of his money. I did not see him fall, but he was not more
than two or three Hundred feet from me. The smoke, and
noise was so heavy, that little could be seen or heard. Peter
Stangeland saw him fall — but we did not get his body till
yesterday. When we found him he was stripped of all his
clothing except his drawers and shirt.

  —   I stood behind a small tree,[15] giving commands to my men,
and heard the balls strike the tree several times. Yesterday
I counted five Balls in the little tree in front of me. One ball
the first evening went through my over coat. During our
hard suffering from frost and hunger, I often had opportunities to feel thankfull to my men — as they would often come
to me and enquire about how I got along and divide a
cracker, or a cup of coffee, when I was willing to take it. —
Many of them came to me with tears in their eys, as they
shook hands with me. It is well worth the suffering I have
had to go through, when I remember how bravely and how
faithfully these men have stood by me — and how well they
have sustained our reput[at]ion for coolness and bravery in
Battle. But I will let some one els do justice to their valor.
I went into Battle with 304 men. I have 13 killed, 70
Wounded and 34 missing. Nearly all the missing were
wounded and afterwards taken prisoners. Out of 9 Field
officers in the Brigade, 3 were killed and one badly wounded.
I have not seen the report, but one half of the Brigade is
gone — mostly wounded. About 150 are killed. My noble
Horse was not shot dead at the time he was hit. I found him
the next morning, and thought I could save him, but had to
leave him when I retreated, and yesterday I found the poor
fellow on the Battlefield with at least a Dozen more Bullets
in him.

    Even Skofstad has been trying to go home for sometime,
and will leave again to morrow. I shall send with him my

---

[15] These words in the original letter have been crossed out.

black horse as I have got a couple of good captured Horses
in my possession that I will try to get. I am also sending
home with him one of the best negro boys that I have yet
found. You will find him honest and faithfull, and he considers himself as belonging to me. I am sure you will like
him. If you have not work enough for him during the winter, you may let him work for Ole if he has anything to do for
him. I want him on my farm when I come home. He will
take good care of the horse and I have told him to get him
broke for a Buggy, and you must get a light Buggy Harness,
and use him for yourself and the children. I also want you
to get me a coat made at the same place I got the other one.
Mr Tracy, in Milwaukee, they have got my measure. Get
me also a Sachell, like the one I had, a couple of the same
kind of shirts you made me, an under shirt and a pair of
Drawers, also a pair of slippers, or light shoes. I happened
to have 2 pairs of Socks & 2 towels in my Saddle roll — this is
all I have left. I have got only my old coat and heavy
Pants on, but I do not want any new Pants. I can not
think of any more to write at present. We shall probably
stay where we are for some time, and should I get to any
place where I could see that you would be comfortable, I,
as well as Doctor Himoe intend to send for our Darlings, to
come and stay with us. I have written several letters to you
since I left Nashville, most of which I suppose you have not
got. We are to move camp again. Good bye my Dearest
Wife. You may let your friends see this letter.

Your HANS

To Gunild, January 8, 1863

IN CAMP NEAR MURFREESBORRO
January 8th 1863

MY DEAR GUNILD.
   I hope that by the time you receive this letter, you will
have heard of my being safly and comfortably situated again.

Even Skofstad started for home yesterday, and took with a letter that I wrote the day before giving a full discription of the great Battle, or at least the part I took in it. We have since moved our camp so that we are now about 3 miles south of Murfreesborro, on what is called the Franklin Pike. The Rebels left in great hurry and have no doubt gone to Chattanooga where we will have our next tussle with them.

Old Rosecranse can, and will whip them every time. He will be the great man in this war yet. I think he is the best, bravest and biggest general we have got. We have lost a great many men in this Battle, perhaps six or eight Thousand killed and wounded, many of them however are not much wounded and will soon be fit for duty. The Battle ground covers several miles and you can fairly say that the ground is covered with dead men and dead Horses. It is no doubt the biggest Battle yet fought during the Rebellion. Our men suffered tremendiously, as we had very little to eat, and were not permitted to have fires, and for two days and night[s] the rain poured down upon us, making the mud almost knee deep. You have no idea up in Wisconsin what we have had to go through. But it is all forgotten again as soon as we get back into our comfortable tents talking over what we saw and did. I can not say that any time during the fight I had any such thing as fear. I seemed to feel certain that there was no ball intended for me. There is only one thing that would have any tendency to make me a coward, and that is when I remember that it would be so terrible hard for you to loose me. During the heaviest fight on Wednesday the 31st I stood for about half an hour behind a small tree, and I heard the Balls strike the tree very often. As I went down on the spot a couple of days ago I found the little tree and found five Balls in it opposite to where I stood.

I have been very bussy to day making out my Report, and just sent it in this evening. I shall send a copy of it, and also a copy of Col. Carlins to the Milwaukee Sentinell or State Journal, so you may look in one of those papers for it.

Col. Carlin pays me a very fine compliment in his report.[16] I have got hold of a very fine Mare to ride instead of the Horse I lost.

The Army is being reorganised and put in order again, and in a short time you will hear of old Rosy heading off towards Chattanooga, and give them another good threshing.

My Regiment is very small now. I have only a little over 200 men left, but I think perhaps I may get my two companies from Island N° 10 now that the Island is evacuated.

The whole country from here to Nashville is completly ruined. Every house is burned and not a fence rail to be seen. What has become of the poor wemen and children I do not know. I begin to feel almost glad to see this destruction, for I have come to the conclusion that nothing will ever bring these people to their senses, and the sooner their places are filled by some others the Better and if the country is ruined and their farms destroyed they certainly can not raise anything for the rebel Armys to live on.

It makes a man pretty hard hearted to be a soldier long. I have got so I almost feel indifferent as to how rebels suffer, although many of them no doubt have been forced and fooled into this war.

We miss McKee considerable, at least I do for he was good company. He was not very popular with the men. D[r] Himoe has had his hands full for sometime now. Our new Doctors have none of them arived. It is very curious that men can be so negligent when it is well known that we need them so badly. I hope *Phelan*, my Darkey will come home safe and that you will be pleased with him. He has been so faithfull to me that I can not doubt but that he will be just as faithfull to you. You may not have much to do for him

[16] Carlin's report is printed in *War of the Rebellion*, series 1, vol. 20, part 1, p. 279–283. Colonel Heg's official report seems not to have been included in the *War of the Rebellion*, but it is printed in the *Wisconsin State Journal* of Madison for January 17, 1863, together with a letter of transmittal to Governor Salomon Colonel Heg's report was dated January 9, 1863.

yet, but you can find enough when spring comes, and when I
come home I will put him to work on my farm.   It is quite
late, and I want to go to bed so I must stop my scribling.
The Regiment is on Picket, and Major Johnson is in command with it.   I am taking it quite easy now.   I will write
often again as soon as the mail begins to run regular.   I have
had no mail at all since we left Nashville, but are looking for
some every day.   You must not fret for me now.   Take good
care of yourself and the children and trust my chances to a
kind Providence.   You can do no good by feeling uneasy for
me.   There is no prospect for any more fighting this month
and perhaps not next.

My Dear One Good Bye — Once more

Your own HANS.

To Gunild, January 10, 1863

CAMP NEAR MURFREESBORO Jan 10th 1863

MY DEAR.

For a couple of days I have been so bussy that I have had
no time to write to you.   I have worked very hard making
out my report and other matters that had to be attended to,
as well as taking a little rest.   I was nearly used up when
this fight was over — but I have had a good long time to lay
still in, and I expect we will lay here at least a week or two.
I have been so quiet in my tent that I have not heard any
news — but to morrow or next day I intend to go up to Murfreesboro and see old Rosecranse.

I shall wait very anxiously for Even Skofstad to come
back, with the articles I wrote for.   I was lucky enough to
find my stove in one of the waggons, and my Cott bed — but
my Blankets and Mattrass are gone.   I have got Blankets
enough again however.   What I need, and what I am most
sory for is my new Suit of Cloths, and the nice shirts you
made.   Luckily I have one of them on me.

I have sent a copy of my Report to the Govornor, and also a copy of Col. Carlins report, both will be published, and I want you to get a copy of those and keep them. I hope you will keep a copy of all corespondence &c. of the 15th that you find in Newspapers. It will be interesting hereafter to have it. I am writing to E. D. Holton of Milwaukee and I see he publishes some of it in the Sentinell. You must take the Sentinel all the time. I would like to send you a copy of Carlins report, but it is too long to write out. I copy what he say[s] about somebody that you have some interest in. He says — "I deem it my duty to call the special Attention of the Genl. comanding the 14th Army Corps (Gen Rosecranse) to Col. Hans C. Heg, 15 Wis Vols. and Col J. W. S. Alexander 21st Ill. vols. While every field officer under my command did his duty faithfully — Col[s] Heg and Alexander in my opinion proved themselves the bravest of the brave. Had such men as these been in command of some of our Brigades we would have been spared the shame of witnessing the rout of our troops and the disgracefull panic encouraged at least by the example and advise of officers high in command." [17]

I can assure you that however badly the troops were beaten on our side at the time he speaks of — The 15th conducted itself with more credit than any other Regiments during the day. I know that you will say that you do not care — if I only was at home again with you. I know you do care though. How would [you] like to have said by the newspapers that Col. Heg ran like a coward? I will be back home again, but not untill I have done some good in this war. I have already done some, but there is much more yet to be done. I hope you will feel satisfied and contented, and be happy to know that I came out of this great Battle with good credit, and did my duty bravly — and that Providence spared

[17] This part of Carlin's report is printed in *War of the Rebellion*, series 1, vol. 20, part 1, p. 282. There are a few minor changes in Heg's version of the statement.

COLONEL HANS CHRISTIAN HEG
[From a portrait in Grand Army Memorial Hall, Madison, Wisconsin.]

my life. Good night my Dear One. Kiss the children for me.

> Your own HANS

To Hilda, January 12, 1863
[Van Doren Mss.]

CAMP NEAR MURFREESBORO Jan. 12th 1863.

MY DEAR LITTLE HILDA,

I have expected to get a nice letter from you, but the mail does not come very regular and I have not got any letter since the big Battle from any of you. Yesterday was Sunday, and it was a very nice warm day. We have no snow down here, and no cold weather. I wished very much yesterday that I could have been at home with you, and seen how you got along.

I have sent home my Black Horse now, and I want Edmund should keep him and give you the Pony. He is just right for you. And I have sent a Negro home to take care of your Horses for you. Ma says in her letters that you are a good girl and I am so glad to hear it. I have been in a big Battle, and the Balls came very thick around me, but I was not hurt, because you were good children and God took care of me so that I could get home again to you. A great many little girls like you, have lost their fathers in this Battle. You must be good to Elmer and to your Mother. The Negro I have sent home is a very good man, and when you get aquainted with him you will like him. I am going to try and get you a present for your Birthday if I can. Next time I will write to Edmund. I have written so many letters to Ma—that I do not owe her any now. Tell Ma that I am well, and I have everything very comfortable. I sent my Black Horse home, because he was getting poor, and I was afraid I might lose him. Good Bye. Your Pa

> HANS.

To Gunild, January 13, 1863
[Van Doren Mss.]

Camp near Murfreesboro. We are resting ourselves and fixing up after the great Battle. *Speaks of his losses:* My Regiment is not what it used to be — I have got about 200 men for duty. *He is boarding at the hospital and living well. Postscript to Nebby.*

To Gunild, January 14, 1863

CAMP NEAR NASHVILLE TENN
Jan 14th 1862 [1863]

MY DEAREST.

To morrow our whole Brigade is ordered to go on Picket for one day. I do not think we go more than a mile or two from camp but as I shall not have chance to write to morrow, so I must do it to night. It is raining very hard this evening, but it is mild as summer. I am very comfortable however in my tent, and I have got some exelent company. Dr Wooster of Racine and Dr Trenckler both came here last night.[18] Wooster stops in my tent with me at present. I went out on a Forage expedition yesterday and returned in the evening. To day I went down to Murfreesboro and called on old Rosy. He shook hands with me as cordially as he generally does and asked how my Rgt stood it after the fight. I send you a very nice piece of Poetry, but you must not think that I am quite as homesick as that represents. I saw that it was reported in the papers that I had lost 7 captains in the Battle, and Dr Wooster said the report came to Wisconsin that the whole Regiment was almost destroyed. Not quite so bad as that. I have yet over 200 men with me here for duty. I suppose when I have fought till all my men are gone that I will get permission to go home to my little

[18] Dr. Oscar Trenkler of Eau Claire was appointed first assistant surgeon of the regiment on December 15, 1862. Dr. Daniel P. Wooster of Racine had been made second assistant surgeon five days earlier. Dr. Wooster resigned on March 2 and Dr. Trenkler on June 1, 1863. *Roster,* 1:804.

family. I am glad to hear that no report came that I was
killed. I was afraid such things might be reported and that
you would feel so bad about it. I am living well and just as
healthy as I used to be. I am getting as fat again as I was
before I got sick. I am only waiting for Even Skofstad to
come back and bring me those things that I wrote to you
about. I am quite ragged and dirty — but as there is no
Ladies down here to shine up to so that it makes but very
little difference.

I have nothing more to write about and must therefor
stop.

I hope you have seen my report printed by this time —
and I know you will feel happy to know that I did my duty
and came through safe.

Good night my Dear Gunild,

Your Own HANS

To Gunild, January 17, 1863
[Van Doren Mss.]

*Camp near Murfreesboro. Refers to his many letters telling
about the recent battle. Commanded the brigade on picket
duty. Sadly in need of new clothes. Interested in Wisconsin reports of battle. Postscript to Edmund.*

To Gunild, January 19, 1863
[Van Doren Mss.]

*Camp near Murfreesboro. The letter is incorrectly dated
1862. Heg reports little to do except picket or escort duty.*
Many of our wounded men have died since the Battle. The
weather and everything els has been unfavorable for sick and
wounded persons. *He acknowledges gifts of articles from
the Soldiers' Aid Society in Norway. Again refers to the
battle and his own escape.* I am going to return home all
safe to you and my little ones after I have done my duty in
this war.

To Gunild, January 21, 1863
[Van Doren Mss.]

Camp near Murfreesboro. Letter is incorrectly dated 1862.
Yesterday I had quite a Spat with Jeff. C. Davis — our
Divission Commander — he is a proslavery General, and he
is down on the Abolitionists. I had some plain talk with
him, and told him what I thought of proslavery Generals —
I have no good feeling for him, and I have made up my mind
that I will not go into another Battle under his command.
*Heg and Carlin have asked Rosecrans to relieve Davis from
his command of the division.* I shall not remain in the
service longer than till next fall, I dont think, whether the
war closes or not.

To Hilda, January 22, 1863
[Van Doren Mss.]

*Camp near Murfreesboro. Letter incorrectly dated 1862.
Asks Hilda to try to persuade her mother to get her a music
teacher.* I hope by this time my Horse has come home,
and also my Negro Boy Phelan.

To Gunild, January 23, 1863
[Van Doren Mss.]

Camp near Murfreesboro. Every Battle I have been in, I
have gone into with a certain conciousness that I would
come out of it all right. *Refers to his luck:* I have always
been fortunate, and you know I never look on the dark side
of any thing. *Sentimental recollection of days when he
peddled cranberries. Heg calls this letter his love letter to
Gunild.*

To Gunild, January 26, 1863
[Van Doren Mss.]

*Camp near Murfreesboro. Commanded brigade on picket.
Hopes for promotion and for favorable influence of Nor-*

wegians in Wisconsin. Violent outburst against all the traitors at the North. I send you a nice piece of poetry.

To Gunild, January 29, 1863
[Van Doren Mss.]

Camp near Murfreesboro. No letters from home. What
is the matter? *Dr. Wooster, ill, has left. Dr. Himoe may
go to a Nashville hospital.* I see that I did not make as
much as I might by selling your Gold. It seems that gold
keeps going up all the time. *As to the war:* Everything is
very quiet with us. I do not believe this Army can move
very soon.

SUPPLEMENT

*The following three communications were written by Colo-
nel Heg to E. D. Holton, a prominent merchant of Milwaukee, and by him communicated to the Milwaukee Sentinel.
The first is unsigned; the second is written over the initials
"H. C. H."; and the third bears the signature "Index." In-
ternal evidence leaves no doubt, however, that all three are
from the pen of Colonel Heg. The letters form an interesting supplement to those written to Mrs. Heg.*

From a Letter by Colonel Heg, December 15, 1862
[*Milwaukee Sentinel*, December 23, 1862]

A private letter from an officer of the Scandinavian regiment dated " near Nashville, Dec. 15th," says:
" We are still lying face to face with the enemy, little or
nothing being done on either side. Rosecrans is evidently
trying to bring on an attack from them. We have orders to
move tomorrow — I suppose it means to the front. It seems
to be a settled opinion among our officers that a stand will
be made between here and Murfreesboro. I have doubted
it, for the reason that I could not see what the enemy could
gain by fighting here, unless they really suppose that they

can get possession of Nashville. It is rumored to-day that Pemberton is on his way to reinforce Bragg at this place; if so, he will undoubtedly make an attack soon. We have all sorts of rumors from Virginia. Papers are very scarce, and we get none but the Louisville *Journal*.

The entire tone and spirit of this army seems to have undergone a wonderful change since I left it in November. Change of commanders has made a different army of it. There is none of that insubordination and marauding that existed to such a terrible extent while we were in Kentucky. There is system and management everywhere — even in our mail arrangements. If this army meets with defeat, I shall be terribly disappointed; I do not think it possible unless from causes not under men's control.

I have never known the health of the troops as good as at present, especially amongst the old volunteers.

Very truly your friend, Etc.

A Letter by Colonel Heg, December 21, 1862 [19]

[*Milwaukee Sentinel*, January 5, 1863]

Camp near Nashville, Dec. 21, '62

Dear Sir: — It is Sunday, and everything is so quiet and still that I will endeavor to write a letter — not that I can entertain you with anything interesting, but more particularly to pass off time which, during a monotonous camp life, generally drags heavy. No troops in the field really needed rest any more than my regiment, after a continuous march of over 1,100 miles, during a hot and dusty summer; still, a quiet camp life is only an enjoyment till you are rested. It soon becomes tedious, and men long for changes and excitements incident to active operations. Such is the case with the troops here in general. I do not believe that any army exists anywhere that is better organized, better taken care of, and more systematically managed, than are the troops

[19] The newspaper uses the heading " Private letter from Rosecrans' Army."

of Gen. Rosecrans' command. The only redeeming trait of
Gen. Buell, as was contended by many, was his order and
system. I heard of that long before I knew anything of him
personally. I failed to discover any such quality in him in
the management of his troops. Whether he was to blame,
or some one else, it can never be contradicted that a looser
disciplined army could hardly be expected to hold together.

With the exception of a few of the new regiments, who are
suffering from camp fever and measles, I can say that there
is hardly any sickness in camp.

I can see no immediate prospect of moving on the rebel
forces said to be between here and Murfreesboro. I still
believe they will not make any stand here, but on our advance will fall back towards Chattanooga. We cannot with
safety advance any distance until we can rely on the river
for supplies. — The prospect for a rise is not flattering.
There has been no rain here to speak of since my return.
The days are most beautiful; just cold enough to be pleasant. We have generally a strong wind from the South or
West, with a bright, clear sky.

Last Thursday I was ordered to take two regiments and
a battery, and go outside of our lines, with 125 forage wagons,
to collect forage for our animals. There are very stringent
orders on the subject of foraging. (I send a copy enclosed.)
Forage is taken for the Government wherever it is found,
but we generally prefer to get it from out-and-out rebels.
I found a large field, containing two hundred acres of corn
unhusked, and upon making enquiries at the negroe quarters
I ascertained that the magnificent brick building standing
on a fine eminence to the left was the former residence of the
rebel owners. — A Mrs. May, with two sons and a daughter — all married — had resided there, or rather the female
portion of Mrs. May's family had stayed there, till recently — the two sons and son-in-law had joined the rebel
army long ago. When I asked the fat negroe proprietress
of the establishment where I halted, where and how she had

procured so much elegant furniture — for her log cabin was filled with sofa chairs, bureaus, tables, bedsteads, and large expensive mirrors — she answered that " Misses gib de brack folks all de nice things when she gone away, and tell dem to take good care of it till she come back " — evidently fearing the " Yankees " might break open her house and destroy her *nice things.*

One hundred and twenty-five wagons, with four men to each wagon, will gather a good deal of corn in one day, and by three o'clock we had spoiled the corn field of Mrs. May quite badly. All our wagons were filled, excepting eight, which I sent up to a man by the name of Williams, who was reported to have several hundred bushels of sweet potatoes. It went against the grain for the old man to open his cellar for us; but he, too, was reported as a prominent rebel, although his wife was from New York, and strongly denied that they had ever sympathized with the rebellion.

We may talk about being tired of this war, and of suffering from it, but the suffering on our part has no comparison with that of those poor, deluded wretches that live on the lines where the armies are moving. How dearly, and how justly too, many are paying the penalty of their folly!

While looking at the splendid residences, and improved farming land lying within our lines about Nashville, owned by rebels, and in many instances like Mrs. May's plantation, no other tenants on them than the negroes they have not been able to bring away with them, it has often occurred to me that government should make use of them immediately.

When we remember that our armies have always suffered for want of vegetables; that thousands upon thousands of acres of the prettiest land in the world — virtually belonging to the government — is lying idle, and at the same time our camps are crowded with blacks, seeking liberty and employment, it seems that government ought to avail itself of these circumstances. An energetic person with the proper authority from Washington, I think, could collect negroes, and by their labor put land under cultivation, next season, the fruits

of which would be of great benefit to the army, and at the
same time give employment to the negroes that we are forced
to turn away from us.   If the emancipation after the first of
January next shall be carried into effect, the negroes will
have to be taken care of in some way by the government, at
least for a while, by employing them on the confiscated plan-
tations, where at the same time they ought to be educated
to take care of themselves, and made to understand their
duties as freemen.   This has worked well, I believe, in South
Carolina, and it ought by all means to be adopted here in
the West.

I must close.   My opportunities for writing are poor.   I
am, however, well and comfortably situated — have a good
tent, stove in it, and plenty to eat.

Very truly yours,

H. C. H.

Colonel Heg to E. D. Holton, January 9, 1863 [20]

[*Milwaukee Sentinel,* January 21, 1863]

Camp near Murfreesboro,

January 9, 1863

Friend Holton: —

I find that I am no prophet; for, contrary to all my expec-
tations, we have had one of the bloodiest battles of the rebellion here.   I could see no good reason why the rebels should
make a stand here, unless they were really in hopes of capturing Nashville.   It is evident now that they had not only
strong hopes of effecting this, but actually felt sure of completely destroying Gen. Rosecrans' army.   I am satisfied
that they had concentrated a much larger force than we had
in the field.

Their deserted camps are stretched over an immense area
of ground, and they had no doubt arranged themselves in fine

[20] The newspaper caption is " Interesting Private Letter from the Fifteenth
Regiment."   Note Colonel Heg's allusion, in his letter of January 10 to Mrs.
Heg, to his correspondence with E. D. Holton.

style. Every tent had its fire-place and chimney of brick. The woods for miles around are covered with these vacant fire-places.

We have fought one of the bloodiest battles yet on record on this continent. I will attempt to give you a short description of what I saw myself, and by adding it to what you may get from other sources, perhaps it may be interesting:

The army under Rosecrans moved from Nashville on the 26th of December, in three *corps de armes*, denominated the right, left, and center. The center moved on the Murfreesboro Pike, the right and left supporting on each side. My command was in the right wing, commanded by Gen. McCook, and his force was composed of Johnson's, Sheridan's, and Davis' divisions, I think. I am not certain whether Rousseau's division is attached to this corps or not.

Our division (Davis) met the enemy at Nolansville, drove them, and captured some of their artillery — changed our direction from them towards Murfreesboro, and on the 30th of December, ran into the enemy in force, about three miles from that place.

We were well satisfied that the last day of the year 1862 would be a bloody one, for we were satisfied that the enemy, instead of leaving his stronghold, was receiving reinforcements every hour.

During the night I lay with my regiment within four hundred yards of the enemy's line, and within half a mile of the main body. At daylight I saw solid columns of troops moving through the woods toward our right, without making any demonstrations toward us. Johnson's division was stationed on our right, and a little to our rear. Soon we heard lively musket fire in the direction of his column, which grew heavier and heavier, and fast getting into our rear. It was an indication to us that we were being outflanked, but still we had no information of it. The truth is, there lay nearly twenty thousand of the best soldiers the world has ever seen, destined to be the victims of the imbecility, treachery, or whatever else it may have been, of one of our Generals.

Gen. Johnson was not with his command when he was attacked. His men had not even been called out of bed. His artillery horses were half a mile off at a creek, watering. In that condition, the concentrated force of the rebels, under command of Bragg, Hardee, and Buckner, found our right flank. And, what was still worse, no intimation was given us of the state of affairs, only as we judged from the direction of the firing, as it kept getting into our rear. The reports will show how desperately some of our troops fought, only to find that when they had beaten the enemy in front, heavy bodies of the rebel troops would assail them in the flank or rear.

When I look at the real condition of things it seems almost a wonder that the entire army was not completely butchered or captured. Nothing prevented it but the fact that the rebels at first feared that the movement was one of Rosecrans' old tricks to draw them into a trap, and consequently they pressed us slowly and cautiously giving us time to get out of the way. The whole of the right wing then fell back on the center, followed by the jubilant and victorious rebel horde — but here they ran against a snag. Column after column came dashing towards the turnpike, like ocean waves against a solid rock. The turnpike and railroad run parallel, and about 200 yards apart, where old Rosy made his stand, the railroad making a deep cut through a hill. — In this cut he would mass his infantry and station his artillery on the hill, which had command of the country around. Here at several times, I understood, he had concentrated from forty to fifty pieces of artillery, and as the rebels came pouring on in their drunken revelry, they were slaughtered like sheep in a pen, and our infantry would pour out of the railroad cut as if they came out of the ground. I have noticed in all the engagements I have been in that the rebel troops are always supplied with whisky while in action, I think they intend always to fight while under the influence of liquor. This accounts partly for the recklessness they generally display during their first charges, and it is also a notable fact that they

never fight well after the first day. Rosecrans was himself
on the field; I saw him while riding to and fro at furious
rates, the sweat pouring down his face, and his clothes spat-
tered over with blood, and I could not help expressing my
gratitude to Providence for having at last given us a man
that was equal to the occasion. A General in fact as well as
in name. When the sun set on the last day of the year
1862, victory was on our side. Although we had lost many
men and considerable artillery, the enemy had battered its
brains out against our solid centre. But they were not satisfied; they knew we had lost heavily; their cavalry had succeeded in destroying much of our supply train coming out of
Nashville, and they even flattered themselves that Rosecrans
would withdraw during the night. On the 1st of January
they made several charges at different points on our lines,
but by that time we were well protected by temporary breast-
works and rifle pits, and all their attacks resulted in our
favor.

On Friday afternoon, the 2d, they made their last desperate attack, waiting till about an hour and a half before
sundown, in order to have the advantage of the night in case
of failure. Our lines wavered at first, but it was only temporary, the rebels were forced to give away in disorder.
Two hours of daylight at this time would have given us the
whole rebel army. But darkness set in and with it a heavy
rain, which continued during the whole of next day. Before
the persuit was given up, however, we captured a great many
prisoners and one or two batteries. From that time they
began to pack up and leave. One of my captains was a prisoner at Murfreesboro at that time; he represents the excitement there as perfectly terrible. Many of the prisoners they
had captured from us escaped during the excitement, even
without being paroled.

That we have gained a splendid victory is very certain;
what will result from it can only be conjectured. They have
undoubtedly fallen back on Chattanooga, but they have at
all events lost Tennessee. It will not be possible for this

army to move again immediately, for there are many repairs
to be made — in fact much of the army will have to be re-
organized.   There are a great many officers whose shoulder
straps should be torn off and given to others who deserve it.
It is very nice to be a good General or a good soldier, while
all is quiet, or even in engagements, while victorious; but to
conduct a command in retreat, and during defeat, then is the
time that qualities are called upon.   I am better satisfied
than I have been before, that many of our generals are made
of very inferior stuff, and that before we reach the object we
are striving for, many of them will have to be sent to the
rear.

As for the generality of the soldiers, there are, perhaps,
none better in the world than ours are becoming.   It takes
a few months of severe hardships to make fighting soldiers.
Men just out from a luxurious home have not the proper
fighting quality in them.   They may be brave, and all that
sort of thing, but until they have tasted the realities of soldier
life, I will not give much for their valor or bravery.

The army is in excellent spirits, and when Rosecrans has
filled up the gaps, and made the necessary changes and repairs, you will again here of our entering victoriously into
East Tennessee.

I have written in a hurry, a few of the facts as I have
found and seen them.   I shall be happy if I can communicate
anything of interest to you, and shall be glad to do it whenever I find anything worth writing about.   But of 308 men
I took into action, I lost 119 killed, wounded, and missing.
I send my report as well as the report of my brigade commander, to Wisconsin for publication.

By the way the Col. commanding our brigade, is a young
officer from the regular service, and he is looked upon by
Rosecrans as one of the best officers in the army.   Such he
is in fact, I wish I could say as much for our division commander, but I can not.

Very truly yours,

" Index "

V. CAMP LIFE NEAR MURFREESBORO

To Gunild, February 10, 1863

Franklin, Tennessee. Is in command of brigade. Head-quarters established at house of Mr. Merrill. He is a very rich planter and has a beautiful establishment here, but they are very hard up for anything to eat &c — as this place has been in the hands of the rebels so long. *As to the general situation:* The rebels are leaving Tennessee and going south. We are also recieving very large reinforcements and I do not believe these old troops that have seen so much hardships and fighting as we have will be called on to go to the front soon. Franklin is a very pleasant place, somewhat larger than Waupun, and with some Union men living in it.

To Gunild, February 14, 1863

Camp near Murfreesboro. I am once more back in my old tent and at our old camp, having been gone just two weeks. *Heg refers to a letter received from Holton in Milwaukee.*[1] I am too ragged to show myself anywhere.

To Gunild, February 16, 1863

CAMP NEAR MURFREESBORO
Febry 16th 1863.

MY DEAREST.

I promised you in my last to write a long letter next time, and to day I am alone the Regiment having gone as an escort to a foraging train, and having caught cold so as not to feel very well, I am left at home.

Time is wearing away quite rapidly. It is already past the middle of this month, and we are beginning to see signs

---

[1] E. D. Holton is mentioned in Heg's letter of January 10, 1863.

188

of spring. The weather is warm, and the Birds and Frogs
are singing as they do up in Wisconsin in April. If I had you
and the children with me I could live and enjoy myself first
rate in such a climate as this is.

The same complaint as usual — I get no mail from home.
Yesterday, a large mail came, but nothing for me. To day
we had a small mail, but it is all the same. I got a letter
from Ole dated Febry 2ᵈ when I came back from Franklin,
but he says not a word about how you are getting along.

But I am getting used to most anything. I think I can
bear this too. Before the Battle I got the mails very regular
and your letters came through in about 6 or 8 days, but it
seems all disarranged since. The Waterford boys are all in
the same fix that I am. The Paymaster is here and preparing to pay us off for four months. I shall send my money to
Holton with the same instructions as I did before. I have
written a couple of letters to Ole, asking him to tell me if he
can loan out my money on a good Mortgage to any body, or
if he knows of any way of investing it in anything safe and
paying. If there is any way that you could find to loan out
the money I am sparing, as youd to Thosten, you had better
do it. I can not give you any news. Everything moves on
as usual. There does not seem to be much prospect of moving yet, though we will not remain here longer than can be
helped. Rosecranse will let the rebels know soon where he
is — and you may make up your mind to hear some more
good victories again.

The only discouraging thing we get down here are the reports of the *Northern Rebels*. I begin to fear them as much
as I do the *Southern Rebels*. I wrote Ole a wholesome letter
to day in regard to the course their party is taking — *misserable, cowardly Skulks*. It is not enough that they are allowed to stay at home, sleeping on their Featherbeds, living
in Luxury and making money, but they must use every opportunity they have to help the enemy we are fighting. Let
them now just drive it far enough to start a civil war at

home, and when they have tried that a while I presume they will be satisfied.

This war will not last for ever, thank God, and we will not all be killed. Some of us will be back sometime, and if those misserable party men will not be called upon to account for the aid and assistance they have rendered the enemy while we have laid down here away from home trying to defend the goverment and the country, then I am mistaken.

I have seen several Rebel Papers from the south lately. They are very much pleased at what the Northern Rebels are doing.

The Rebel Army would not hold together but a very short time now if it was not for the prospect that they hold out to them that the Democrats up north are getting up a civil war amongst us at home. I hope for Oles sake that he has good sense enough to keep away from his party, now that it is openly declaring itself in favor of treason.

Jacob that has taken care of my Horse, is discharged. He has been quite sick. I think when he goes home, he will go by Waterford. He feels very much pleased. Even, or Holmen is not here yet. Are they ever intending to come back?

They will lose a good deal of their debts down here by being away now while the men are being paid off.

I am so anxious to hear from you. But there is no use in being impatient.

I shall probably send home about 700 Dollars if we are paid for 4 months.

No more this time — only once more Good Bye.

                                    Your Own
                                    HANS C.

Get a music teacher for Hilda if possible.

MY DEAR EDMUND

It is so long since I got any letter from you, that I am very anxious to hear what you have to write. How is the Pony? How are the Sheep up on the Farm? Are they going to build

the Rail Road by our Farm?   You must write to me and give
me as much news as possible.   I forgot to tell Ma in my letter on the other side that [I] want she should employ a music
teacher for Hilda if there is one to be got.   I have got me
another fine Horse for the one I lost, — and I am trying to
get hold of one more.

Be a good Boy, and I will come home to you before a great
while.

YOUR FATHER.

DEAR LITTLE HILDA.

I saw a little girl down at Fran[k]lin, that was three or 4
years older than you are, who played the Piano for me, every
night that I stayed there.   I wished I could have heard you
play.   She was not as nice a girl as *my Hilda* but she played
first rate.

I want you to practice, and you must have your Mother
get you a teacher than can give you lessons.

Write to me again, as often as Ma writes.   Good By.

Your

PA PA

To Gunild, February 17, 1863

[Van Doren Mss.]

*Camp near Murfreesboro.   Heg is glad to know that his wife
is thinking of buying a house.   It now appears that* Dr.
*Himoe will be stationed at a Murfreesboro hospital.   Hopes
that Gunild will come down.*

To Gunild, February 18, 1863

[Van Doren Mss.]

*Camp near Murfreesboro.   Advice to Gunild about the chil-
dren's pony.*   I saw a man that knows all about my land up
in Minnesota — from his description of it I think it will be
very valuable, he says there will be a rail road by it finished
in less than a year.   *On Clausen:*   I got a fine letter from

Clauson to day—he is willing to come back to the Regiment as Chaplain, if his health will permit him. I will try and urg him to do so—his company was indeed pleasant. *Comment on people of Norway Township:* After all the people of Norway, are about the only Norwegians, that have any sense of what their duty is.

To Gunild, February 20, 1863
[Van Doren Mss.]

Camp near Murfreesboro. Chiefly about purchase of house in Waterford. I want you to have the House and Lot Deeded directly to you. Have the deed read M<u>rs</u> Gunild Heg, Wife of Col. Hans C. Heg. . . .

To Gunild, February 22, 1863
[Van Doren Mss.]

Camp near Murfreesboro. Dr. Himoe has been ordered to report to Murfreesboro. Urges Gunild to come down for a visit.

To Gunild, February 25, 1863
[Van Doren Mss.]

Camp near Murfreesboro. Dr. Himoe is in charge of Hospital No. 2 at Murfreesboro. An election in the regiment: Maj Johnson of course was chosen for Lt Col—and Capt. Wilson of Co. H. was the choice of the officers for major— he is my choice—and I am glad to see him promoted. *Postscript to Hilda.*

To Gunild, February 28, 1863
[Van Doren Mss.]

Camp near Murfreesboro. Apologizes for chiding Gunild because she had written disheartening letters. Is commanding brigade. Postscript to Hilda.

To Gunild, February 28, 1863
[Van Doren Mss.]

Camp near Murfreesboro.   Col. Carlin went home this morning, and I am again in command of the Brigade — Carlin will
be gone about a month.   *Was serenaded by band of Twenty-
first Illinois last night.*   I learn that old Rosy — objects to
letting any wemen come down here, so I fear you could not
get here if you should wish to come down.

To Gunild, March 3, 1863
[Van Doren Mss.]

*Camp near Murfreesboro.   Reports visit of paymaster and
is sending three hundred dollars to Gunild by express in care
of Holton.*   I gave Ole permission to let the Waterford boys
use my Brass Band Instruments.   I hope you will see that
they are not allowed to be used by any of the Secesh Copperheads, or at any of their meetings — and that you will let me
know if they are used for that.   *Inquires about new house and
adds,* I would like to have you get, say 10 Dollars worth of
Apple, Cherry, Plumb, Current and Goos berry trees, to set
out on the old Farm.   *Gives directions as to setting out
these.*   We get all our news from the Newspaper from the
north, and I suppose you know more about the war than I do.

To Gunild, March 5, 1863

CAMP NEAR MURFREESBORO
March 5th 1863.

MY DEAR.
I have not time to write a long letter this time.   I am ordered on Picket with my Brigade to morrow, and have to be
on hand at 8 oclock to morrow morning.   Yesterday I had a
very nice little exploit.   I was ordered by Gen. Mc.Cook to
take my Brigade and go out in a certain direction & engage
the enemy, and to try and capture his Pickets, which have

been stationed some 5 miles from ours. After marching
about 6 miles we got in sight of the enemys cavalry, and had
quite a little skirmish, but none of our men were hurt.   After
driving them as far as I cared about I turned around and
took another road to the left, and moved cautiously through
the woods.   The rebels seeing us go back, thought evidently
that we had gone back to camp — but I had now figured
around till I knew exactly where to find the Picket that I
intended to hunt for.   When I got within a mile of where I
knew the Picket stood, I left two of the regiments and the
Battery, and took the other two Regiments, and marched
them through the brush up to the road back of the Pickets
and got clear up to the road before I was seen.   I had no
Cavalry with me, but I was now about 20 or 30 Steps behind
the two rebel Sentinels, who were on guard, both sitting on
their Horses and not seen by them.   I had two smart young
fellows close by my side, one a Norwegian, by the name of
Hans, who waits on me in my tent, and takes care of my
horses, the other one is a Yankee.   I asked these fellows if
they were able to ride up and scare them so that they would
not fire, and to catch them so as not to make any alarm.
They said they could — and off they went as fast as their
Horses could carry them, and in less than a minute they had
the two fellows and their horses & guns — without firing a
gun.   I knew that a little farther back must be an other station of about 10 men, and my plan was to catch these two
fellows, without giving notice to the rest, and then run up
and capture them before they could get away.   This I partly
succeeded in, having got the first two, I ordered out a company from one of the Regiments to go carefully down the
road, and try to get close up to these fellows and not fire at
them unless they should attempt to run.   The company got
within 10 paces of them, and then fired, and the rebels run
like wild fellows — but we got all their horses, saddles and
guns, and one of the men.   This was done at a place only 3
miles from a large rebel camp where there was 4000 rebel sol-

diers, and after having acomplished this, I started for camp — the men feeling in the very best kind of spirits.

When I returned to camp, McCook sent for me and gave me his compliments.

It is one of the best things that have been done here since the Battle. We came to camp with 10 Horses and three Prisoners — but the idea of capturing a cavalry Picket Post, with infantry is what is interesting. It is seldom acomplished.

We came back to camp before dark, although we marched about 22 miles.

The weather is quite cold down here, and the ground is drying up — and we will soon be getting more to do than we have had.

The Doctor got a letter from home as late as the 25th of Febry. Andrea says Even leaves on the 25th. It has been so all along. Why dont you send my cloths by express? Even will never start, and if he comes now, he will not be able to get here. I hope Morgan, or some other Rebel will get him. I could even afford to lose the cloths he has along, to have the pleasure of seeing him catched, for serving me as he has done. It is outragious to go the way I am doing, and you know I can not go and buy another suit till I know whether he is comming or not. I must go to bed.

Good night to all of you.

Your own
HANS C.

I bought a p^r of Pants a few days ago — and paid 14 Dollars for them.

To Gunild, March 7, 1863

CAMP NEAR MURFREESBORO
March 7th 1863 —

MY DEAR GUNILD.

I have very little time to write. I am kept on the move

nearly all the time. Yesterday I was away all day on a scout & had a lively time & got into camp at 5 this morning — and I have just now recd. orders to march again imidiately — with (3) days rations — which means that we will be gone that many days.[2]

The Brigade to which *Utly* of Racine belongs, has been badly whipped near Franklin and I suppose it is expected for us to make up for it some way.[3] I have had good luck so far commanding the Brigade — and I trust I shall be able to succeed.

The men are becomming very much attached to me — and will fight under me as long as anybody. I am taking good care of myself — and you must have no fears on my account. Even has tellegraphed to me from Louisville that he can not get a Pass without getting *papers* from me. I have not time to make them out now — and I do not know how soon I will be able to do it. I have ordered Doctor Himoe to write to him — and tell him to send my cloths to me by express — if he can not come down himself.

I got no letter from you to day. I suppose Even has some. Good bye my Dear — I have no time to write more.

Your Own
Háns C.

To Gunild, March 15, 1863
[Van Doren Mss.]

Camp near Murfreesboro. Moving about the last two weeks. But the best of all was to get back to camp to day and find my nicely filled sachel of clothing. *Gives advice about building a barn. Again speaks of leaving the service in the fall.*

[2] A report of March 7, 1863, by Colonel Heg, telling of the movements of the second brigade on March 6 and 7, appears in *War of the Rebellion*, series 1, vol. 23, part 1, p. 138–139. He describes a sharp fight between his troops and enemy cavalry some eight miles from Murfreesboro.

[3] William L. Utley's report of the episode in question, which he wrote as the colonel of the Twenty-second (not the Fifty-second) Wisconsin, appears in *War of the Rebellion*, series 1, vol. 23, part 1, p. 106–111. His regiment was surrendered; his report was written after his return from Libby Prison.

To Gunild, March 16, 1863
[Van Doren Mss.]

Headquarters, second brigade, near Murfreesboro. The Rebels are leaving Vicksburg — and generally getting discouraged. *A new sutler shop:* Even and Christen are putting up thier Sutler Shop to day and will begin to sell goods this after noon.

To Hilda, March 16, 1863
[Van Doren Mss.]

Sorry to hear she has been sick. Thanks her for pin cushion. Tells about his new mare: She is the nicest little riding horse there is to be found, and if you will only learn to ride till I get back, then I will give her to you for your riding horse. *Suggests that she can get a new play house built for herself. Postscript to Nebby.*

To Gunild, March 23, 1863

HEAD QUARTERS 2^d BRIGADE
March 23^d 1863

MY DEAR GUNILD

We have been out on outpost duty for a few days and consequently I have not been able to write to you for that time. I wrote to Edmund, day before yesterday in answer to the very nice long letters I received from you, and Hilda and him.

Carlin has not got back yet. His leave of Absense has been extended 12 days and he will not be here till the 4th of April. We have just commenced arranging our camp, and I tell you I am getting up the nicest camp this Brigade has ever had. We expect Rosecranse to come out and see us in a few days and I propose to show him that our camp is in good order. But we may not remain here very long. I had an order this morning to keep the troops in readyness for a Battle. Still I hardly think that the rebels will attack us.

I hope they will, for we are right well prepared for them now, and we must fight somewhere before there is an end to this rebellion. No better place could be found for us than right where we are. I am going to see Rosecranse in the course of a day or two, and ask him for a favor. I think I am entitled to something better, than to go back to the little Regiment again.

My camp is only one mile from Murfreesboro but I have not had time to go down and see Doctor Himoe since I got back. He has nice times now — A good house — plenty to eat, and two *Wemen* with him. If I was as nicely fixed as he is, I would not think of sending for my *Wife*. I am dressing up in fine style since I got my new cloths, and I got them just in time too. It was too bad to look so ragged and dirty and then to command a Brigade.

We have had several little skirmishes with the enemy, and whipped them every time, but no real Battles, except the one near Franklin where they captured Utley, and his Regiment.

I did not send my last package of money by Express, but I sent it a couple of days ago by one of the State Agents of Illinois — who is to send it to Holton in Milwaukee. I hope you have got a good Deed on the Hovey Property by this time. Christian has gone up to Nashville after Goods.[4] They have sold out all they brought with them, and made a good deal of money. There is no good reason why they can not get rich down here, if they are carefull. Christen is getting healthy. Even is here putting up his Suttlers Store. They will probably have their goods on hand in a day or two. . . .

To Gunild, March 27, 1863

Camp near Murfreesboro. Apologizes for tone of recent letter. Tells of review of his brigade by General Rosecrans. Old Rosy — as he rode up to the little 15th, the first thing he said — was, that "There" is a Regiment that suits me.

[4] Christen, or Christian, Hattlestad. See Heg's letter of June 27, 1863.

Col Hegs old Regiment is in a fine condition. *Later the general said that Heg's brigade camp* was the best in the Division. This camp is exclusively my own, as I have laid it out and ordered it arranged — all through. *Heg hopes to get the general's recommendation for a star.* Everything begins to look brighter now. We are sure to clear out this Rebellion during the summer — and I will be home with you in the fall.

To Hilda, March 30, 1863
[Van Doren Mss.]

Camp near Murfreesboro. I hope you are taking music lessons, and getting to be a good player. *Postscripts to Nebby and Gunild. To Gunild:* Carlin has returned and I am back again to the Regiment. *Prospective fighting:* It is my opinion that there will be some fighting down here before long. The Rebels are getting very hard up for Provissions, and many of thier men are deserting and comming to our camps.

To Hilda, April 1, 1863
[Van Doren Mss.]

Camp near Murfreesboro. Sends her four twenty-five cent pieces and suggests that she give one for candy to General Ellsworth — Nebby, whose name was Elmer Ellsworth Heg.

To Gunild, April 1, 1863

CAMP NEAR MURFREESBORO
April 1st 1863

MY DEAREST —

This is the 1st of April and I would like to play April fool on you, but I will not this time. Next April I will try and be around where I can come a trick on you. I have written one long letter to each of the children except Nebby and maybe I shall have to write a little to him too. I have given up all idea of having you come down here now. You will have to wait till I get a Star — on my Shoulder. I shall try and have you come down to let you sleep with a *General* then. But I do not know — I think An Eagle is prettier than a Star — what do you say? I bought a very pretty pair of Shoulder Straps, and with my new Dress I am cutting quite a shine. I hardly knew how to act with clean cloths on.

I am very healthy. I have got a Major for the Regiment now — Capt Wilson of Co. H. I see you are afraid the copperheads will be troublesom. But I will prophesy that they will not live long. It will not be long before nearly every one of them will deny that they ever had any such thoughts as to oppose this war. The conscript law will fix them — And we have lots of brave and loyal soldiers. As soon as we have cleaned out the Rebels, we will attend to these fellows that are staying at home scaring our wemen and children. I have undertaken to write several letters home to be published, but my feelings toward these misserable fellows that are proving to be traitors, is such that I have not hardly been able to write decently. I have been afraid my bitter feelings would make me go too far.

A Copperhead down here amongst the soldiers is regarded as a great deal worse man than a real Rebel and dispised much more, for we know they are cowards.

I can not tell you anything new. I think I shall go up to Nashville soon, and stay a day or two. I have lost the *tooth* that I had put in several years ago, and I took my knife and made one myself of wood — that I have worn for over three weeks, but I want to go up and get a new one now.

It was very cold yesterday but it is warmer again to day. I shall have to come home as soon as Ole Luraas goes away, of course.

Good Bye my Dear. Take care of your self, and do not allow the Blues to get hold of you too much. Good Night My Dear.

Your own
HANS C.

To Gunild, April 5, 1863

[Van Doren Mss.]

Camp near Murfreesboro. Has just returned from Nashville. Escorted two nurses to Nashville. Visited dentist. I ordered some pictures taken at Nashville — and I expect to get them here by the last of this week. *Considers an offer to buy his farm. Thinks it worth twenty-five dollars an acre. Comments on wife of "Count de Tankerville" as described in Peterson's Magazine. Considers her* true and brave. I know that when this war is over we may begin to expect real greatness as a Nation. It will be then that America will be developed in her full Bloom. *On the duration of the war —* we must fight till we have beaten the Rebels if it should take 10 years — or we must fight till they are used up — no matter how long it takes. *Speaks of Gunild's house and adds,* I hope to be able to make you a little Queen somewhere yet. *Exasperated because Edmund is afraid to ride the pony.*

To Gunild, April 7, 1863

[Van Doren Mss.]

Murfreesboro. If Charleston is taken I think we will soon be able to give the rascals a few more blows that will be thier death. *Anticipates attack.* We are preparing for the Rebels to come and attack us here. I really hope they will. It would be a great deal the best for us. Our Pickets see them most every day. *Is planning to send her some trophies.* I send a flower in this letter that I picked on President Polks grave at Nashville.

To Hilda, April 10, 1863

[Van Doren Mss.]

Murfreesboro. Compliments her for her nice letters, which he expects to receive as often as once a week. Sends five dollars for a dress. Many inquiries about children.

To Gunild, April 11, 1863
[Van Doren Mss.]

Camp near Murfreesboro. We have had some excitement here to day. The Rebels captured the train that went up to Nashville yesterday and took several Prisoners and all the money they could find. Chrissten started on that train for Nashville yesterday and had about two Thousand Dollars with him — mostly belonging to himself and Even and we have had great fears that he was gone up the spout — but a few Minutes ago — We got a tellegraph Dispatch that he was all right — he was captured, but it seems he got away with his money all safe. It took a big load off from Evens Shoulders — besides he also had a good deal of Money along for some of the boys. *Comments on news from home:* I am glad to hear that Edmund is attending the german school. I like very well that he should learn German — and you may let him go all summer if he wishes to. But do not let him go a part of the time to one, and a part of the time to another. If he is going to the german school — let him keep on if it is a good one. *The war:* Yesterday & the day before there was some cannonading towards Franklin. *An enclosure:* I send you a copy of the Ladies Union League of Madison. *Suggests that one be organized at Waterford.*

To Gunild, April 12, 1863

MURFREESBORO April 12ᵗʰ 1863

MY DEAR.

I must write again to day, although I wrote last night. This is Sunday, and it is a very beautifull day indeed. Everything is still and it looks almost as it used to do at home on Sundays in the Spring. I got a letter from Bache to day that I send enclosed with this.[5] You will see from that, that

[5] The reference is undoubtedly to Søren Bache, the Muskego pioneer, who had returned to Norway in 1847. See *ante,* p. 3–5, and Blegen, *Norwegian Migration to America,* 129.

LADIES' UNION LEAGUE,
MADISON, WISCONSIN.

PREAMBLE.

In the history of every nation, crises are liable to arise, wherein the patriotic services and sacrifices of the whole people, without regard to condition or circumstance, are essential to the perpetuity of the government—wherein ability should be recognized as the sole measure of duty.

If in our conviction that the American Republic is to-day passing through such a crisis, and that upon the success of the Government in putting down the rebellion, which so disturbs the peace, and threatens the liberties of the country, depends not only the future existence of the Republic under which we live, but likewise the progress of liberal ideas, and the growth of free institutions in all the nations of the world.

In this condition of our national affairs, the women of America, not less than the heroic men who are fighting our battles, are most imperatively called upon for all such services and sacrifices as are consistent with their position and relations as women and as may in any degree subserve the cause of our beloved country.

In addition to and in no way interfering with the "Aid Societies" already widely established, and doing much toward alleviating the sufferings incident to a state of war, there appear three ways in which earnest and judicious efforts may promote this desired end:

1st. By retrenchment in household and personal expenses, to the end that the material resources of the Government, may as far as possible, be devoted to the entire and thorough vindication of its authority.

2d. By strengthening, in the hearts of citizens at home, the sentiment of love and reverence for the National Government, and of establishing in them an unwavering determination, that the war so wickedly waged against the Union of these States, shall not cease, until the rebellion shall have been utterly crushed out, and the integrity of the Republic re-established upon a sure and enduring basis.

3d. By keeping before our soldiers now engaged in, or hereafter to be called into the service of the country, indubitable evidences of the earnest sympathy and untiring co-operation of all true American women, and that it is our purpose to do our whole duty to their families.

Now, therefore, we, ladies of Madison, recognizing the value of united effort, in order that our duties, as above indicated, may the more effectually be performed, do hereby associate ourselves together under the name and style of "The Ladies' Union League of the city of Madison," and in our associate proceedings agree to be governed by the following Constitution, together with such rules and regulations as the League may, in its wisdom, from time to time adopt:

CONSTITUTION.

ARTICLE ONE.

The name and style of this association shall be "The Ladies' Union League of the city of Madison."

ARTICLE TWO.

All ladies who shall subscribe to the Preamble and Constitution hereby ordained, and wear such badge as the League may prescribe, shall be the members thereof.

ARTICLE THREE.

The officers of this League shall consist of a President, two Vice Presidents, a Secretary, Treasurer, and an Executive Committee of three, all of whom, except the Executive Committee, shall be elected by ballot, and hold their respective offices for a term of three months, and until their successors are elected.

ARTICLE FOUR.

The President shall preside at the meetings of the League, and may call special meetings thereof when, with the concurrence of two members of the Executive Committee, it may be deemed expedient. In the absence of the President, the Vice Presidents respectively, in the order of their rank, shall exercise the prerogatives, and perform all the duties of the President. The duties of the Secretary and Treasurer shall be such as are common to such officers in all like associations. The Executive Committee shall act in connection with the President, and with her shall constitute the standing business committee of the League. All duties of officers, committees and members of the League, not herein defined, shall be prescribed from time to time by vote or resolution.

The proceedings of this League shall be conducted according to parliamentary usage.

ARTICLE SIX.

Any member of this League who shall violate the pledges and provisions of this Constitution and the Preamble thereto, may be expelled by a vote of a majority of its members: Provided, That no member shall be expelled until written charges have been preferred, and notice given to the person so charged, who shall have the privilege of a fair and impartial hearing.

ARTICLE SEVEN.

No money shall be drawn from the treasury except upon an order authorized by the Executive Committee, which order shall be signed by the President and countersigned by the Secretary.

ARTICLE EIGHT.

The regular meetings of the League shall be held on —— day of each week, unless otherwise ordered by a vote of the members, and at such place as may be determined by the executive committee. A majority of the members present at any meeting shall constitute a quorum for the transaction of business.

ARTICLE NINE.

This Constitution may be amended by a vote of two-thirds of the members present at any regular meeting, notice of the proposed amendments having been given specifically in writing, two weeks previous, and recorded in the minutes of the proceedings.

NOTE.—It is the intention of this League to endeavor to secure the formation of similar associations in all sections of the State.

MRS. E. S. CARR, Secretary.

Mrs. H. G. Morris,
Pres.

LADIES' UNION LEAGUE: A BROADSIDE
[Enclosed with Colonel Heg's letter of April 11, 1863.]

when we get ready to take that trip over to Norway we will find some there that knows us.

I had another letter from a Person in Bergen and one from Dreutzer who is consul to one of the cities there. They seem to think since the Battle of Stone River that the 15th Wisconsin is quite an institution.[6]

Christen sent a letter down from Nashville to day, giving us an account of his experience amongst the Rebels. I suppose he has already written home how they treated him. He saved his money by putting it in his Boots. I saw him the night before he left and I told him what he ought to do in a case of that kind. That I had put what money I had at Stones River in my Boots and that was all that saved him I expect. He had about two Thousand Dollars.

There is nothing new. No fighting in prospect. There will probably be something to do here soon.

I told you in my letter yesterday and the day before about the money I have sent home. I think you have enough to pay for the house and some besides. I have now in my hands 300 Dollars, belonging to some of the soldiers here, that I will send home in a few days and put it in the Bank for you and I will pay them next pay day.

I have also got about 75 Dollars left to live on. Lieut. Brown of Co E. is going home in a day or two. I am going to send a little Box with him — in which I will put a few articles that has been picked up on the Battle field of Stones River. A Pipe for Hans Wood — and a Parasol for Hilda — that I bought up in Nashville — also a few Pictures that you may give to some of your best friends.

You may let your friends see Baches letter. I will write to him again as soon as I get time to do so.

Good Bye my Dear.

Your Own HANS

[6] It is of interest to note that O. E. Dreutzer, the American consul at Bergen, published in 1863 a circular in which he explained American conditions for the benefit of prospective emigrants and combated the report, then being circulated in Norway, that the Civil War meant the failure of American democracy. *Cirkulære fra de nordamerikanske Staters Consulat i Bergen* (Bergen, 1863. 16 p.).

To Gunild, April 15, 1863
[Van Doren Mss.]

Camp near Murfreesboro. To go on picket guard in after-noon. Expresses concern that children should have good education. Wants Hilda to take music lessons. I expect if we ever visit Norway, she must go along — and I want her to be a little lady. *The children must learn Norwegian.* Tell them that if they do not learn to speak Norwegian they can not go with us.

To Gunild, April 17, 1863

Sunday [April] 17th 1863.

My Darling.

I am going out on *Out Post* for 4 or 5 days, to a place about 4 miles from here with my Brigade — and I may not get time to write to you while I am out there so I will drop you these lines this morning. Everything is just as quiet as usual. I am in fine health. D[r] Himoe has not got leave of absence yet, and I do not know yet whether he will or not. If old Rosey will give me permission to let you come down, I will have you come with the Doctor. You would not be in my way at all, on the contrary I am fixed so that you could stay here just as comfortable and nice as anywhere. The fact is I could have had you here all the spring just as well as not, but I have all the time been afraid we would have a fight.

Old Rosey has issued a pretty strong order against *Wemen* and I may not be able to get permission for you.

I have not time to write any more — My Dear One. Take things easey, and be in good spirits. Do not work too hard. Good Bye my own Dear Wife.

from Your
Hans.

To Gunild, April, 1863

Camp near Murfreesboro. The day is not indicated in date line. On picket post two miles from camp. We have just received an order from the War Department, to consolidate all Regiments that have less than 500 men, and make them up into companies of 100 each — and all extra officers together with the Col. and Major are to be mustered out or allowed to resign. *He still has 560 men, and thus does not come under order, but writes that* it is too discouraging to stay and have hardly more than a good company to command.

To Gunild, April 20, 1863
[Van Doren Mss.]

Murfreesboro. Glad to hear that Gunild has at last moved into her own house. Eager for family and local news. Asks for description of his Minnesota land. Thinks he may sell it to some officer. Advice to Gunild about building a barn.

To Gunild, April 23, 1863
[Van Doren Mss.]

*Camp near Murfreesboro. Reports that Rosecrans has got permission to consolidate only such Regiments as he thinks ought to be co[n]solidated, Mine will not of course go into the list. I have more than the necessary number now, and if I had not, he would not allow this Regiment to be con-*solidated. *Says that he has heard that the general would not accept his resignation if it were submitted. He will wait until fall. Plans to build house on farm. Asks Gunild to send him some maple syrup.* We get buckwheat flour here and I have my regular Buckwheat Cakes for Breakfast. We get Eggs for 75 cents a Dozen.

To Gunild, April 24, 1863

[Van Doren Mss.]

Murfreesboro. Says he will think no more about resigning until next fall. I want you to keep all the sheep you have left. I would like to have had about one Hundred this spring. Wool will no doubt be worth a Dollar a pound.— You must see that they are sheared and that the wool is well done up—and also that the lambs, if there are any are taken care of. I want no Bucks with them during the summer. *Plans on partnership in store with Ole if he goes home in fall. But he would be perfectly contented in army if Gunild were with him.* I begin to think no Soldier ought to be married. It helps to make him a coward. *Refers again to maple syrup, which is worth from three to four dollars a gallon.* I have no doubt but we will remain here for some time, perhaps for the most part of the summer, if the Rebels do not drive us away, and that we believe they can not do at all.

To Gunild, April 25, 1863

[Van Doren Mss.]

Murfreesboro. Much about tediousness of camp life. Expresses regret over impatience displayed in earlier letters. Our money is beginning to be valuable again and there will soon be only a small premium on gold then goods will be cheaper. *Sundry other matters.*

To Gunild, April 26, 1863

[Van Doren Mss.]

Murfreesboro. Reports on amounts of money he has sent home since the battle. He has been recommended for commission as brigadier general by Carlin, Davis, and McCook. Will go home in fall unless made brigadier. Speaks of various articles he has sent home. Inquiries on several matters. Are they organising a Brass Band up at Waterford?

To Gunild, May 1, 1863

NEAR MURFREESBORO
HEAD QU^{rs} 3^d BRIGADE
May 1st 1863

MY DEAR GUNILD

In my last I told you that I would write to you again as soon as I got fully installed into my new place. Well yesterday we moved. I have taken command of the Brigade and fixed up my Head Quarters in grand style. Dr Himoe is my Brigade Surgeon — Hauff is my Adjt. General — Albert Skofstad is my Inspector General. The rest of my staff you do not know and there is no use of my giving you their names.

I have three Regiments, One Battery and a comp. of Cavalry, and Rosey has promised me one more Regiment in a short time. I have a splendid tent and so have the staff officers. We are just arranging a mess for six or eight of us. All there is wanting now is to have *you* here with me. What a time I could have if you could only come down and visit with me about 2 or 3 weeks and see how we live — and see the great Battle Field of Stones River. If everything remains quiet when Christen goes up to Wisconsin I am going to tell you to come down with him. I will at all events get ready *passes* for you and send [them] up with him, and I can not see why you and Nebby could not come down here. May be you could even leave him at home.

There are a great many officers wives here. Many of them have been here since the Battle of Stones River. Sophia would take care of Edmund and Hilda. I think if I could see you down here a while, I can stand it to be away from home till next fall without getting homesick.

Everything is quiet again here — no fighting. I have a good deal to do in organizing my new command. The fact is I have been put in command of this Brigade for the purpose of making it more efficient — and I am going to try my

best to do it. Gen. Carlin issued a very complimentary
order to our Regiment when we left his Brigade. The order
will be published in some of the newspapers at home.

Even started for Louisville to day. They are doing a
big bussiness as usual. They will make thems[e]lves rich if
they have good luck and take care of their money. I have
written all the news I have. I am daily looking for a letter.
Direct hereafter to Col. Hans C. Heg 3^d Brigade 1st Divission
20th A. C. Dept. of the Cumberland.

I would give a good deal to see you — my own Dear One.
I dreamt I saw you last night, and you seemed so happy to
find me. Good Bye my Love

Your Own HANS.

To Gunild, May 3, 1863
[Van Doren Mss.]

Headquarters, Third Brigade. A Sunday morning. I suppose you would like to [see] old Rosey — and I send you enclosed herein the old fellows Photograph. *On a history of
the regiment:* I also send you enclosed a letter that I got
yesterday — off course I complied with the request, and went
down and had my Photograph taken. I have ordered a
sketch of the history of the Regiment, to be made out by
Lt. Col Johnson — and he has also volunteered to write a
short sketch of my life. This Book will be published soon.
Judge Fitch goes to Philadelphia this week to have the Book
published — it will be a splendid Book containing Photographs of nearly all our Generals and thier Staffs.[7] *On prospects for moving:* I expect likely we will be sent out on scouting expeditions now and then but I do not think this Army
will move for good, till Hooker fights down on the Potomac.

[7] John Fitch, *Annals of the Army of the Cumberland* (Philadelphia, 1863).
There is an interesting brief sketch (p. 229–233) entitled " The Scandinavian
Regiment and its Colonel," and the photograph of Colonel Heg, to which reference is made in his letter, appears opposite p. 218. A second edition of Fitch's
book appeared in 1864. Copies of both editions are in the library of the Minnesota Historical Society.

To Gunild, May 4, 1863
[Van Doren Mss.]

Third Brigade. Refers to checks for $700 and $300 which he has sent home and which she has not reported as received. Has sent her his photograph; is waiting for hers. Refers again to sketch for Judge Fitch. Receives two Wisconsin newspapers regularly, Emigranten and the State Journal. What a misserable institution that Emigranten is getting to be.

To Gunild, May 7, 1863

Headquarters, Third Brigade, First Division. In from picket yesterday. Good news from Army of Potomac. I received a very complimintary order from Gen. McCook yesterday. *He explains that General Rosecrans' inspector on the day the brigade was on picket duty found the brigade well instructed in its duties and the men and officers vigilant. The report came from Rosecrans to Colonel Heg via General McCook and was read on dress parade.* You ought to have heard the Boys cheer last night as the order was read to them. Such little things helps very much to give spirit to the troops. *Hopes that Gunild will come down. Tells her to bring a riding dress.* I have got the nicest little riding Horse for you down here that you ever saw. *Heg adds as a postscript a copy of the order referred to in his letter.*

To Gunild, May 8, 1863
[Van Doren Mss.]

Third Brigade, First Division, Murfreesboro. Acknowledges pictures of Edmund and Hilda. Asks for Gunild and Nebby's. There is heavy fighting on the Potomac. I hope to God it may be favorable for us — if it is, then we may look for peace by fall. *Is worried about money sent home. Refers again to prospective trip to Norway after war is over.*

To Gunild, May 9, 1863
[Van Doren Mss.]

Headquarters, Third Brigade. Acknowledges box with pictures of Gunild and children. Excited about reports from Virginia. Reports usually have to be discounted. Tremendious Slaughter, *and* Terrible Fighting — and when we get the real facts there are a few Men and horses killed and wounded — 15 thousand Prisoners taken and they gradually grow smaller and smaller — till you get about as many hundred. *Has applied for permission to detail recruiting party to Wisconsin.* I see by to days papers that the President is going to put the Conscription Law into force. *Heg is pleased* — now Copperheads and all will have to come in.

To Gunild, May 10, 1863 [8]
[Van Doren Mss.]

Third Brigade. Sends picture of his Inspector General. Optimistic about recent war news. Old Rosy sends report that Richmond has been taken. Postscript to Hilda.

To Gunild, May 12, 1863
[Van Doren Mss.]

Headquarters, Third Brigade. I have got a fine little Tent about 12 feet square, with a good Floor in it my bed on one side — a table in one end, and a couple of chairs. This I call my parlor. It is as clean and nice as any Parlor you ever saw. *Serenaded by band of second brigade on preceding evening. Much about possibility of Gunild's visit.*

[8] Students of the history of the Fifteenth Wisconsin will be interested in knowing of a valuable collection of some twenty unpublished letters and a diary written by Harvey Britton, first sergeant of Company B. The letters, addressed to a brother, Albert Britton of Union, Wisconsin, run from May 10, 1863, to April 28, 1864. The diary was kept in 1864; its last entry was made on September 17 of that year; Britton was then a prisoner at Andersonville; he died there of scurvy on October 11. The letters and diary are in the possession of Mrs. H. L. Howard of Chicago, a niece of Sergeant Britton. They were brought to my attention through the courtesy of Mr. Birger Osland of Chicago, and Mrs. Howard has very graciously permitted me to examine the originals.

To Gunild, May 14, 1863

3ᵈ BRIGADE, MURFREESBORO May 14ᵗʰ 1863
MY DARLING WIFE.

I am just ready to go out on Picket to day, and will drop you a few lines while the rest of the boys are getting their Horses ready to go with me. I have to visit the line once during the day. This takes about three hours — and in the mean time we generally stop at some of the farm houses to see the *Ladies* and get a few Flowers — or Strawberries for they are getting ripe now. Our officers are getting to be great favorites with the girls down here — by the way. There are 5 or 6 of our men down at Island N° 10 who have got married to some of the wemen down there. One fellow wrote a letter to Hauff the other day telling him he was married, to a Secesh widdow. Her husband went into the rebel Army two years ago — and she *supposed* he is dead — not having heard anything from him for a very long time. The people living around here are not as strong Secesh as they used to be, in fact I am pretty sure many of the young ladies would be right glad to marry some of our gay and handsome looking officers and the *old Ladies* seem to be very willing for thier daughters to get on good terms with our boys. So it goes — and I suppose that if it was not for that pretty little woman up in Waterford — some of these Secesh would be picking up this fellow too. But I do not expose myself much. The Boys come in every little while after their Scouts through the country, with their heads and hearts all full of *Secesh* love stories. Dʳ Himoe has not got his leave of Absence yet, and I do not know whether he will get it or not. I am still flattering myself that if he goes home he will bring you down with him. I am going up to ask Rosey personally for permission to have you visit me.

It would be pleasant for a good many to see you down here — besides the pleasure it would be to me. The officers around Head Quarters say that if you should come they would not allow you to stay up in town—they would fix up any kind of an arangement to make you comfortable here.

To day I expect to get a letter or two from home. I must stop, the mail is ready. Good Bye my own Dear one. Keep the Blues off, and dont work too hard.

Yours as ever—

HANS

To Gunild, May 20, 1863

HEAD Q^r 3^d BRIGADE ON SHELBYVILLE ROAD
6 MILES FROM MURFREESBORO
May 20th 1863.

MY DEAR.

I have not had a chance to write to you since Sunday when we moved out here and I have not had any letter from home since that time either. I have got my whole Brigade here on our Post duty, and we have a real fine pleasant place. The Rebels are in sight of our Pickets, and nearly every day our boys exchange shots with them. Yesterday I sent out a small cavalry company and a part of the 15th Wis—and had quite a Brush with them. The boys when they came back told me they were certain that they had killed some and wounded several. In the afternoon several Union Ladies came up through the rebel lines from Shelbyville, and they told us that we had scared them pretty bad, and killed 2 and wounded 6—and shot the horse under the Col. commanding the Picket. So much for our little fight—we lost nothing.

Every day there comes up a lot of wemen and children from Shelbyville—which is 20 miles from here.They are all very strong Union—and they seem to be perfectly delighted to get inside of our lines.

They tell us that the people of Shelbyville are very strong Union men. Bragg has his head quarters there, and is wait-

ing for us to come up and fight him. I have got a Tellegraph office right by my tent, and send in dispatches to Murfreesboro whenever I have anything to comunicate. The
wire is carried in a Waggon and set up almost as fast as we
march. They have their instrument in the waggon with
them and can send dispatches from any place they stop.

Things are very quiet around this Army — no movements
of any importance that I can hear of.

I shall expect to get a letter to day. I dreamt of you last
night, and when I awoke this morning I felt quite homesick.

The mail is ready to leave. I must stop. Will write
again in a day or two. I expect to go back to camp to morrow or next day.

Good Bye my Darling.
Your Own
HANS.

To Gunild, May 22, 1863
[Van Doren Mss.]

Doctor Himoe leaves for home to morrow, on leave of absence, and I send this by him. I hope to morrow to be able
to get a pass from Gen¹ Rosecranse for you to come down
and visit me. *Explains that the doctor will return about
June 10 or 11 and that Christen Hattlestad will go to Wisconsin about July 1. The two might act as her escorts, coming and going.*

To Gunild, May 24, 1863
[Van Doren Mss.]

*Third Brigade. A Sunday morning. Has seen General
Rosecrans, who advised him not to have Gunild come down.
The general expected to fight soon. As to farming:* I do not
want you to sell any of the Sheep. I would like to have the
farm stocked with Sheep altogether.

To Gunild, May 27, 1863
[Van Doren Mss.]

Headquarters, Third Brigade. Sends her a print from the plate in Fitch's book. I took this Picture one morning when I was down at Roseys Head Quarters, unexpectedly, and hardly had my head combed at the time. *As to food:* we are now getting everything that we want here from the Commissary Department, very cheap. We get Peaches put up in Cans, and Smoked Herring, Eggs — Lemons &co — at what they cost in Louisville or a little over — Dry Peaches and Apples — Salt fish and Smoked Salmon. All is bought by the goverment and sent down to be sold to officers at cost prices. If they carry out this plan all the time it will use up the Sutler bussiness some. *Postscript to Nebby.*

To Gunild, May 27, 1863
[Van Doren Mss.]

Murfreesboro. We have had first rate News from Vicks-burg, and it begins to look as if we were going to do something there.

To Gunild, May 31, 1863
[Van Doren Mss.]

Tell Dr Himoe that Dr Trenkler has sent in his resignation, and that he ought to find a Surgeon for the Regiment while he is up there.

To Hilda, June 1, 1863
[Van Doren Mss.]

Murfreesboro. I have got a fine Riding Horse for you that I call "Flora." I am keeping it to bring home for you to ride when the war is over. She is the prettiest thing there is down here, and is very gentle and never runs away.

To Gunild, June 6, 1863

HEAD QR. 3ᵈ BRIGADE June 6ᵗʰ 1863.

DEAR GUNILD.

I came back to camp last night, after having been out in a little skirmish with the enemy on the Shelbyville Pike. On Thursday morning, the rebels attacked Carlins Brigade, which is out about 4 miles from here on out Post duty, and at noon I was sent out to help him. But we did not get a chance to do anything. I got near enough with one of my Regiments to see them and they threw a few cannon shot at us, but hurt nobody. Carlin lost one man — and the cavalry had a few men wounded, but it was a small thing. At Franklin however we heard very heavy firing all day, and I have heard that we whipped them there, but I do not know the particulars. Everything is quiet to day — and I guess it is nothing more than a feeler sent out by the rebels to find out we have sent any reinforcements to Grant, or els it is done to make us believe they intend to attack us, while they really are sending their Army down to Vicksburg. I suppose the Doctor will start on his way down here, day after to morrow which will be Monday. And we will look for him about Wednesday or Thursday. I have been promised an other Regiment for my Brigade — the 8ᵗʰ Kansas is at Nashville, and I have been promised that it shall be ordered down to my Brigade. They have a splendid Brass Band, and it is now the largest Regiment in the service. You know I have told about that Regiment before. It was with us all last summer.

I have not time to write you a long letter this time, but I will do better in a day or two. To morrow we will go on Out Post, in place of Carlin, but as I take my tents and everything els along: so I can write letters from there just as well as from here. I wrote to Edmund and Hilda a few days ago. I suppose they are pleased now because you could not come down with Himoe. I have bought me a splendid Horse but paid a big price 160 Dollars. I have run out of money, but Mathews has some on hand, and I have borrowed considerable of him. The Sutlers will let me have all the money I need, so you need have no uneasiness but I will get along. The Paymaster is expected every day and will pay us for two months. I will have 4 months pay due at the end of this month.

The mail is ready to leave and I must stop. Good by my own Darling. I dreamt about you last night, and I did think you *kissed* me so sweetly.

Goodbye my Own Dear One

Yours Ever

HANS.

To Gunild, June 8, 1863

[Van Doren Mss.]

On outpost, four miles from Murfreesboro. I got your letter of June 1st day before yesterday, and I am very sory to hear that you have lost Turk. I would rather have lost fifty Dollars. — Cant you find out who killed him — it would be some satisfaction when I come home to pay him up for it. *Gunild seems to believe that her husband is going to be killed and he reassures her.* A person that goes into the war, always expecting to be killed, is generally sure to be so. *Discusses finances and his property at Waupun.* I have called my new horse <u>Turk</u> in honor of the Dog that you lost.

To Gunild, June 9, 1863

[Van Doren Mss.]

Headquarters, Third Brigade. The Doctor came back yesterday and reports everything well. — *Heg is* going to have one more Regiment for this Brigade in a day or two.

COLONEL HEG IN THE SPRING OF 1863

[From John Fitch, *Annals of the Army of the Cumberland*, 218 (Philadelphia, 1863).]

To Gunild, June 11, 1863
[Van Doren Mss.]

Third Brigade. Is planning to place someone other than Ole Luraas on his farm in the fall. Has received the Eighth Kansas as an addition to his brigade. Sends her photographs of two of his officers, Tandberg and Clement. Is still on outpost duty. We see the Rebels every day — and exchange Papers with them very often. There is no firing between our Pickets. One of the Rebs sent me a Paper last night and wrote a note one [*sic*] his paper saying that they had a rumor in thier camp that another big fight had come off at Vicksburg.

To Hilda, June 13, 1863
[Van Doren Mss.]

Five miles from Murfreesboro. Acknowledges letters from her. Interested in her music, riding, etc. Sends a picture of one of his lieutenants, O. R. Dahl.

To Gunild, June 13, 1863
[Van Doren Mss.]

I have hardly anything to write about, only to tell you that I am well. *Tells her how proud he is of his brigade.* I see your wool crop has turned out poor. *Advises her to sell soon* — I do not think it will get any higher than it is now.

To Gunild, June 15, 1863
[Van Doren Mss.]

Outpost five miles from Murfreesboro. Comforts Gunild, who has written of her lonesomeness. Advice as to farm, rent, and sundry matters. Write to me often, I love so much to hear from you.

To Gunild, June 17, 1863

[Van Doren Mss.]

Third Brigade. Returned from outpost duty yesterday and is in old camp. Visited with General McCook. The news in yesterdays papers from the Potomac looks rather scaly. *Has written to Dr. Moore of Waupun, asking him to come as first assistant surgeon.* There is nothing new here. *Touches on sundry home matters.*

To Gunild, June 19, 1863

[Van Doren Mss.]

Third Brigade. Chiefly about finances at home. Comments on war news from Maryland and Pennsylvania. Yesterday I saw two men hung. They were Citizens and Rebels who had murdered another Citizen and taken his money, the man they murdered was a Union man. *Comment:* It looked pretty hard to see men hung — I have seen men shot, but it does not look as bad as to see them hung. *Sundry other matters.*

To Gunild, June 23, 1863

[Van Doren Mss.]

Third Brigade. After some comment on mortgages and debts, Colonel Heg writes, You are very much troubled about things that generally come out all right. *Discusses plans for a store building to be put up for Ole and himself in partnership or for himself alone. Speaks of possibility that he will resign commission.* I hardly expect to stay in the army longer than till fall. *Asks Gunild to look up an article or letter that appeared in the Chicago Tribune for June 20.*[9]

[9] In an article headed "From Rosecrans' Army," a *Tribune* correspondent tells, on the date indicated, of a visit to Colonel Heg's headquarters on the Shelbyville Pike and praises the troops and the colonel's management.

SUPPLEMENT

A letter written by Colonel Heg on February 15, acknowledging gifts from a soldiers' aid society in his own community, is of interest as an expression of his general views on the war.

Colonel Heg to [Thomas?] Adland, February 15, 1863
[*Milwaukee Sentinel,* March 30, 1863]

Headquarters Fifteenth Wis. Vols.
Near Murfreesboro Tenn., Feb 15

Mr. Adland, Esq.— My Dear Sir: —

The many valuable donations that have been received by the sick and wounded of my Regiment, from the Soldiers' Aid Society of Norway and Raymond, through the efforts of your and other friends there, ought to have been acknowledged by me long ago. That I have neglected it is no reason why I should continue to do so.

The Box I received from your Brother, I succeeded in getting through myself, and it was immediately turned over to the hospital. It was nearly all on hand and used for the wounded after the battle. What there has been forewarded to us since has mostly gone directly to the hospital at Nashville, where a large number of our wounded and sick are, at present.

Not to say anything of the comforts and blessings your liberal donations have bestowed upon the sick and suffering soldiers who so bravely have fought for a cause common to us, but aside from all that, your kindness speaks to the heart of every soldier in the Army. What are men exposing their lives and health for in this great struggle, but a cause in which we are all interested?

What encouragements for men to undergo what they are daily called on to do here, but that they know their efforts are appreciated by friends at home? And what better evidence can be furnished that your hearts are with them than the valuable tokens of your kindness and generosity in careing for the sick and wounded? Our army is bound to crush this terrible rebellion, if the people of the North will only stand by the army, and by all their power encourage the soldiers.

And here let me add that I know from experience that there is nothing equal to encouragement from home. You can do a great deal of good, not only by the efforts in which you have been so liberal, but I would ask you to encourage our soldiers by your kind letters. If a mother has a son, or a wife a husband in the army, her encouragement to him to do his duty, is worth more than anything else; her continual complaints, and whinings, asking him to "come home" etc., has more to do with creating discouragement and finally sickness and disease than the hardships he has to endure.

I can see no daylight in any other direction than a suppression of the rebels by us. It is nothing else than simply this. Death and destruction to us, and our government, or their subjugation. The latter must be accomplished, no matter what the sacrifice may be — life, property, or anything else.

Hoping that the members of your society will continue to labor in the good cause they are engaged, and that you will on behalf of the Fifteenth Wisconsin, tender our friends our sincere thanks for your kind remembrances and favors, and trusting hereafter to be able to prove ourselves worthy of them I remain,

Very truly yours,

HANS C. HEG,

Col. Fifteenth Wis. Vols.

VI. THE CHICKAMAUGA CAMPAIGN

To Gunild, June 23, 1863

HEAD QUARTERS 3ᵈ BRIGADE
June 23ᵈ 1863.

MY DEAR WIFE.

We are now under marching orders and will probably move by to morrow morning or in a short time at least. It looks more like moving now than ever before. Where we will go I do not know of course, but we have laid still so long that it is high time that we had something to do. I hope you will not feel uneasy about me now if you should not hear from me for a few days. I will write just as often as possible — but it will be very uncertain if we move ahead. And unless you get a Tellegraph dispatch you need not have any uneasiness about my safty. The boys are in good spirits and fine order for march or fight. My Brigade is in as fine trim as any of them and will compare well with any in the whole Army.

I have nothing new to write. I intended to have written to Edmund and Hilda, but if we move by to morrow morning, then I shall not have time. I have everything that I need to eat, &c. My money is getting rather short — but we will be paid before long no doubt. I am better off without money in an action than with it so I have plenty to eat. I can borrow all the money I shall want.

I received a tellegraph Dispatch from James McFarland to day, from Louisville. He could not get here without a pass. I had a pass tellegraphed to him. His Brother he says is sick at Nashville.

I will close this, as I have a good deal to attend to — And if we do not move during the night I will write again.

Good bye darling.
Your Own HANS.

To Gunild, June 24, 1863

Wednesday Morning June 24th 1863.

DEAR GUNILD

We did not move yesterday.   We will start in a few hours.
In the meantime we are waiting for some other Divission to
go ahead of us.   There is nothing new yet, but probably will
be something to do in a day or two.

Good Bye my Darling.

Your Own —

HANS C.

To Gunild, June 27, 1863

HEAD QU^r 3^d BRIGADE
June 27th in the evening.

MY DEAR WIFE

I have an opportunity to send a few words home, and will
do so.   Off course you know that the Army is moving.   We
left Murfreesboro on the 24th.   So far we have driven Braggs
Army before us.   Our Divission has had one fight and lost
about 30 or 40 wounded — mostly slight.   But my Brigade
did not get into the fight.   I had charge of the Waggon train
on that day.   Other Divissions have had skirmishes with
Braggs force & some of them have lost as high as 150 killed
& wounded.   We have captured a good many Prisoners, and
driven them every time.   A Big Battle will no doubt be
fought before many days.   I have no doubt of our success.
We have a splendid Army and Bragg is afraid of us.   I got
your letter of June 20th to night.   We still get the mail regular but you must not expect to hear from me as often as you
have.   I can only write whenever the mail goes.   I am well
and in a splendid trim for a fight.   You must have no uneasiness on my account.   It will do no good.   I will take as
good care of myself as possible, and trust to good fortune for
the rest.

Christen Hattlestad is back at Murfreesboro. He will get all kinds of stories back there, if he writes any of them home. You must take it with much allowance.

I have no news except what I have written. It is raining like fun and the roads are very bad.

I have plenty of good cloths, and keep dry, and lots of men to help take good care of me and my Horses. Old Rosey is with us himself. No more at present. Good night my own darling.   Good By.

Your Own
HANS

We are now about 16 or 18 miles south of Murfreesboro.

To Gunild, June 29, 1863

3ᵈ BRIGADE AT MANCHESTER.
June 29ᵗʰ 1863.

MY DEAR WIFE

I have again an opportunity to write. The mails follow us regularly and leaves us every day nearly, so I am in hopes to be able to write as often almost as I did at Murfreesboro.

We have advanced very slow. It has rained every day since we left, and to day it has poured down all day. Yesterday we had a terrible day. We started off in the Morning, just as it began to rain, and as we marched behind a large train of waggons we moved only a short distance before it got dark — and it rained most of the day. After dark I moved the Brigade about 8 miles, through mud that reached half ways to the mens knees, and got into camp at about 1 oclock at night. I had just time to get a tent up when another heavy shower commenced. Off course, I am generally pretty comfortable. I have a good "Indi Rubber Blanket" and two good Horses. I have not been wet once since I started. But the men, poor fellows are having a severe time of it. They have had such nice times at Murfreesboro for six Months now that it comes really hard for them, but it can

not last very long. It must stop raining soon. It is not
very warm, still the rain is warm enough to make it a good
deal more pleasant than it was at the Battle of Stone River.
I find that it makes some difference to be in command of a
Brigade. I have better opportunities to protect myself
against such bad weather as we have had this last week anyway — for I have plenty of good tents. The Regiments have
given up all tents, but One for Head Quarters — But there
are many responsibillities that I did not have while in command of the Regiment. After all I find that it mostly depends on getting good men to assist me. Albert Skofstad is
getting to be one of the best Officers to be found in the Army.
He has learned a great deal since I put him in his new place
and I think he would soon be capable of taking command of
a Regiment. I have worked him very hard. My Adjutant,
Capt Hauff is a splindid man for that post, but in some respects not so practical as Albert.

Rosecranse is with us — and we will be at Tallahoma by to
morrow if we do not have to fight too much. It is not known
what the Rebels will do. We have already captured a good
many prisoners. Had two or three pretty severe fights with
them, but no real Battle yet.

The Roads are awfull and we have to move slow. The
main body of the Army is in front of us. I do not know how
far ahead, but I think some 6 or 8 miles. Tallahoma is about
12 miles from here. If there is no Battle fought at that place
we will no doubt have a fight at Chattanooga.

Dont feel uneasy for me. Soldiering is getting to be an
old thing with me now, and I know very well how to take
care of myself. I am in strong hopes of a great victory here.
Old Rosey is the only General we have, who I have undoubted
confidence in. You must write as often as possible. I think
the mail will reach me tollerable regular.

To morrow we muster for pay — being the last day of the
month. Time is passing off a good deal faster when on a
march than while laying still in camp.

Doctor Himoe is all right. His waggons still are with him, and he has all the tents and baggage with him that he needs. I got your last letter dated June 20. I was very glad to see that you are so cheerfull. I hope you will visit amongst your friends and try to pass off the time as comfortable as possible. As soon as we are established at Chattanooga if everything goes well—I will apply to old Rosey for leave to visit you. But there is not much use in making any calculations here, for we do not know one day what may turn up the next.

Well I have nearly filled up my sheet of paper, and I will stop. Tell my Dear Hilda that I like her new Dress first rate. But I have not time to write to her. I hope you will not neglect to let her take music lessons. I have more anxiety about having Edmund & Hilda receive a good education than anything els. Good Bye my Dear One. I did not sleep much last night and I am just going to Bed.

Good night — Your own
HANS

To Gunild, July 3, 1863

WINCHESTER TENN. July 3ᵈ 1863.

MY DARLING.

We have been out 10 days now, and driven Bragg before us for some distance. He dares not fight us. We skirmished with his forces yesterday & to day. I took several prisoners. We have had no big fight, and may not have any for some time. I got your letter of the 24ᵗʰ to day. I am glad to hear from you so often. I told you in one of my last letters what proposition I had made to Ole about building a store on my lot. I wrote to him afterwards and told him I did not want him to do anything about it till I get home. I shall try to be at home in August or 1ˢᵗ of Sept. He may go to work and make estmate & draw up a plan, but I have told him I do not want him to do anything about it till I come home.

I wrote to Dr Moore of Waupun about comming here as

assistant Surgeon of the 15th. To day I got a letter from him stating that he will come imidiately. I have written to the governor to get him appointed.[1] I hope he will come soon. He will be good company to me. His wife is dead he tells me. I thought it was some other Mrs Moore that was dead, but I am sory to hear that it was your old friend. Do not feel uneasy for me. You will see me safe out of this. I am doing well. We have had some hard times, but nothing serious. It has been very rainy and muddy. If we stay here a day or two, which I think we will — Gen. McCook told me so to day, then I will write every day. I am very glad to get such encouraging letters from you and I hope you will be brave enough to be a *generals* wife — one of these days. I love to be out doing something. Laying still in camp was very tedious and time went very slow.

I hope you will do all you can to have Edmund and Hilda tend school. You may tell my little Rat — Nebby — that I am shooting the Rebels for him now.

So you begin to like the Black Horse. I knew you would like him. I have got two more down here now that I think a great deal of. One is a mare, that I am going to bring home for Hilda when I get out of the Army.

Good night my Dear. The boys have all gone to bed. I must go too. If you have a map you will find this place about 14 miles south of Tallahoma.

> Good Bye Darling —
> Your own
> HANS

To Gunild, July 4, 1863

WINCHESTER TENN. July 4th 1863

MY DEAR WIFE

This has been the 4th of July and a very quiet one indeed. It has rained again as usual, but the men have made them-

---

[1] The doctor referred to seems not to have been appointed. His name does not appear in the regimental roster.

selves very comfortable resting after the severe and muddy march.[2] Gen. Mc. Cook got up a splendid Dinner to day, and Old Rosey came down to see him. We had a fine Dinner party composed of three major Generals with Old Rosecrans at the head — Two Brigadier Generals — Carlin and Garfield,[3] two Colonels of us and several of the Staff Officers. The Dinner was splendid and we had plenty of music — two Brass Bands being on hand.

This place is about as large as Burlington and full of Secesh wemen. There are several acadamies here and a great many young ladies attending school. But they are bitter Secesh. Our Army will soon bring them to terms. We are taking all Thier Beef Cattle, Cows, Sheep and Corn. All their Potatoe patches are suffering. If we stay here two or three weeks they will not have much left to live on. Old Rosey feels fine. We have done a nice thing and lost a very few men. Braggs army is very much discouraged.

We got dispatches to day at noon dated at Washington this morning at 8 oclock, giving good news from our Army there. I think matters have never looked so favorable to us as they do at present. If our Army in the East can only whip Gen. Lee — We are all right.

I send you enclosed one more picture. It is that of a young fellow, who acts as my Aid De Camp. He and Albert stop together and are great friends. I think it is very probable that we will remain here a few days — maybe weeks. Our mail goes and comes quite regular and I will write you often while we remain in camp. There may be some trouble between here and Murfreesboro in getting our mail through on account of Guirillas — but not for the present I think. I hope you have had a pleasant 4th of July, and I trust the

[2] A report of July 6, 1863, by Colonel Heg as commander of the third brigade summarizes his marches from June 24, when the brigade left the camp near Murfreesboro, to July 3, when it encamped at Winchester. "The march," he wrote, " has been one of unusual hardship and fatigue, on account of the almost constant rain and muddy roads." *War of the Rebellion*, series 1, vol. 23, part 1, p. 482.

[3] Heg on this occasion dined with a future president of the United States — James A. Garfield, who served as chief of staff in the Chickamauga campaign.

next 4ᵗʰ I may be able to be with you. I have not had time
to call and see any of the citizens of this place. I have remained very quietly in my camp. I have nothing more to
write about. I am well and hearty. Time is wearing off
tollerable fast and I hope before long to have a chance to see
you again. Only I hate the idea of parting with you so
much. Good night my own darling. I must go to bed. My
love to the children.

Good night.
Your Own
Hans

To Gunild, July 7, 1863
[Van Doren Mss.]

Headquarters, Third Brigade, Winchester. I got your letter
of the 28ᵗʰ of June yesterday. Your dream does not hold
good — I have got both of legs yet, and they are as sound as
ever. You must not frighten yourself with any fancy
dreams. *On the campaign:* The Rebels have gone over the
mountain and we can not follow them for several weeks — I
suppose. *Discusses possible sale of some of his property.* I
am glad you have got a music teacher for Hilda. *Touches
on finances and other matters.* We live very well now.
Apples begin to be ripe — Blackberries are plenty — and we
get Honey — Potatoes and Fresh Meat in abundance. The
Turkeys and Chickins are all gone. *Tells about a Vermont
family living at the house next to his headquarters.*

To Gunild, July 9, 1863

3ᵈ Brigade July 9ᵗʰ 1863.

Dear Gunild.

We have not been able to get any mail for several days, so
I have not heard from you since your letter of the 27ᵗʰ. To
day we expect to get a mail through. The difficulty has been

THE HEG MONUMENT AT CHICKAMAUGA

INSCRIPTION ON THE HEG MONUMENT AT CHICKAMAUGA

to get over Elk River which has raised so high during this heavy rain that Teams can not cross — and the Rebels burned the Bridge before they left. We are just as badly off for something to Eat as for the mail. The only thing we have had, is corn bread — baked out of Water and Meal without anything els in it. I was lucky enough to get hold of a lot of Honey and we have also killed a few Pigs so we have not starved. We have plenty of Coffee but no Sugar. We have scoured the whole country for corn and all sorts of eatables, but it is now perfectly cleaned out. How the people will live — I can not understand. We have taken nearly all there is to be found. The news we have had lately is so good that we have had a regular jubilee over it.[4] Night before last a number of the officers were invited up to Gen. Davis where we had lots of Music and *whiskey* — but I got an order while I was up there to take two of my Regiments and start at 2 °clock in the night and go up in the mountains to hunt for Rebels.

I did so, and after a pretty hard march up some of the roughest places I ever saw, I at last found a *Cave* in the rocks where I believe there was about 10 or 15 of them. We had to crawl on our hands & Feet to get to the place but they heard us and jumped away from us. We captured 8 Horses and two Mules — a Lot of Hams — Guns — and clothing — and one Prisoner, and got back to camp about 4 oclock in the afternoon Very tired. If the news that we have received lately is true, We must soon have an end to the war. And Then — Oh, wont it be pleasant to meet again? I look for peace by the 1ˢᵗ of January next anyway.

I am afraid you have not had any letters from me for sometime. The mail has run very irregular — on account of the heavy rain. I send this enclosed in a letter to Hilda. You will have to consider yourself under obligation to her for this.

[4] The allusion is to the capture of Vicksburg by General Grant and to the battle of Gettysburg.

There is nothing new from us. The enemy has gone accross the mountains and we do not see any of them on this side. I captured a mail Bag full of letters yesterday — and the boys around Head Quarters have had a very nice time reading love letters — &c. I must close — and I will promise to write again soon and often. Good [bye] my Dear.

From
Your Own,
HANS.

To Hilda, July 9, 1863

[Van Doren Mss.]

Winchester, Third Brigade. I am so glad to hear that you are a good girl, and also to hear that you are taking music lessons and going to School. I want my girl to be one of the nicest and smartest little Lady to be found. *Considers it probable that war will soon end.* I hear that Nebby is such a hard little case — I shall have to make an officer of him. I expect a letter from you soon.

To Gunild, July 13, 1863

[Van Doren Mss.]

Winchester, Tennessee, Third Brigade. On the day before, a Sunday, he dined with his neighbor from Vermont on pancakes and maple syrup. Tells of young lady from Vermont, a niece of D. A. J. Upham of Milwaukee, who is painting a sketch of his headquarters to take with her to Wisconsin. Comments again on belief that war is coming to a close. You have no idea of how good we have felt over the good News we have had for the last two weeks. *More about his idea of a store.* I shall probably apply for a furlough about the 1st of September. — I think I shall have no trouble in getting leave for at least 20 days. I send you a New[s]paper that we are printing at this place.

To Gunild, July 15, 1863
[Van Doren Mss.]

Third Brigade. Same place. Doing nothing. Thinks it doubtful that his letters will reach her now as it is reported that Morgan is playing hob with the Rail Roads in Ohio and Indiana. *Busy with picketing. Message to Nebby.* I borrow Books from some of my citizen neighbors and have plenty interesting to read.

To Gunild, July 16, 1863

Third Brigade, Winchester, Tennessee. Comments on letter received from Ole. Thinks he may be home by New Year's. The news we have been receiving for some time back is so good that I can not help but think that the war must soon come to a close. I should not be surprised if we had no more hard fighting. Braggs Army is deserting very fast, and he will soon have very little force left. *Does not care about the rank that he returns with, whether it is colonel or general,* so that I am able to say that I stood at my post till the war ended.

To Gunild, July 19, 1863
[Van Doren Mss.]

Third Brigade. Denies that he has given up the idea of going home in the fall, but he will not leave if there is an advance. If there is not, he will get a twenty-day leave. Writes in some detail about plans for his return on leave.

To Gunild, July 21, 1863
[Van Doren Mss.]

Third Brigade, Winchester, Tennessee. Has done nothing about leave, owing to absence of Rosecrans. Discusses plans for meeting Gunild in Chicago. Other details. I visited with Col. Hobart and Col. Starkweather last Sunday we had a big time together, they are camped about 4 miles from here. To day or to morrow they will come up to visit me.

To Gunild, July 24, 1863
[Van Doren Mss.]

Headquarters, Third Brigade. Tells of visit of Stark-weather, Hobart, and other Wisconsin officers. I did not have any thing good to treat them to, but we had a very fine time together. We drank a few Bottles of wine &co. *Has just been paid off — $760. Discusses finances and other matters. Is sending papers from tax assessor for her to fill out.* I pay tax on my sallary down here, and the rest I dont know anything about.

To Hilda, July 26, 1863
[Van Doren Mss.]

Third Brigade, Winchester, Tennessee. Promises that if she learns to write well, he will get someone to teach her how to paint. Sends money for candy for Nebby. But you must tell him that he must not hurah for Jeff. Davis, or I will not be his Pa Pa any longer.

To Gunild, July 28, 1863
[Van Doren Mss.]

Winchester. Little or nothing to do. Has appointed Mathews commissary in place of Jim Larson. Has written plainly to Ole about his " Copperheadism." If he is going to remain the tool of the Copperheads I will have as little to do with him as I can.

To Gunild, August 5, 1863
[Van Doren Mss.]

Winchester. Hopeful of getting leave. Will know in a day or two. Will telegraph from Nashville. Suggests that she

*meet him in Chicago. General McCook has endorsed his
application for leave.*

To Gunild, August 7, 1863

HEAD QUARTERS 3ᵈ BRIGADE
Aug 7ᵗʰ 1863.

MY DEAR WIFE —

I must write again this morning so as to keep up my usual
letters.

My Leave of Absence has not returned, and I am pretty
sure already that I can not go home just now. We shall
probably move from here before long — perhaps in a day or
two, and I will not go if that is the case.

Tanberg got Leave of Absence yesterday for 20 days, and
goes to morrow. We have also got orders to send three officers and six men from each regiment home to get the drafted
men down here.

If I get Leave of Absence and go home I will get it to day
or to morrow. But even if I get it, I shall go up and see old
Rosey what prospects there are for the Brigade remaining
here. I can not afford to go away from the Brigade if we are
to move towards Chattanooga. It is understood very well
now that I have the best Brigade in this Divission. I do not
know but I can say in the Corps — and for me to go away
from it when it is a prospect of something to do, after I have
worked, and made the Brigade what it is, would not be right.
If I do not come home I suppose you will be very much disappointed, but I told you not to be — for I know how uncertain these things are.

It does not seem to be much prospects for any fighting
ahead. The Rebels have been very much used up. But we
will have warm weather to march in. It has been very cool
and pleasant all summer, but it is getting hot now.

I am very healthy. I have never been better than I am
at present.

Mrs Genl Mc. Cook is here.   Yesterday I had an introduction to her by the Genl.   She is a very pretty little woman.

Yesterday was the Presidents Thanksgiving day and we had a lively time.   After our *celebration* broke up we started for camp, and the rain began to pour down.   We got as wet as rats.   Last night our Bands were all out, and I had amongst the rest, a big *Serenade*.[5]

I tell you we have lively times down here whenever we can.   There is only one thing I miss that is my own Dear wife.   If I had you and Nebby here I should be perfectly contented.   I will write again before we move.

Good bye my Darling.

Your own
HANS.

To Gunild, August 8, 1863
[Van Doren Mss.]

Winchester.   General Rosecrans has declined to give him a leave.   No news except that we are preparing for the move. He is having his photograph taken at the request of some of his men.   Regrets that he could not have gone to Wisconsin for the state convention.

To Gunild, August 10, 1863

Winchester.   Rosecrans will give him leave as soon as he can be spared.   But now I can not.   I have a pretty important command, and the best Brigade in the Corps.   I have got the reputation of taking good care of my men and I am anxious to show them that I can take care of them in the field as well.   *Paraded his brigade yesterday.*

[5] In the summer of 1863, after the battle of Gettysburg and the fall of Vicksburg, President Lincoln issued a proclamation setting apart August 6 as a " day for national thanksgiving, praise, and prayer."

To Gunild, August 12, 1863
[Van Doren Mss.]

Winchester. Asks her not to feel too much disappointed because he did not get leave. When he saw there were pros-pects of moving, he did not want to leave under any circum-stances. *Has recommended Willard as an officer in a Negro regiment. He himself could get a very strong recommenda-tion for promotion, but he is not working that way.* When Old Rosey feels like asking for my promotion I will get it — and I will know then that I have earned it.

To Gunild, August 13, 1863
[Van Doren Mss.]

Headquarters, Third Brigade, Winchester, Tennessee. Is sending this letter and various gifts by Christen Hattlestad, who is starting for home. Sends her some pictures of him-self, taken as he sat in an open tent. Discusses plans for farm. I want the farm all, or nearly all sowed to grass — and, keep sheep & cattle on it. *His service:* It is just 18 months to day since I was mustered into the United States Service. I have to day served just one half of my time — which is three years.

To Gunild, August 17, 1863

WINCHESTER Aug 17ᵗʰ 1863.

MY OWN DARLING.

We are again ready to move and shall start to day at 2 o'clock.[6] Which way we will move from here, I do not know yet, but we are of course going towards Tennessee River. The Troops have all been moving for several days. I am glad to get off for several reasons. We have laid here till it began to be tedious and times go faster when we are stirring

---

[6] The orders to Heg to move the third brigade are printed in *War of the Rebellion*, series 1, vol. 30, part 3, p. 51, 59.

around, but the main reason is that as soon as we have made
this move, and get through this campaign, I shall get leave of
Absence to go home. I could not get it till we made this
move. I may not be able to write to you as regular as I have
done while here. You will know the reason when you hear
that we are marching, but I will keep you posted whenever I
have an opportunity. I shall expect you to meet me in Chicago when I get on my way home. I will tellegraph from
Nashville as I said before — and let you know exactly when
to come. I have been living first rate while we have laid
here. The only thing that has troubled me, was lazyness, as
I have had very little to do and I have been anxious to see
you.

I sent you Two Hundred Dollars by Christen and I have
paid up my debts for the big Horse I bought. I have got
about 150 Dollars left with me. I bought me a very fine
Gold Watch a few days ago. It is very expensive, but I
thought a Gen. could not be without a good watch, so I
traded off my old one and gave my note for one Hundred
Dollars to boot. I have got a good one now. I think it
worth at least 150. or 200 Dollars. If I get into a fight then
I shall leave it with Doctor Himoe.[7]

I have not time to write much more. The mail is ready to
leave.

I sent some money to Edmund & Hilda by letter, but have
not heard if they got the letter. I have a good many Photographs to send, and will put a couple in this letter.

Edmund & Hilda must be good children now till I come
home and I will get them some nice presents. The one that
is the best of them will get the prettiest.

Good Bye my own Dear one. Do not feel uneasy on my
account.

Your Own
HANS

[7] The watch of which Colonel Heg writes is now in the possession of the
State Historical Society of Wisconsin.

To Gunild, August 21, 1863

STEVENSON ALABAMA
Aug 21st 1863.

MY OWN DEAR WIFE —

I have not been able to write to you since leaving Winchester. We are now here — within 5 miles of the Tennessee River. I have got my Brigade in a good camp. We had a very pleasant trip this time — no rain — but it was warm and a very rough road in crossing the Cumberland Mountains. The Mountains are full of Bushwhackers — and a few of our men were shot at, but no body killed. We left Winchester on Monday, traveled very slow and reached here yesterday — which was Thursday.

I have no news. I am in good health and fine spirits. The cars run to this place regularly. The [mail] comes every day I understand. The Rebels are right on the other side of the River. As soon as we get ready to cross, I expect we may have a little fighting to do. I have had no letters from you by the last two or three mails.

The Boys are all well. Christen I suppose has got home by this time & I suppose he is going in partnership with Ole. He and Ole will not agree very long — See if they do. I know both of them. I am going to make another application for leave of Absence as soon as Col. Martin of the 8th Kansas comes back. He is a good officer & the only one that they consider capable of taking command of this Brigade in my absence, out of the Col[s] on duty.

I will write again as soon as I have more time & leasure.
Good Bye my own Darling.

Your Own
HANS

To Gunild, August 22, 1863
[Van Doren Mss.]

Stevenson, Alabama. Anticipates fighting as soon as we cross the Tennessee River. He is glad to hear that the crops

*have been good and gives advice as to their disposition. Is
anxious to know about nominations for state officers in Wisconsin. Has been trying to help Sorenson to get the nomination for prison commissioner.*

To Gunild, August 25, 1863
[Van Doren Mss.]

Stevenson, Alabama. We are having some firing along the
line nearly every day and we may probably have some fighting before we take Chattanooga. *Routine:* We have lots of
music and all sorts of amusements. I have two Brass Bands
in my Brigade. They call at my tent very often to Serenade, and have a Glass of Beer or something of that kind.
On the whole I am having it as pleasant as any one can wish
in the Army. I have had very little trouble with any of my
officers or men, I think they are generally satisfied with my
way of doing things. *Writes again about the prospects for
promotion.*

To Gunild, August 30, 1863

On Top of Sand Mountain
8 miles from Stevenson
Sunday Aug 30ᵗʰ 1863.

My Dear Gunild.

I got your letter of Aug. 24 to day. I am glad you are
all well, but sory to hear that you are having trouble with
the wheat. Put it in the Mill if you can. Now I must tell
you what we have been doing. Friday afternoon I recᵈ orders to be ready to move imidiately. My Brigade was to
have the honor of crossing the Tennessee River in advance of
the Army and to lay the Pontoons. We marched to the River
that night — 4 miles — I was up all night and made prepara-
tions for the mornings work. The Rebel Pickets being in
sight on the other side of the River, and near enough so we

could talk to them. At 7 oclock in the Morning all was ready. My whole Brigade in the Boats. We went over expecting every moment to be shot at, But all went well. We were the first accross the River and moved right up on the Mountain without any fighting a[nd] very little skirmishing.[8] A few Rebs were captured. In the afternoon, Old Rosey and McCook paid us a visit — feeling good. I am now stationed here five miles away from any other forces. It was quite a compliment to our Brigade to have the advance.

I have very little time to write to day. You must not expect me home till we take Chattanooga.

I am going to suprise you. The first thing you know you will have a lover drop in on you and ask to sleep with you over night. Good Bye my Darling

I depend upon you for my agent to run my Pet-Farm. You dont tell me anything about what Christ brought home — or if he brought anything at all.

Yours
HANS

To Gunild, September 1, 1863

ON TOP OF SAND MOUNTAIN
HEAD QUARTERS 3^d BRIGADE.
Sept 1st 1863.

DEAR GUNILD.

Excuse my paper — I have to use the best [I] got. We are still at the same place I wrote from on the 30th but will

---

[8] On August 30 General McCook forwarded to Heg a compliment from General Garfield on " the promptness and success " of this action. *War of the Rebellion,* series 1, vol. 30, part 3, p. 973. McCook himself, in a report of October 2, wrote, "At 4 a. m., August 29, the pontoons were ready for the construction of the bridge over the Tennessee River. Heg's brigade, of Davis' division, of this corps, was placed in the boats and crossed to the opposite bank to cover its construction, to drive away the enemy's pickets, and to seize the heights of Sand Mountain. This duty was well performed, and the bridge completed at 1 p. m." *Ibid.,* series 1, vol. 30, part 1, p. 485. An interesting account of the crossing of the Tennessee is given by Harvey Britton in a letter of September 2 to his brother Albert. Britton Papers, in the possession of Mrs. H. L. Howard of Chicago. See also Heg's account in the *Milwaukee Sentinel,* September 19, 1863, and reprinted *post,* p. 246.

probably move to morrow.[9]   The whole Army is in motion I think, and perhaps before you get this, you will have heard that we have taken Chattanooga.   I hope so.   I do [not] think there will be much fighting before we have it.   Martin Skofstad came down last night.   I have only time to write a very few words to day.   We are very bussy packing up some of our things and sending them back, as they are ordering the most of our Teams back to Stevenson on account of the bad roads.   I get three waggons however for my Head Quarters.   I can take along all I have got.   If you do not hear from me as often as you expect, dont feel uneasy.   I am all right.   Doctor Himoe the same.

Good Bye my Darling.   I will drop in to see you sometime when you dont expect me.

Your own
HANS.

To Gunild, September 4, 1863

WILLS VALLEY ALABAMA
Sept 4th 1863

MY DEAR WIFE.

I have opportunity again to drop you a few lines.   We are on the march, but where we are going no one knows, but old Rosey.   We are already quite a little piece down into Alabama.   You can find a place by the name of Lebanon laid down on the map — it is the County Seat of DeCalb County Alabama — about 30 or 40 miles south of Chattanooga.   Well we are going towards that place to day.

I think we are getting perfectly around Chattanooga and Bragg will find himself as badly flanked here as he did at Tulahoma.

I am in fine health — enjoying myself first rate.   If it was not that I have a good deal of anxiety for you I would have nothing to trouble me.   I hope you will get along.   You are

[9] A brief dispatch by Colonel Heg written on August 31, 1863, at " Lieutenant Wood's Signal Station " is in *War of the Rebellion*, series 1, vol. 30, part 3, p. 254.

able now to take care of yourself. I shall be at home as soon
as this campaign is over. I could give you a good deal of
news — the most of which would only be sickening to tell —
how the people here are suffering by the rebels. The people
are nearly all loyal but very poor. Men wemen and children
have been shot and hung by the hundred. After seeing and
hearing these people tell their tales of suffering and grief and
then to think that there is men even in Wisconsin who sym-
pathise and aid the infernal brutes, is almost enough to make
a mans blood boil. I have never felt so glad to be a soldier
as I have since I came into these mountains where we could
do so much good to the poor down trodden people. There
are hundreds here that have laid in hollow log and caves for
months hiding themselves, and their wemen have been hung
till they were compelled to tell where their husbands were.
One woman came into camp yesterday whose husband had
been shot a few weeks ago, after he had been compelled to
dig his own grave — she said she came in with her boy to
sell some chickens and get some coffee — but the main thing
she came for she said, was to see the old Flag. Some of our
boys brought her a Flag — she took it and geathered it up
in her hands and kissed it while the tears rolled down her
cheek. It was [a] touching sight. I could give any lot of
heartrending stories but I must stop. We move to day at
2 o'clock P. M. Good bye my own Dear one. Kiss the children for me.

> Your own
> HANS

To Gunild, September 6, 1863

> HEAD QUARTERS 3ᵈ BRIGADE
> WILLS VALLEY, ALABAMA
> Sept 6ᵗʰ 1863.

DEAR WIFE.

A couple of days ago I wrote you a letter, but I have it
still in my coat pocket, not having been able to send it.

The mail I understand goes to morrow, and Even also goes to Louisville and there will be plenty of opportunity to send, and I will send you both at once. I recieved your letter of Aug 28th day before yesterday. I am glad to see that you are so cheerfull, and that you are doing so well in taking care of my wheat &c. I know you can get along well enough if you only think so. The Horses you must keep till I get home and I will dispose of them some way so they will not be any trouble to you. I learn that Horses are very high up in Wisconsin — and I am sure they will be very high all over the country before the war is over. Our present campaign will be over before very long, and as soon as it is I can get permission to go home. My Brigade as well as your humble servant is doing well and I think gaining favors the older we get in the service.

I am having good times. The marching has not been very hard. The boys are all in good condition. The country is full of fruit, Apples and Peaches — Sweet Potatoes and chickens, and we are living very well.

You will probably see an article published in the Milwaukee Sentinel from this Brigade signed H.H. You may guess who wrote it.[10]

This country is full of poor people — and they are all loyal — but very ignorant. They have been butchered, and hung like animals. It is awfull to hear them relate their stories. One old woman came down to my Head Q[rs] yesterday. She has 6 children the oldest 12 years old. She is nearly dead with consumption, and little over two weeks ago they took her husband right before her eys, and tied him with a rope, and then shot him. She had nothing to eat, and she left my tent with a small bag of Flour, some coffee and a good chunk of the Maple Sugar you sent me — and I have never met any one feeling happier than she did. Her

---

[10] The article was an account of "Rosecrans' Army Crossing the Tennessee." It was printed in the *Milwaukee Sentinel* for September 19, 1863, over the initials "H. H." See *post*, p. 246.

husband was shot because he was a Union man — and her husbans brother was shot a few days afterwards for the same reason.

She was perfectly happy now, she said that she had been able to meet us and tell us how she had been treated. She knew we would pay them back, and that was all she wished to live and see. Some of the houses of those men that have helped to torment these poor fellows have already gone .up in smoke — and more will be apt to follow.

We hear cannonading every day, but we do not get any news just now as to what is going on. There are no Rebels very near us at present. I expect we will move again to morrow. I am always better contented when we are moving, and time passes off very fast. Gen Davis has his wife along. She calls on me now and then. She is a young, fine intelligent Woman but not handsome. My love to the children. Do not feel uneasy for me. Take matters as cooly as possible. This war will soon be over. I may not be able to write very often. If anything is wrong with me you will get tellegraph Dispatch from Gen. Rosecranses H^d Qu^{rs}.

Good Bye My Darling.

Your own
HANS

PS. We have received news from Washington that our two companies at Island N° 10, will come here soon.

To Gunild, September 15, 1863
[Van Doren Mss.]

Wills Valley, Alabama. We have been on a scout, and it has been impossible to write. I am all right and doing well. *Gives opinion that the* campaign is about over, and as soon as it is you may look for me. *Adds:* We have had a hard campaign — but little fighting. *Postscript:* We came from "Georgia" yesterday.

To Gunild, September 15, 1863

HEAD QUARTER WILLS VALLEY
Sept 15th 1863.

MY DEAR GUNILD.

I barely had time this morning to scratch of[f] a few lines to send you by one of the men going home. I had orders to march at day break to day, and was all ready, but soon after Sun rise I received orders to remain in camp to day — and I am improving it by writing letters, answering old ones &c.

We started off accross Look out Mountain a few days ago, my Brigade taking one road and Carlins another. We found the enemy in pretty heavy force. I captured a few but go[t] no fight out of them. Carlin also captured a few but had no fight. Gen Stanley was along with his cavalry, and had a lively brush with them, giving them a good threshing.

We have taken Chattanooga and the enemy is retreating towards Atlanta, I think. Some of our Generals still think they are near by here and preparing to give us Battle somewhere among these mountains. I think they are mistaken. The Rebs were glad to get away from us. We are too much for them, although I have no doubt but that they have more men than Rosecranse. The news from all parts are good.

Charlston will soon be either in ruins, or in our hands — and the Rebellion played out.

I have had pretty hard times since we left Stevenson. It has been very dusty and warm, and we have marched pretty hard sometimes up and down the mountains, but my health has been good. You write a very cheerfull letter. I am glad to hear that you are doing so well. Sop. and Ole wrote to me at the same time. I think Ole feels bad on account of my lectures on his Copperheadism. He says he had expected to have gone in partnership with me in the Store, but it seems that I did not trust him he says. I think he has very good reason to say that I do not trust him, after

Head Qurs 3d Brigade —
19 Miles from Chattanooga
Sept 18th 1863

My Dear —

Once more I have an opportunity
to write a few words. We have continued
to march since I last wrote, and are still
laying here ready at a moments notice
for anything. The Rebels are in our front
and we may have to fight him a Battle — if
we do it will be apt to be a big one —

Do not feel uneasy for me, I am well
and in good spirits. and trusting to my
usual good luck — I shall use all the caution
and Courage I am capable of and leave
the rest to take care of itself — The soldiers
are in tollerable good condition, many
of ours however have marched hard
and had rough time for the last two weeks
and aught to have a few days rest
before fighting — Our train is not with us.
but I have one Head quarter waggon
with me and get along well — Even has gone
home I understand, Martin is here in
his place, but stays with the waggons — I
have let him have a Hundred Dollars
my money to use, till I get my furlaugh
to go home — The mail reached us
yesterday, but I got nothing from Joe
or O. Mitchel wrote me a few lines —
and I got several Newspapers — some
of them I see have accounts of my
Brigade crossing the Tennessee River.
The Rebels were here where we are
camped yesterday, and got one of their

COLONEL HEG'S LAST LETTER

[Original in possession of State Historical Society of Wisconsin. See other
side of this insert for second page of letter and signature.]

Colonels killed in a skirmish —
Albert Skofstad has been sick.. but
he is better. — I have a good Buggy that
belongs to me, and he rides in that. —
We use it whenever any of us are sick
and we carry our dinner in it —
Old Roseys Head Quarters are only a
few miles from here. — I think, if it is
true that the Rebels have not gone, that
he will give them one of the biggest
whippings they ever had. — Burnsides Army
is close by us. and can assist us any
time I think. — Thus far Roseys Army
has gained a tremendous victory —
by forcing Bragg to leave Chattanooga.
I can of course say nothing about
it. prospects of getting home — but as
soon as this present Campaign is
ended — I am certain of being able
to come. — We have had such hard
work, marching over these Mountains that
we are entitled to some rest — The "Gen."
will call and see you the first thing
You know probably surprise you.
my love to the Children —
Good Bye my Darling —
write often, but do not expect
to hear from me very often till
the Campaign is over
Your own
Hans

having put nearly half of all I am worth in his hands without a cent for security.

We are laying here without any prospect of staying very long. I am in hopes to be ordered up to Chattanooga soon so I can get my Leave of Absence grant[e]d.

I must write several letters, & I must close this one. Your last two letters reached me two days before the mail, because you directed them to the Brigade instead of the Regiment. Good Bye my Dear. Write often.

Your own
HANS

To Gunild, September 18, 1863

HEAD QURS 3^d BRIGADE —
19 MILES FROM CHATTANOOGA
Sept 18th 1863

MY DEAR —

Once more I have an opportunity to write a few words. We have continued to march since I last wrote, and are still laying here ready at a moments notice for anything. The Rebels are in our front and we may have to fight him a Battle — if we do it will be apt to be a big one.

Do not feel uneasy for me. I am well and in good spirits — and trusting to my usual good luck. I shall use all the caution and courage I am capable of and leave the rest to take care of itself. The soldie[r]s are in tollerable good condition. Many of ours however have marched hard and had rough time for the last two weeks and ought to have a few days rest before fighting. Our train is not with us — but I have one Head quarter waggon with me and get along well. Even has gone home I understand. Martin is here in his place, but stays with the waggons. I have let him have a Hundred Dollars of my money to use, till I get my furlough to go home. The mail reached us yesterday, but I got nothing from you. Old Mitchel wrote me a few lines —

and I got several Newspapers — some of them I see have accounts of my Brigade crossing the Tennessee River. The Rebels were here where we are camped yesterday, and got one of their Colonels killed in a skirmish. Albert Skofstad has been sick, but he is better. I have a good Buggy that belongs to me, and he rides in that. We use it whenever any of us are sick and we carry our Dinner in it.

Old Roseys Head Quarters are only a few miles from here. I think, if it is true that the Rebels have not gone, that he will give them one of the biggest whippings they ever had. Burnsides Army is close by us, and can assist us any time I think. Thus far Roseys Army has gained a tremendeous victory by forcing Bragg to leave Chattanooga.

I can of course say nothing about the prospects of getting home — but as soon as this present campaign is ended — I am certain of being able to come. We have had such hard work marching over these mountains that we are entittled to some rest. The "*Gen.*" will call and see you the first thing you know — probably surprise you. My love to the children.

Good Bye my Darling — write often, but do not expect to hear from me very often till the campaign is over.

Your Own
HANS

SUPPLEMENT I

The following account, published in the Milwaukee Sentinel, is probably the "article" referred to by Colonel Heg in the letter that he wrote to his wife on September 6.

"Rosecrans' Army Crossing the Tennessee"
(Correspondence of the Sentinel)
[*Milwaukee Sentinel*, September 19, 1863.]

On Saturday morning August 29th I had the pleasure of witnessing one of those rare scenes that now and then occur in the campaigns of modern warfare. The crossing of the advance Brigade of old Rosy's Army in boats, prior to the laying of the Pontoon Bridge across the Tennessee.

Col. Heg was notified on Friday afternoon that his brigade was designated for the advance, and ordered to move immediately to the river, bivouack for the night, and at early dawn throw his brigade across, drive the enemy from the opposite bank and occupy the summit of the mountain. Wisconsin is represented in this by the 15th (the Scandinavian) Regiment and the 8th Battery.

This was glorious news for the boys, who have repeatedly won high praise and commendation from Headquarters for their efficiency in all those things that constitute good soldiers, now came a new opportunity to test their prompness as well as courage.

The enemy's pickets were stationed on the south bank.

The river here is less than 500 yards wide, and the pickets of both parties held frequent conversations with each other during our stay at Stevenson.

The moving of the pontoons and troops to the river bank was effected during the night as quietly as possible, and as daylight spread over the mountain tops of Cumberland on Saturday morning, there lay the disjointed mass of boats, timbers and materials that was to bridge the beautiful Tennessee, scattered along its bank, and the brigade drawn up in line, concealed by the bushes, with the battery posted to the right and left to be used in case of necessity.

Soon the troops were seen to move by details to their several boats. Oars and oarsmen were provided — the boats gradually slid down the steep embankment, and before a person had time to realize the beauty of the sight, the word "Forward" was given. — My pen will fail to describe the reality of the scene before me. The beautiful scenery of the country, the mountain tops glittering in the sunshine, the thick misty cloud just rising from the still blue waters of the river, forced to leave its night couch by the rays of the rising sun, the sharp command "Foreward," as it resounded along the river bank, and was taken up by the mountain echo. All this requires a better pen than mine to portray. There was something grand and beautiful in this sight, something emblematic of the great cause in which we are engaged. The dawn of the day among the peaks of the Cumberland mountains, the disappearance of the dark mist that had spread itself over the country, coupled with the significant command "Foreward," the stars and stripes floating over the boats bearing the valiant soldiers of our army "Foreward," driving before them the enemies of our country, of liberty, civilization and intelligence. All this, I say, was so inspiring that I almost forgot how terribly those men were exposed, should the enemy be in condition to take advantage of the opportunity; but he was not. The boats all landed without a single accident, only a few shots were exchanged with him after we had gained a footing on the opposite shore. He was evidently bewildered and confounded, as he did not expect us to cross here, or certainly not on so short notice. The troops advanced in line of battle for a distance of over a mile, and then commenced ascending the mountain. A few of the enemy's pickets were captured, the balance hurried on, spreading terror among the rebel sympathizers, and glad tidings of deliverance to the hundreds of loyal mountaineers, who were concealing themselves in the mountains, to avoid imprisonment and butchery.

As soon as it was known at Headquarters that we had succeeded so admirably, "Old Rosy" started to pay us a visit, together with McCook and others, he took a trip over the "Pontoon" which was in readiness by 12 o'clock, M., and came to see the troops and compliment them on their successful crossing. The boys think all the world of "Old Rosy," and it makes them feel proud to be complimented by him.

H. H.

SUPPLEMENT II

The following account of Mrs. Heg is taken from an informing letter written to the editor of this volume by Mr. Tollef Sanderson of Harmony, Minnesota, on April 18, 1935. The information embodied in the letter was derived by Mr. Sanderson from his mother, Mrs. Sophia Jacobson Sanderson, who is a niece of Mrs. Heg.

Mrs. Hans Christian Heg

Mrs. Hans C. Heg was Gunhild Einong, a daughter of Jacob and Anne Einong. They immigrated to the United States in 1842 [*1843?*] and spent thirteen weeks on the ocean. The mother was taken ill with typhoid fever, died, and was buried at sea. There were five daughters, Aslaug, Mrs. Hans Tweito; Anne, Mrs. John Evenson [Molee]; Gunhild, Mrs. Hans C. Heg; Gurina, Mrs. Elias Stangeland; and Susanna, a twin sister of Anne who also died and was buried at sea. There were three brothers, John, Ole, and Austin. Ole died in his youth. The family left a good farm home in Norway. The father bought tickets for ten people and also paid for eight "forties" of land when he arrived in Wisconsin. They came to Milwaukee by lake and canal travel and settled in Muskego, Waukesha County. When the father died a few years later, there was a small farm and a sum of money for each child. The women were good pioneer women, patient, thrifty, and industrious, although the family had been accustomed to having servants in Norway. John was a successful farmer in Fillmore County, Minnesota, and Austin was a typical old-time miner who went west at the time of the California gold rush. Mrs. Tweito and Mrs. Evenson were married in the famous Heg barn at Muskego. John and Austin used the name of Jacobson instead of Einong.

It is not known just when or where Gunhild Einong first met Colonel Heg, but most likely it was at Muskego, since

that was the home of both.   They were married in 1851 and
had four children.   One daughter died in infancy and is
buried in the Norway cemetery beside the father.   Mrs. Heg
lived with the children in Waterford until she moved to Beloit in order to put them through college.   It was the ambition of Colonel and Mrs. Heg to educate their children, and
on his last visit home they had discussed this matter.   My
mother remembers distinctly Mrs. Heg telling that Colonel
Heg advised her, if necessary, to sell all their property in
order to educate the children.   Hilda, the late Mrs. Charles
Newell Fowler of Elizabeth, New Jersey, studied in Germany
and later taught music in a school for girls.   Elmer became
a physician in Seattle, and Edmund (James E.) was a newspaper man in Chicago [and Wisconsin].

Mrs. Heg was financially independent and did not work
especially to earn the money necessary for the education of
her children.   My own father lived at her home when he attended Beloit College, but we do not know that any others
stayed there.   Mrs. Heg was a very quiet and reserved
woman, capable, sensible, simple and plain in her likes, a
very good manager, and a good business woman.   She was
well read and interested in the affairs of the day.   She was
a good conversationalist,— in a quiet manner, however.   In
later life she accepted only thirty dollars [a month] in pen-
sion, although the government offered her more.   She thought
that amount sufficient. . . .

Mrs. Heg and Mrs. Fowler visited at the home of Mrs.
Heg's brother John (my grandfather) here in Fillmore County
about sixty-seven years ago.   They apparently came by rail-
way to Prairie du Chien and thence either overland by stage
coach to Elliota or Lenora or by river to Brownsville, a mar-
ket point in those days. . . . Mrs. Heg also visited here
about forty years ago and it is through these visits that my
mother retains memories of her.   My father and sister visited Mrs. Heg and her daughter at Elizabeth in 1914 or 1916.

INDEX

INDEX